Acclaim for

The Spell of the Sensuous

"Forges a thoroughly articulate passage between science and mysticism. . . . Speculative, learned, and always 'lucid and precise' as the eye of the vulture that confronted him once on a cliff ledge, Abram has one of those rare minds which, like the mind of a musician or a great mathematician, fuses dreaminess with smarts."

—*Village Voice Literary Supplement*

"This is a landmark book. Scholars will doubtless recognize its brilliance, but they may overlook the most important part of Abram's achievement: he has written the best instruction manual yet for becoming fully human. I walked outside when I was done and the world was a different place."

—Bill McKibben,
author of *The End of Nature*

"Abram manages, almost magically, to stir in us a long-lost memory: deep in our bones, in our blood, in the air we breathe, we know that the world lives and speaks to us. . . . He shows that it is possible to reawaken the animistic dimension of perception and feeling without renouncing rationality and intellectual analysis. . . . A joy to read and a brilliant gift to our rapidly darkening world."

—*Shambhala Sun*

vistas that will be fruitfully explored for years, indeed for generations, to come."

—Joanna Macy,
translator of Rainer Maria Rilke's
The Book of Hours

"*The Spell of the Sensuous* does more than place itself on the cutting edge where ecology meets philosophy, psychology, and history. It magically subverts the dichotomies of culture and nature, body and mind, opening a vista of organic being and human possibility that is often imagined but seldom described. Reader beware, the message is spell-binding. One cannot read this book without risk of entering into an altered state of perceptual possibility."

—Max Oelschlager,
author of *The Idea of Wilderness*

"This book by David Abram lights up the landscape of language, flesh, mind, history, mapping us back into the world."

—Gary Snyder,
author of *Mountains and Rivers Without End*

"Nobody writes about the ecological depths of the human and more-than-human world with more love and lyrical sensitivity than David Abram."

—Theodore Roszak,
author of *Where the Wasteland Ends*

"Disclosing the sentience of all nature, and revealing the unsuspected effect of the more-than-human on our language and our lives, in unprecedented fashion, Abram generates true philosophy for the twenty-first century."

—Lynn Margulis, originator of the Gaia Hypothesis,
author of *What Is Life?*

David Abram

The Spell of the Sensuous

David Abram, Ph.D., is an ecologist and philosopher whose writings have had a deepening influence upon the environmental movement in North America and abroad. A summa cum laude graduate of Wesleyan University, he holds a doctorate in philosophy from the State University of New York at Stony Brook and has been the recipient of fellowships from the Watson and Rockefeller Foundations and a Lannan Literary Award for Nonfiction. He is an accomplished sleight-of-hand magician and has lived and traded magic with indigenous magicians in Indonesia, Nepal, and the Americas. This is his first book.

The Spell of the
Sensuous

The Spell of the Sensuous

PERCEPTION AND LANGUAGE
IN A MORE-THAN-HUMAN WORLD

David Abram

VINTAGE BOOKS

A DIVISION OF RANDOM HOUSE, INC. • NEW YORK

FIRST VINTAGE BOOKS EDITION, FEBRUARY 1997

Copyright © 1996 by David Abram

All rights reserved under International and Pan-American
Copyright Conventions. Published in the United States by
Vintage Books, a division of Random House, Inc., New York,
and simultaneously in Canada by Random House of Canada
Limited, Toronto. Originally published in hardcover by Pantheon Books, a division of Random House, Inc., New York,
in 1996.

Permissions acknowledgments are on page 313.

The Library of Congress has cataloged the Pantheon edition
as follows:
Abram, David.
The spell of the sensuous: perception and language in a
more-than-human world / David Abram.
p.   cm.
Includes bibliographical references and index.
ISBN 0-679-43819-X
1. Philosophy of nature.   2. Body, Human (Philosophy).
3. Sense (Philosophy).   4. Perception (Philosophy).
5. Human ecology.   I. Title.
BD581.A25   1996   95-31466
128—dc20
CIP
Vintage ISBN: 0-679-77639-7

Book design by Chris Welch

Random House Web address: http://www.randomhouse.com/

Printed in the United States of America
20 19 18 17 16 15

to the endangered and vanishing ones

Contents

Preface and Acknowledgments

Humans are tuned for relationship. The eyes, the skin, the tongue, ears, and nostrils—all are gates where our body receives the nourishment of otherness. This landscape of shadowed voices, these feathered bodies and antlers and tumbling streams—these breathing shapes are our family, the beings with whom we are engaged, with whom we struggle and suffer and celebrate. For the largest part of our species' existence, humans have negotiated relationships with every aspect of the sensuous surroundings, exchanging possibilities with every flapping form, with each textured surface and shivering entity that we happened to focus upon. All could speak, articulating in gesture and whistle and sigh a shifting web of meanings that we felt on our skin or inhaled through our nostrils or focused with our listening ears, and to which we replied—whether with sounds, or through movements, or minute shifts of mood. The color of sky, the rush of waves—every aspect of the earthly sensuous could draw us into a relationship fed with curiosity and spiced with danger. Every sound was a voice, every scrape or blunder was a meeting—with Thunder, with Oak, with Dragonfly. And from all of these relationships our collective sensibilities were nourished.

Today we participate almost exclusively with other humans and with our own human-made technologies. It is a precarious situation, given our age-old reciprocity with the many-voiced landscape. We still *need* that which is other than ourselves and our own creations. The simple premise of this book is that we are human only in contact, and conviviality, with what is not human.

Does such a premise imply that we must renounce all our complex technologies? It does not. But it does imply that we must renew our acquaintance with the sensuous world in which our techniques and technologies are all rooted. Without the oxygenating breath of the forests, without the clutch of gravity and the tumbled magic of river rapids, we have no distance from our technologies, no way of assessing their limitations, no way to keep ourselves from turning into them. We need to know the textures, the rhythms and tastes of the bodily world, and to distinguish readily between such tastes and those of our own invention. Direct sensuous reality, in all its more-than-human mystery, remains the sole solid touchstone for an experiential world now inundated with electronically-generated vistas and engineered pleasures; only in regular contact with the tangible ground and sky can we learn how to orient and to navigate in the multiple dimensions that now claim us.

✢

THIS BOOK HAS BEEN WRITTEN WITH TWO GOALS IN MIND. I HAVE hoped, first, to provide a set of powerful conceptual tools for my colleagues in the broad world of environmental activism—for conservationists, wilderness advocates, community organizers, bioregionalists, nature writers, conservation biologists, ecopsychologists, and all others who are already struggling to make sense of, and to alleviate, our current estrangement from the animate earth. Yet I have also wished to provoke some new thinking within the institutional realm of scholars, scientists, and educators—many of whom have been strangely silent in response to the rapid deterioration of wild nature, the steady vanishing of other species, and the consequent flattening of our human relationships.

In light of these twin aims, I have tried to maintain a high standard of theoretical and scholarly precision, without, however, masking the passion, the puzzlement, and the pleasure that flow from my own engagement with the living land.

The reader will discover, for instance, that there are *two* introductory chapters to the book. There is, first, a "Personal Introduction," which details some of the unusual adventures that first led me to raise the various questions addressed in this work. This chapter focuses upon my encounters and reflections while living as an itinerant sleight-of-hand magician among traditional, indigenous magicians in rural Asia. Second, there is a "Technical Introduction," outlining the theoretical approach brought to bear upon the questions addressed herein. More specifically, this chapter discusses the development, in the twentieth century, of the tradition of "phenomenology"—the study of direct experience. Originally intended to provide a solid foundation for the empirical sciences, the careful study of perceptual experience unexpectedly began to make evident the hidden centrality of the earth in all human experience; indeed, phenomenological research began to suggest that the human mind was thoroughly dependent upon (and thoroughly influenced by) our forgotten relation with the encompassing earth.

While sensorial experience, philosophical reflection, and empirical information are thoroughly entwined throughout this book, those readers who have little patience with philosophical matters should feel free to leap across the technical introduction (Chapter 2)—perhaps touching briefly down to explore those subsections whose titles provoke their curiosity. Others may wish to dance across parts of Chapter 3, which necessarily contains a few somewhat technical sections regarding the bodily nature of language. Toward the end of Chapter 3 a very brief summary will set the stage for what follows.

MANY COMRADES LENT THEIR SUPPORT TO THIS PROJECT. AMONG those whose curiosity and kindness helped engender this book are the bioregional animateur Chris Wells, ecological cellist Nelson Denman, seeress Heather Rowntree, dreamtracker R. P. Harbour, Julia Meeks, Francis Huxley, Sam Hitt, Vicki Dean, Rich Ryan, Stella Reed, and the rest of the All-Species clan of northern New Mexico.

The various reflections in this work were honed in passionate conversations with friends in diverse places, among them David Rothenberg, Arne Naess, Rachel Wiener, Bill Boaz, Gary Nabhan, Ivan Illich, Christopher Manes, Drew Leder, Max Oelschlager, Lynn Margulis, Dorion Sagan, James Hillman, Chellis Glendinning, Laura Sewall, Rick Boothby, Baird Callicott, Starhawk, Rex and Lisa Weyler, Valerie Gremillion, Tom Jay, and the greathearted Thomas Berry. Mountain-wizard Dolores LaChapelle and letter-scribe Amy Hannon gave essential encouragement in the earliest stages. Among those who read through parts of the earliest manuscript, Peter Manchester, Anthony Weston, Paul Shepard, and John Elder all offered fine insights.

Philosopher Edward Casey provided fellowship and guidance, as did the wild salmon-sage Freeman House. Historian Donald Worster provided encouragement and inspiration. The Buddhist scholar-poet Stan Lombardo offered unexpected hospitality, as did prairie-stewards Ken Lassman and Caryn Goldberg. Christian Gronau and Aileen Douglas shared their keen insights into the worlds of other animals. Rachel Bagby provided soul sustenance.

My editors were both a pleasure to work with. Jack Shoemaker deserves my warm thanks for his immediate enthusiasm with the book, and for taking time out from the bustle of setting up a new publishing house in order to read and refine the manuscript. Dan Frank provided patient guidance through the publishing maze, and many keen-sighted suggestions. He has my gratitude, as does his assistant Claudine O'Hearn. Thanks, as well, to my agent Ned Leavitt.

Generous grants from the Foundation for Deep Ecology and from the Levinson Foundation, as well as a year-long fellowship from the Rockefeller Foundation, greatly aided the researching and writing of this book.

Few people are gifted with great artists for parents, as I have been. Blanche Abram and Irv Abram, pianist and painter, provided much tactical help during the crafting of this work. I thank them for their encouragement, and for the intuition of beauty that they carefully granted to their children.

Finally, I extend a gratitude beyond words to my closest friend and ally, Grietje Laga, whose graceful intelligence deepens all my thoughts, and whose gentle magic ceaselessly returns me to my senses. Her company has made this whole adventure ever so much more wonderful.

AS THE CRICKETS' SOFT AUTUMN HUM
IS TO US
SO ARE WE TO THE TREES
AS ARE THEY
TO THE ROCKS AND THE HILLS

—Gary Snyder

The Spell of the
Sensuous

The Ecology of Magic

A PERSONAL INTRODUCTION TO THE INQUIRY

LATE ONE EVENING I STEPPED OUT OF MY LITTLE HUT IN THE rice paddies of eastern Bali and found myself falling through space. Over my head the black sky was rippling with stars, densely clustered in some regions, almost blocking out the darkness between them, and more loosely scattered in other areas, pulsing and beckoning to each other. Behind them all streamed the great river of light with its several tributaries. Yet the Milky Way churned beneath me as well, for my hut was set in the middle of a large patchwork of rice paddies, separated from each other by narrow two-foot-high dikes, and these paddies were all filled with water. The surface of these pools, by day, reflected perfectly the blue sky, a reflection broken only by the thin, bright green tips of new rice. But by night the stars themselves glimmered from the surface of the paddies, and the river of light whirled through the darkness underfoot as well as above; there seemed no ground in front of my feet, only the abyss of star-studded space falling away forever.

I was no longer simply beneath the night sky, but also *above* it— the immediate impression was of weightlessness. I might have been able to reorient myself, to regain some sense of ground and gravity, were it not for a fact that confounded my senses entirely: between the constellations below and the constellations above drifted countless fireflies, their lights flickering like the stars, some drifting up to join the clusters of stars overhead, others, like graceful meteors, slipping down from above to join the constellations underfoot, and all these paths of light upward and downward were mirrored, as well, in the still surface of the paddies. I felt myself at times falling through space, at other moments floating and drifting. I simply could not dispel the profound vertigo and giddiness; the paths of the fireflies, and their reflections in the water's surface, held me in a sustained trance. Even after I crawled back to my hut and shut the door on this whirling world, I felt that now the little room in which I lay was itself floating free of the earth.

Fireflies! It was in Indonesia, you see, that I was first introduced to the world of insects, and there that I first learned of the great influence that insects—such diminutive entities—could have upon the human senses. I had traveled to Indonesia on a research grant to study magic—more precisely, to study the relation between magic and medicine, first among the traditional sorcerers, or *dukuns,* of the Indonesian archipelago, and later among the *dzankris,* the traditional shamans of Nepal. One aspect of the grant was somewhat unique: I was to journey into rural Asia not outwardly as an anthropologist or academic researcher, but as a magician in my own right, in hopes of gaining a more direct access to the local sorcerers. I had been a professional sleight-of-hand magician for five years back in the United States, helping to put myself through college by performing in clubs and restaurants throughout New England. I had, as well, taken a year off from my studies in the psychology of perception to travel as a street magician through Europe and, toward the end of that journey, had spent some months in London, England, exploring the use of sleight-of-hand magic in psychotherapy, as a means of engendering communication with distressed individuals largely unapproachable by clinical healers.[1] The success of this work suggested to me that sleight-of-hand might lend itself well to the curative arts, and I became, for the first time, interested in the relation, largely forgotten in the West, between folk medicine and magic.

It was this interest that led to the aforementioned grant, and to my sojourn as a magician in rural Asia. There, my sleight-of-hand skills proved invaluable as a means of stirring the curiosity of the local shamans. For magicians—whether modern entertainers or indigenous, tribal sorcerers—have in common the fact that they work with the malleable texture of perception. When the local sorcerers gleaned that I had at least some rudimentary skill in altering the common field of perception, I was invited into their homes, asked to share secrets with them, and eventually encouraged, even urged, to participate in various rituals and ceremonies.

But the focus of my research gradually shifted from questions regarding the application of magical techniques in medicine and ritual curing toward a deeper pondering of the relation between traditional magic and the animate natural world. This broader concern seemed to hold the keys to the earlier questions. For none of the several island sorcerers that I came to know in Indonesia, nor any of the *dzankris* with whom I lived in Nepal, considered their work as ritual healers to be their major role or function within their communities. Most of them, to be sure, *were* the primary healers or "doctors" for the villages in their vicinity, and they were often spoken of as such by the inhabitants of those villages. But the villagers also sometimes spoke of them, in low voices and in very private conversations, as witches (or "lejaks" in Bali), as dark magicians who at night might well be practicing their healing spells backward (or while turning to the left instead of to the right) in order to afflict people with the very diseases that they would later work to cure by day. Such suspicions seemed fairly common in Indonesia, and often were harbored with regard to the most effective and powerful healers, those who were most renowned for their skill in driving out illness. For it was assumed that a magician, in order to expel malevolent influences, must have a strong understanding of those influences and demons—even, in some areas, a close rapport with such powers. I myself never consciously saw any of those magicians or shamans with whom I became acquainted engage in magic for harmful purposes, nor any convincing evidence that they had ever done so. (Few of the magicians that I came to know even accepted money in return for their services, although they did accept gifts in the way of food, blankets, and the like.) Yet I was struck by the fact that none of them ever did or said anything to counter such disturbing rumors and speculations, which circulated quietly through the regions where they lived. Slowly, I came to recognize that it was through the agency of such rumors, and the ambiguous fears that such rumors engendered in the village people, that the sorcerers were able to maintain a basic level of privacy. If the villagers did not entertain certain fears about the local sorcerer, then they would likely come to obtain his or her magical help for every little malady and disturbance; and since a more potent practitioner must provide services for several large villages, the sorcerer would be swamped from morning to night with requests for ritual aid. By allowing the inevitable suspicions and fears to circulate unhindered in the region (and sometimes even encouraging and contributing to such rumors), the sorcerer ensured that *only* those who were in real and profound need of his skills would dare to approach him for help.

This privacy, in turn, left the magician free to attend to what he acknowledged to be his primary craft and function. A clue to this function may be found in the circumstance that such magicians rarely dwell at the heart of their village; rather, their dwellings are commonly at the spatial periphery of the community or, more often, out beyond the edges of the village—amid the rice fields, or in a forest, or a wild cluster of boulders. I could easily attribute this to the just-mentioned need for privacy, yet for the magician in a traditional culture it seems to serve another purpose as well, providing a spatial expression of his or her symbolic position with regard to the community. For the magician's intelligence is not encompassed *within* the society; its place is at the edge of the community, mediating *between* the human community and the larger community of beings upon which the village depends for its nourishment and sustenance. This larger community includes, along with the humans, the multiple nonhuman entities that constitute the local landscape, from the diverse plants and the myriad animals—birds, mammals, fish, reptiles, insects—that inhabit or migrate through the region, to the particular winds and weather patterns that inform the local geography, as well as the various landforms—forests, rivers, caves, mountains—that lend their specific character to the surrounding earth.

The traditional or tribal shaman, I came to discern, acts as an intermediary between the human community and the larger ecological field, ensuring that there is an appropriate flow of nourishment, not just from the landscape to the human inhabitants, but from the human community back to the local earth. By his constant rituals, trances, ecstasies, and "journeys," he ensures that the relation between human society and the larger society of beings is balanced and reciprocal, and that the village never takes more from the living land than it returns to it—not just materially but with prayers, propitiations, and praise. The scale of a harvest or the size of a hunt are always negotiated between the tribal community and the natural world that it inhabits. To some extent every adult in the community is engaged in this process of listening and attuning to the other presences that surround and influence daily life. But the shaman or sorcerer is the exemplary voyager in the intermediate realm between the human and the more-than-human worlds, the primary strategist and negotiator in any dealings with the Others.

And it is only as a result of her continual engagement with the animate powers that dwell beyond the human community that the traditional magician is able to alleviate many individual illnesses that arise *within* that community. The sorcerer derives her ability to cure ailments from her more continuous practice of "healing" or balancing the community's relation to the surrounding land. Disease, in such cultures, is often conceptualized as a kind of systemic imbalance within the sick person, or more vividly as the intrusion of a demonic or malevolent presence into his body. There are, at times, malevolent influences within the village or tribe itself that disrupt the health and emotional well-being of susceptible individuals within the community. Yet such destructive influences within the human community are commonly traceable to a disequilibrium between that community and the larger field of forces in which it is embedded. Only those persons who, by their everyday practice, are involved in monitoring and maintaining the relations *between* the human village and the animate landscape are able to appropriately diagnose, treat, and ultimately relieve personal ailments and illnesses arising *within* the village. Any healer who was not simultaneously attending to the intertwined relation between the human community and the larger, more-than-human field, would likely dispel an illness from one person only to have the same problem arise (perhaps in a new guise) somewhere else in the community. Hence, the traditional magician or medicine person functions primarily as an intermediary between human and nonhuman worlds, and only secondarily as a healer.[2] Without a continually adjusted awareness of the relative balance or imbalance between the human group and its nonhuman environ, along with the skills necessary to modulate that primary relation, any "healer" is worthless—indeed, not a healer at all. The medicine person's primary allegiance, then, is not to the human community, but to the earthly web of relations in which that community is embedded—it is from this that his or her power to alleviate human illness derives—and this sets the local magician apart from other persons.

The primacy for the magician of nonhuman nature—the centrality of his relation to other species and to the earth—is not always evident to Western researchers. Countless anthropologists have managed to overlook the ecological dimension of the shaman's craft, while writing at great length of the shaman's rapport with "supernatural" entities. We can attribute much of this oversight to the modern, civilized assumption that the natural world is largely determinate and mechanical, and that that which is regarded as mysterious, powerful, and beyond human ken must therefore be of some other, nonphysical realm *above* nature, "supernatural."

The oversight becomes still more comprehensible when we realize that many of the earliest European interpreters of indigenous lifeways were Christian missionaries. For the Church had long assumed that only human beings have intelligent souls, and that the other animals, to say nothing of trees and rivers, were "created" for no other reason than to serve humankind. We can easily understand why European missionaries, steeped in the dogma of institutionalized Christianity, assumed a belief in supernatural, otherworldly powers among those tribal persons whom they saw awestruck and entranced by nonhuman (but nevertheless natural) forces. What is remarkable is the extent to which contemporary anthropology still preserves the ethnocentric bias of these early interpreters. We no

longer describe the shamans' enigmatic spirit-helpers as the "superstitious claptrap of heathen primitives"—we have cleansed ourselves
of at least *that* much ethnocentrism; yet we still refer to such enigmatic forces, respectfully now, as "supernaturals"—for we are unable to shed the sense, so endemic to scientific civilization, of nature
as a rather prosaic and predictable realm, unsuited to such mysteries.
Nevertheless, that which is regarded with the greatest awe and wonder by indigenous, oral cultures is, I suggest, none other than what
we view as nature itself. The deeply mysterious powers and entities
with whom the shaman enters into a rapport are ultimately the same
forces—the same plants, animals, forests, and winds—that to literate, "civilized" Europeans are just so much scenery, the pleasant
backdrop of our more pressing human concerns.

The most sophisticated definition of "magic" that now circulates
through the American counterculture is "the ability or power to alter
one's consciousness at will." No mention is made of any *reason* for
altering one's consciousness. Yet in tribal cultures that which we call
"magic" takes its meaning from the fact that humans, in an indigenous and oral context, experience their own consciousness as simply
one form of awareness among many others. The traditional magician cultivates an ability to shift out of his or her common state of
consciousness precisely in order to make contact with the other organic forms of sensitivity and awareness with which human existence is entwined. Only by temporarily shedding the accepted
perceptual logic of his culture can the sorcerer hope to enter into relation with other species on their own terms; only by altering the
common organization of his senses will he be able to enter into a rapport with the multiple nonhuman sensibilities that animate the local
landscape. It is this, we might say, that defines a shaman: the ability
to readily slip out of the perceptual boundaries that demarcate his or
her particular culture—boundaries reinforced by social customs,
taboos, and most importantly, the common speech or language—in
order to make contact with, and learn from, the other powers in the
land. His magic is precisely this heightened receptivity to the meaningful solicitations—songs, cries, gestures—of the larger, more-
than-human field.

Magic, then, in its perhaps most primordial sense, is the experience of existing in a world made up of multiple intelligences, the in-

tuition that every form one perceives—from the swallow swooping overhead to the fly on a blade of grass, and indeed the blade of grass itself—is an *experiencing* form, an entity with its own predilections and sensations, albeit sensations that are very different from our own.

To be sure, the shaman's ecological function, his or her role as intermediary between human society and the land, is not always obvious at first blush, even to a sensitive observer. We see the sorcerer being called upon to cure an ailing tribesman of his sleeplessness, or perhaps simply to locate some missing goods; we witness him entering into trance and sending his awareness into other dimensions in search of insight and aid. Yet we should not be so ready to interpret these dimensions as "supernatural," nor to view them as realms entirely "internal" to the personal psyche of the practitioner. For it is likely that the "inner world" of our Western psychological experience, like the supernatural heaven of Christian belief, originates in the loss of our ancestral reciprocity with the animate earth. When the animate powers that surround us are suddenly construed as having less significance than ourselves, when the generative earth is abruptly defined as a determinate object devoid of its own sensations and feelings, then the sense of a wild and multiplicitous otherness (in relation to which human existence has always oriented itself) must migrate, either into a supersensory heaven beyond the natural world, or else into the human skull itself—the only allowable refuge, in this world, for what is ineffable and unfathomable.

But in genuinely oral, indigenous cultures, the sensuous world itself remains the dwelling place of the gods, of the numinous powers that can either sustain or extinguish human life. It is not by sending his awareness out beyond the natural world that the shaman makes contact with the purveyors of life and health, nor by journeying into his personal psyche; rather, it is by propelling his awareness laterally, outward into the depths of a landscape at once both sensuous and psychological, the living dream that we share with the soaring hawk, the spider, and the stone silently sprouting lichens on its coarse surface.

The magician's intimate relationship with nonhuman nature becomes most evident when we attend to the easily overlooked background of his or her practice—not just to the more visible tasks of curing and ritual aid to which she is called by individual clients, or to the larger ceremonies at which she presides and dances, but to the content of the prayers by which she prepares for such ceremonies, and to the countless ritual gestures that she enacts when alone, the daily propitiations and praise that flow from her toward the land and *its* many voices.

ALL THIS ATTENTION TO NONHUMAN NATURE WAS, AS I HAVE MEN-tioned, very far from my intended focus when I embarked on my re-search into the uses of magic and medicine in Indonesia, and it was only gradually that I became aware of this more subtle dimension of the native magician's craft. The first shift in my preconceptions came rather quietly, when I was staying for some days in the home of a young "balian," or magic practitioner, in the interior of Bali. I had been provided with a simple bed in a separate, one-room building in the balian's family compound (most compound homes, in Bali, are comprised of several separate small buildings, for sleeping and for cooking, set on a single enclosed plot of land), and early each morn-ing the balian's wife came to bring me a small but delicious bowl of fruit, which I ate by myself, sitting on the ground outside, leaning against the wall of my hut and watching the sun slowly climb through the rustling palm leaves. I noticed, when she delivered the fruit, that my hostess was also balancing a tray containing many lit-tle green plates: actually, they were little boat-shaped platters, each woven simply and neatly from a freshly cut section of palm frond. The platters were two or three inches long, and within each was a lit-tle mound of white rice. After handing me my breakfast, the woman and the tray disappeared from view behind the other buildings, and when she came by some minutes later to pick up my empty bowl, the tray in her hands was empty as well.

The second time that I saw the array of tiny rice platters, I asked my hostess what they were for. Patiently, she explained to me that they were offerings for the household spirits. When I inquired about the Balinese term that she used for "spirit," she repeated the same explanation, now in Indonesian, that these were gifts for the spirits of the family compound, and I saw that I had understood her cor-rectly. She handed me a bowl of sliced papaya and mango, and disappeared around the corner. I pondered for a minute, then set down the bowl, stepped to the side of my hut, and peered through the trees. At first unable to see her, I soon caught sight of her crouched low beside the corner of one of the other buildings, carefully setting what I presumed was one of the offerings on the ground at that spot. Then she stood up with the tray, walked to the other visible corner of the same building, and there slowly and carefully set another offering on the ground. I returned to my bowl of fruit and finished my breakfast. That afternoon, when the rest of the household was busy, I walked back behind the building where I had seen her set down the two offerings. There were the little green platters, resting neatly at the two rear corners of the building. But the mounds of rice that had been within them were gone.

The next morning I finished the sliced fruit, waited for my hostess to come by for the empty bowl, then quietly headed back behind the buildings. Two fresh palm-leaf offerings sat at the same spots where the others had been the day before. These were filled with rice. Yet as I gazed at one of these offerings, I abruptly realized, with a start, that one of the rice kernels was actually moving.

Only when I knelt down to look more closely did I notice a line of tiny black ants winding through the dirt to the offering. Peering still closer, I saw that two ants had already climbed onto the offering and were struggling with the uppermost kernel of rice; as I watched, one of them dragged the kernel down and off the leaf, then set off with it back along the line of ants advancing on the offering. The second ant took another kernel and climbed down with it, dragging and pushing, and fell over the edge of the leaf, then a third climbed onto the offering. The line of ants seemed to emerge from a thick clump of grass around a nearby palm tree. I walked over to the other offering and discovered another line of ants dragging away the white kernels. This line emerged from the top of a little mound of dirt, about fifteen feet away from the buildings. There was an offering on the ground by a corner of my building as well, and a nearly identical line of ants. I walked into my room chuckling to myself: the balian and his wife had gone to so much trouble to placate the household spirits with gifts, only to have their offerings stolen by little six-legged thieves. What a waste! But then a strange thought dawned on me: what if the ants were the very "household spirits" to whom the offerings were being made?

I soon began to discern the logic of this. The family compound, ike most on this tropical island, had been constructed in the vicinity of several ant colonies. Since a great deal of cooking took place in the compound (which housed, along with the balian and his wife and children, various members of their extended family), and also much preparation of elaborate offerings of foodstuffs for various rituals and festivals in the surrounding villages, the grounds and the buildings at the compound were vulnerable to infestations by the sizable ant population. Such invasions could range from rare nuisances to a periodic or even constant siege. It became apparent that the daily palm-frond offerings served to preclude such an attack by the natural forces that surrounded (and underlay) the family's land. The daily gifts of rice kept the ant colonies occupied—and, presumably, satisfied. Placed in regular, repeated locations at the corners of various structures around the compound, the offerings seemed to establish certain boundaries between the human and ant communities; by honoring this boundary with gifts, the humans apparently hoped to persuade the insects to respect the boundary and not enter the buildings.

Yet I remained puzzled by my hostess's assertion that these were gifts "for the spirits." To be sure, there has always been some confusion between our Western notion of "spirit" (which so often is defined in contrast to matter or "flesh"), and the mysterious presences to which tribal and indigenous cultures pay so much respect. I have already alluded to the gross misunderstandings arising from the circumstance that many of the earliest Western students of these other customs were Christian missionaries all too ready to see occult ghosts and immaterial phantoms where the tribespeople were simply offering their respect to the local winds. While the notion of "spirit" has come to have, for us in the West, a primarily anthropomorphic or human association, my encounter with the ants was the first of many experiences suggesting to me that the "spirits" of an indigenous culture are primarily those modes of intelligence or awareness that do *not* possess a human form.

As humans, we are well acquainted with the needs and capacities of the human body—we *live* our own bodies and so know, from within, the possibilities of our form. We cannot know, with the same familiarity and intimacy, the lived experience of a grass snake or a snapping turtle; we cannot readily experience the precise sensations of a hummingbird sipping nectar from a flower or a rubber tree soaking up sunlight. And yet we do know how it feels to sip from a fresh pool of water or to bask and stretch in the sun. Our experience may indeed be a variant of these other modes of sensitivity; nevertheless, we cannot, as humans, precisely experience the living sensations of another form. We do not know, with full clarity, their desires or motivations; we cannot know, or can never be sure that we know, what they know. That the deer does experience sensations, that it carries knowledge of how to orient in the land, of where to find food and how to protect its young, that it knows well how to survive in the forest without the tools upon which we depend, is readily evident to our human senses. That the mango tree has the ability to create fruit, or the yarrow plant the power to reduce a child's fever, is also evident. To humankind, these Others are purveyors of secrets, carriers of intelligence that we ourselves often need: it is these Others who can inform us of unseasonable changes in the weather, or warn us of imminent eruptions and earthquakes, who show us, when foraging, where we may find the ripest berries or the best route to follow back home. By watching them build their nests and shelters, we glean clues regarding how to strengthen our own dwellings, and their deaths teach us of our own. We receive from them countless gifts of food, fuel, shelter, and clothing. Yet still they remain Other to us, inhabiting their own cultures and displaying their own rituals, never wholly fathomable.

Moreover, it is not only those entities acknowledged by Western civilization as "alive," not only the other animals and the plants that speak, as spirits, to the senses of an oral culture, but also the meandering river from which those animals drink, and the torrential monsoon rains, and the stone that fits neatly into the palm of the hand. The mountain, too, has its thoughts. The forest birds whirring and chattering as the sun slips below the horizon are vocal organs of the rain forest itself.[3]

Bali, of course, is hardly an aboriginal culture; the complexity of its temple architecture, the intricacy of its irrigation systems, the resplendence of its colorful festivals and crafts all bespeak the influence of various civilizations, most notably the Hindu complex of India. In Bali, nevertheless, these influences are thoroughly intertwined with the indigenous animism of the Indonesian archipelago;

the Hindu gods and goddesses have been appropriated, as it were, by the more volcanic, eruptive spirits of the local terrain.

Yet the underlying animistic cultures of Indonesia, like those of many islands in the Pacific, are steeped as well in beliefs often referred to by ethnologists as "ancestor worship," and some may argue that the ritual reverence paid to one's long-dead human ancestors (and the assumption of their influence in present life), easily invalidates my assertion that the various "powers" or "spirits" that move through the discourse of indigenous, oral peoples are ultimately tied to nonhuman (but nonetheless sentient) forces in the enveloping landscape.

This objection rests upon certain assumptions implicit in Christian civilization, such as the assumption that the "spirits" of dead persons necessarily retain their human form, and that they reside in a domain outside of the physical world to which our senses give us access. However, most indigenous tribal peoples have no such ready recourse to an immaterial realm outside earthly nature. Our strictly human heavens and hells have only recently been abstracted from the sensuous world that surrounds us, from this more-than-human realm that abounds in its own winged intelligences and cloven-hoofed powers. For almost all oral cultures, the enveloping and sensuous earth remains the dwelling place of both the living *and* the dead. The "body"—whether human or otherwise—is not yet a mechanical object in such cultures, but is a magical entity, the mind's own sensuous aspect, and at death the body's decomposition into soil, worms, and dust can only signify the gradual reintegration of one's ancestors and elders into the living landscape, from which all, too, are born.

Each indigenous culture elaborates this recognition of metamorphosis in its own fashion, taking its clues from the particular terrain in which it is situated. Often the invisible atmosphere that animates the visible world—the subtle presence that circulates both within us and between all things—retains within itself the spirit or breath of the dead person until the time when that breath will enter and animate another visible body—a bird, or a deer, or a field of wild grain. Some cultures may burn, or "cremate," the body in order to more completely return the person, as smoke, to the swirling air, while that which departs as flame is offered to the sun and stars, and that which lingers as ash is fed to the dense earth. Still other cultures may dismember the body, leaving certain parts in precise locations where they will likely be found by condors, or where they will be consumed by mountain lions or by wolves, thus hastening the re-incarnation of that person into a particular animal realm within the landscape. Such examples illustrate simply that death, in tribal cultures, initiates a metamorphosis wherein the person's presence does not "vanish" from the sensible world (where would it go?) but rather remains as an animating force within the vastness of the landscape, whether subtly, in the wind, or more visibly, in animal form, or even as the eruptive, ever to be appeased, wrath of the volcano. "Ancestor worship," in its myriad forms, then, is ultimately another mode of attentiveness to nonhuman nature; it signifies not so much an awe or reverence of human powers, but rather a reverence for those forms that awareness takes when it is *not* in human form, when the familiar human embodiment dies and decays to become part of the encompassing cosmos.

This cycling of the human back into the larger world ensures that the other forms of experience that we encounter—whether ants, or willow trees, or clouds—are never absolutely alien to ourselves. Despite the obvious differences in shape, and ability, and style of being, they remain at least distantly familiar, even familial. It is, paradoxically, this perceived kinship or consanguinity that renders the difference, or otherness, so eerily potent.[4]

❦

SEVERAL MONTHS AFTER MY ARRIVAL IN BALI, I LEFT THE VILLAGE in which I was staying to visit one of the pre-Hindu sites on the island. I arrived on my bicycle early in the afternoon, after the bus carrying tourists from the coast had departed. A flight of steps took me down into a lush, emerald valley, lined by cliffs on either side, awash with the speech of the river and the sighing of the wind through high, unharvested grasses. On a small bridge crossing the river I met an old woman carrying a wide basket on her head and holding the hand of a little, shy child; the woman grinned at me with the red, toothless smile of a beetle nut chewer. On the far side of the river I stood in front of a great moss-covered complex of passageways, rooms, and courtyards carved by hand out of the black volcanic rock.

I noticed, at a bend in the canyon downstream, a further series of caves carved into the cliffs. These appeared more isolated and remote, unattended by any footpath I could discern. I set out through the grasses to explore them. This proved much more difficult than I anticipated, but after getting lost in the tall grasses, and fording the river three times, I at last found myself beneath the caves. A short scramble up the rock wall brought me to the mouth of one of them, and I entered on my hands and knees. It was a wide but low opening, perhaps only four feet high, and the interior receded only about five or six feet into the cliff. The floor and walls were covered with mosses, painting the cave with green patterns and softening the harshness of the rock; the place, despite its small size—or perhaps because of it—had an air of great friendliness. I climbed to two other caves, each about the same size, but then felt drawn back to the first one, to sit cross-legged on the cushioning moss and gaze out across the emerald canyon. It was quiet inside, a kind of intimate sanctuary hewn into the stone. I began to explore the rich resonance of the enclosure, first just humming, then intoning a simple chant taught to me by a balian some days before. I was delighted by the overtones that the cave added to my voice, and sat there singing for a long while. I did not notice the change in the wind outside, or the cloud shadows darkening the valley, until the rains broke—suddenly and with great force. The first storm of the monsoon!

I had experienced only slight rains on the island before then, and was startled by the torrential downpour now sending stones tumbling along the cliffs, building puddles and then ponds in the green landscape below, swelling the river. There was no question of returning home—I would be unable to make my way back through the flood to the valley's entrance. And so, thankful for the shelter, I recrossed my legs to wait out the storm. Before long the rivulets falling along the cliff above gathered themselves into streams, and two small waterfalls cascaded across the cave's mouth. Soon I was looking into a solid curtain of water, thin in some places, where the canyon's image flickered unsteadily, and thickly rushing in others. My senses were all but overcome by the wild beauty of the cascade and by the roar of sound, my body trembling inwardly at the weird sense of being sealed into my hiding place.

And then, in the midst of all this tumult, I noticed a small, delicate activity. Just in front of me, and only an inch or two to my side of the torrent, a spider was climbing a thin thread stretched across the mouth of the cave. As I watched, it anchored another thread to the top of the opening, then slipped back along the first thread and joined the two at a point about midway between the roof and the floor. I lost sight of the spider then, and for a while it seemed that it had vanished, thread and all, until my focus rediscovered it. Two more threads now radiated from the center to the floor, and then another; soon the spider began to swing between these as on a circular trellis, trailing an ever-lengthening thread which it affixed to each radiating rung as it moved from one to the next, spiraling outward. The spider seemed wholly undaunted by the tumult of waters spilling past it, although every now and then it broke off its spiral dance and climbed to the roof or the floor to tug on the radii there, assuring the tautness of the threads, then crawled back to where it left off. Whenever I lost the correct focus, I waited to catch sight of the spinning arachnid, and then let its dancing form gradually draw the lineaments of the web back into visibility, tying my focus into each new knot of silk as it moved, weaving my gaze into the ever-deepening pattern.

And then, abruptly, my vision snagged on a strange incongruity: another thread slanted across the web, neither radiating nor spiraling from the central juncture, violating the symmetry. As I followed it with my eyes, pondering its purpose in the overall pattern, I began to realize that it was on a different plane from the rest of the web, for the web slipped out of focus whenever this new line became clearer. I soon saw that it led to its own center, about twelve inches to the right of the first, another nexus of forces from which several threads stretched to the floor and the ceiling. And then I saw that there was a *different* spider spinning this web, testing its tautness by dancing around it like the first, now setting the silken cross weaves around the nodal point and winding outward. The two spiders spun independently of each other, but to my eyes they wove a single intersecting pattern. This widening of my gaze soon disclosed yet another spider spiraling in the cave's mouth, and suddenly I realized that there were *many* overlapping webs coming into being, radiating out at different rhythms from myriad centers poised—some higher, some lower, some minutely closer to my eyes and some farther—between the stone above and the stone below.

I sat stunned and mesmerized before this ever-complexifying expanse of living patterns upon patterns, my gaze drawn like a breath into one converging group of lines, then breathed out into open space, then drawn down into another convergence. The curtain of water had become utterly silent—I tried at one point to hear it, but could not. My senses were entranced.

I had the distinct impression that I was watching the universe being born, galaxy upon galaxy. . . .

NIGHT FILLED THE CAVE WITH DARKNESS. THE RAIN HAD NOT stopped. Yet, strangely, I felt neither cold nor hungry—only remarkably peaceful and at home. Stretching out upon the moist, mossy floor near the back of the cave, I slept.

When I awoke, the sun was staring into the canyon, the grasses below rippling with bright blues and greens. I could see no trace of the webs, nor their weavers. Thinking that they were invisible to my eyes without the curtain of water behind them, I felt carefully with my hands around and through the mouth of the cave. But the webs were gone. I climbed down to the river and washed, then hiked across and out of the canyon to where my cycle was drying in the sun, and headed back to my own valley.

I have never, since that time, been able to encounter a spider without feeling a great strangeness and awe. To be sure, insects and spiders are not the only powers, or even central presences, in the Indonesian universe. But they were *my* introduction to the spirits, to the magic afoot in the land. It was from them that I first learned of the intelligence that lurks in nonhuman nature, the ability that an alien form of sentience has to echo one's own, to instill a reverberation in oneself that temporarily shatters habitual ways of seeing and feeling, leaving one open to a world all alive, awake, and aware. It was from such small beings that my senses first learned of the countless worlds within worlds that spin in the depths of this world that we commonly inhabit, and from them that I learned that my body could, with practice, enter sensorially into these dimensions. The precise and minuscule craft of the spiders had so honed and focused my awareness that the very webwork of the universe, of which my own flesh was a part, seemed to be being spun by their arcane art. I have already spoken of the ants, and of the fireflies, whose sensory likeness to the lights in the night sky had taught me the fickleness of gravity. The long and cyclical trance that we call malaria was also brought to me by insects, in this case mosquitoes, and I lived for three weeks in a feverish state of shivers, sweat, and visions.

I had rarely before paid much attention to the natural world. But my exposure to traditional magicians and seers was shifting my senses; I became increasingly susceptible to the solicitations of non-human things. In the course of struggling to decipher the magicians' odd gestures or to fathom their constant spoken references to powers unseen and unheard, I began to *see* and to *hear* in a manner I never had before. When a magician spoke of a power or "presence" lingering in the corner of his house, I learned to notice the ray of sunlight that was then pouring through a chink in the roof, illuminating a column of drifting dust, and to realize that that column of light was indeed a power, influencing the air currents by its warmth, and indeed influencing the whole mood of the room; although I had not consciously seen it before, it had already been structuring my experience. My ears began to attend, in a new way, to the songs of birds—no longer just a melodic background to human speech, but meaningful speech in its own right, responding to and commenting on events in the surrounding earth. I became a student of subtle differences: the way a breeze may flutter a single leaf on a whole tree, leaving the other leaves silent and unmoved (had not that leaf, then, been brushed by a magic?); or the way the intensity of the sun's heat expresses itself in the precise rhythm of the crickets. Walking along the dirt paths, I learned to slow my pace in order to *feel* the difference between one nearby hill and the next, or to taste the presence of a particular field at a certain time of day when, as I had been told by a local *dukun,* the place had a special power and proffered unique gifts. It was a power communicated to my senses by the way the shadows of the trees fell at that hour, and by smells that only then lingered in the tops of the grasses without being wafted away by the wind, and other elements I could only isolate after many days of stopping and listening.

And gradually, then, other animals began to intercept me in my wanderings, as if some quality in my posture or the rhythm of my breathing had disarmed their wariness; I would find myself face-to-face with monkeys, and with large lizards that did not slither away when I spoke, but leaned forward in apparent curiosity. In rural Java, I often noticed monkeys accompanying me in the branches overhead, and ravens walked toward me on the road, croaking. While at Pangandaran, a nature preserve on a peninsula jutting out from the south coast of Java ("a place of many spirits," I was told by nearby fishermen), I stepped out from a clutch of trees and found myself looking into the face of one of the rare and beautiful bison that exist only on that island. Our eyes locked. When it snorted, I snorted back; when it shifted its shoulders, I shifted my stance; when I tossed my head, it tossed *its* head in reply. I found myself caught in a nonverbal conversation with this Other, a gestural duet with which my conscious awareness had very little to do. It was as if my body in its actions was suddenly being motivated by a wisdom older than my thinking mind, as though it was held and moved by a logos, deeper than words, spoken by the Other's body, the trees, and the stony ground on which we stood.

ANTHROPOLOGY'S INABILITY TO DISCERN THE SHAMAN'S ALLE-giance to nonhuman nature has led to a curious circumstance in the "developed world" today, where many persons in search of spir-itual understanding are enrolling in workshops concerned with "shamanic" methods of personal discovery and revelation. Psy-chotherapists and some physicians have begun to specialize in "shamanic healing techniques." "Shamanism" has thus come to connote an alternative form of therapy; the emphasis, among these new practitioners of popular shamanism, is on personal insight and curing. These are noble aims, to be sure, yet they are secondary to, and derivative from, the primary role of the indigenous shaman, a role that cannot be fulfilled without long and sustained exposure to wild nature, to its patterns and vicissitudes. Mimicking the indige-nous shaman's curative methods without his intimate knowledge of the wider natural community cannnot, if I am correct, do anything more than trade certain symptoms for others, or shift the locus of dis-ease from place to place within the human community. For the source of stress lies in the relation *between* the human community and the natural landscape.

Western industrial society, of course, with its massive scale and hugely centralized economy, can hardly be seen in relation to any particular landscape or ecosystem; the more-than-human ecology with which it is directly engaged is the biosphere itself. Sadly, our culture's relation to the earthly biosphere can in no way be considered a reciprocal or balanced one: with thousands of acres of nonregenerating forest disappearing every hour, and hundreds of our fellow species becoming extinct each month as a result of our civilization's excesses, we can hardly be surprised by the amount of epidemic illness in our culture, from increasingly severe immune dysfunctions and cancers, to widespread psychological distress, depression, and ever more frequent suicides, to the accelerating number of household killings and mass murders committed for no apparent reason by otherwise coherent individuals.

From an animistic perspective, the clearest source of all this distress, both physical and psychological, lies in the aforementioned violence needlessly perpetrated by our civilization on the ecology of the planet; only by alleviating the latter will we be able to heal the former. While this may sound at first like a simple statement of faith, it makes eminent and obvious sense as soon as we acknowledge our thorough dependence upon the countless other organisms with whom we have evolved. Caught up in a mass of abstractions, our attention hypnotized by a host of human-made technologies that only reflect us back to ourselves, it is all too easy for us to forget our carnal inherence in a more-than-human matrix of sensations and sensibilities. Our bodies have formed themselves in delicate reciprocity with the manifold textures, sounds, and shapes of an animate earth—our eyes have evolved in subtle interaction with *other* eyes, as our ears are attuned by their very structure to the howling of wolves and the honking of geese. To shut ourselves off from these other voices, to continue by our lifestyles to condemn these other sensibilities to the oblivion of extinction, is to rob our own senses of their integrity, and to rob our minds of their coherence. We are human only in contact, and conviviality, with what is not human.

❦

ALTHOUGH THE INDONESIAN ISLANDS ARE HOME TO AN ASTONISHing diversity of birds, it was only when I went to study among the Sherpa people of the high Himalayas that I was truly initiated into the avian world. The Himalayas are young mountains, their peaks not yet rounded by the endless action of wind and ice, and so the primary dimension of the visible landscape is overwhelmingly vertical. Even in the high ridges one seldom attains a view of a distant horizon; instead one's vision is deflected upward by the steep face of the next mountain. The whole land has surged skyward in a manner still evident in the lines and furrows of the mountain walls, and this ancient dynamism readily communicates itself to the sensing body.

In such a world those who dwell and soar in the sky are the primary powers. They alone move easily in such a zone, swooping downward to become a speck near the valley floor, or spiraling into the heights on invisible currents. The wingeds, alone, carry the immediate knowledge of what is unfolding on the far side of the next ridge, and hence it is only by watching them that one can be kept apprised of climatic changes in the offing, as well as of subtle shifts in the flow and density of air currents in one's own valley. Several of the shamans that I met in Nepal had birds as their close familiars. Ravens are constant commentators on village affairs. The smaller, flocking birds perform aerobatics in unison over the village rooftops, twisting and swerving in a perfect sympathy of motion, the whole flock appearing like a magic banner that floats and flaps on air currents over the village, then descends in a heap, only to be carried aloft by the wind a moment later, rippling and swelling.

For some time I visited a Sherpa *dzankri* whose rock home was built into one of the steep mountainsides of the Khumbu region in Nepal. On one of our walks along the narrow cliff trails that wind around the mountain, the *dzankri* pointed out to me a certain boulder, jutting out from the cliff, on which he had "danced" before attempting some especially difficult cures. I recognized the boulder several days later when hiking back down toward the *dzankri*'s home from the upper yak pastures, and I climbed onto the rock, not to dance but to ponder the pale white and red lichens that gave life to its surface, and to rest. Across the dry valley, two lammergeier condors floated between gleaming, snow-covered peaks. It was a ringing blue Himalayan day, clear as a bell. After a few moments I took a silver coin out of my pocket and aimlessly began a simple sleight-of-hand exercise, rolling the coin over the knuckles of my right hand. I had taken to practicing this somewhat monotonous exercise in response to the endless flicking of prayer-beads by the older Sherpas, a practice usually accompanied by a repetitively chanted prayer: *"Om Mani Padme Hum"* (O the Jewel in the Lotus). But there was no prayer accompanying my revolving coin, aside from my quiet breathing and the dazzling sunlight. I noticed that one of the two condors in the distance had swerved away from its partner and was now floating over the valley, wings outstretched. As I watched it grow larger, I realized, with some delight, that it was heading in my general direction; I stopped rolling the coin and stared. Yet just then the lammergeier halted in its flight, motionless for a moment against the peaks, then swerved around and headed back toward its partner in the distance. Disappointed, I took up the coin and began rolling it along my knuckles once again, its silver surface catching the sunlight as it turned, reflecting the rays back into the sky. Instantly, the condor swung out from its path and began soaring back in a wide arc. Once again, I watched its shape grow larger. As the great size of the bird became apparent, I felt my skin begin to crawl and come alive, like a swarm of bees all in motion, and a humming grew loud in my ears. The coin continued rolling along my fingers. The creature loomed larger, and larger still, until, suddenly, it was there—an immense silhouette hovering just above my head, huge wing feathers rustling ever so slightly as they mastered the breeze. My fingers were frozen, unable to move; the coin dropped out of my hand. And then I felt myself stripped naked by an alien gaze infinitely more lucid and precise than my own. I do not know for how long I was transfixed, only that I felt the air streaming past naked knees and heard the wind whispering in my feathers long after the Visitor had departed.

I RETURNED TO A NORTH AMERICA WHOSE ONLY INDIGENOUS species of condor was on the brink of extinction, mostly as a result of lead poisoning from bullets in the carrion it consumes. But I did not think about this. I was excited by the new sensibilities that had stirred in me—my newfound awareness of a more-than-human world, of the great potency of the land, and particularly of the keen intelligence of other animals, large and small, whose lives and cultures interpenetrate our own. I startled neighbors by chattering with squirrels, who swiftly climbed down the trunks of their trees and across lawns to banter with me, or by gazing for hours on end at a heron fishing in a nearby estuary, or at gulls opening clams by dropping them from a height onto the rocks along the beach.

Yet, very gradually, I began to lose my sense of the animals' own awareness. The gulls' technique for breaking open the clams began to appear as a largely automatic behavior, and I could not easily feel the attention that they must bring to each new shell. Perhaps each shell was entirely the same as the last, and *no* spontaneous attention was really necessary. . . .

I found myself now observing the heron from outside its world, noting with interest its careful high-stepping walk and the sudden dart of its beak into the water, but no longer feeling its tensed yet poised alertness with my own muscles. And, strangely, the suburban squirrels no longer responded to my chittering calls. Although I wished to, I could no longer focus my awareness on engaging in their world as I had so easily done a few weeks earlier, for my attention was quickly deflected by internal, verbal deliberations of one sort or another—by a conversation I now seemed to carry on entirely within myself. The squirrels had no part in this conversation.

It became increasingly apparent, from books and articles and discussions with various people, that other animals were not as awake and aware as I had assumed, that they lacked any real language and hence the possibility of thought, and that even their seemingly spontaneous responses to the world around them were largely "programmed" behaviors, "coded" in the genetic material now being mapped by biologists. Indeed, the more I spoke *about* other animals, the less possible it became to speak *to* them. I gradually came to discern that there was no common ground between the unlimited human intellect and the limited sentience of other animals, no medium through which we and they might communicate with and reciprocate one another.

As the expressive and sentient landscape slowly faded behind my more exclusively human concerns, threatening to become little more than an illusion or fantasy, I began to feel—particularly in my chest and abdomen—as though I were being cut off from vital sources of nourishment. I was indeed reacclimating to my own culture, becoming more attuned to its styles of discourse and interaction, yet my bodily senses seemed to be losing their acuteness, becoming less awake to subtle changes and patterns. The thrumming of crickets, and even the songs of the local blackbirds, readily faded from my awareness after a few moments, and it was only by an effort of will that I could bring them back into the perceptual field. The flight of sparrows and of dragonflies no longer sustained my focus very long, if indeed they gained my attention at all. My skin quit registering the various changes in the breeze, and smells seemed to have faded from the world almost entirely, my nose waking up only once or twice a day, perhaps while cooking, or when taking out the garbage.

In Nepal, the air had been filled with smells—whether in the towns, where burning incense combined with the aromas of roasting meats and honeyed pastries and fruits for trade in the open market, and the stench of organic refuse rotting in the ravines, and some-times of corpses being cremated by the river; or in the high moun-tains, where the wind carried the whiffs of countless wildflowers, and of the newly turned earth outside the villages where the fragrant dung of yaks was drying in round patties on the outer walls of the houses, to be used, when dry, as fuel for the household fires, and where smoke from those many home fires always mingled in the outside air. And sounds as well: the chants of aspiring monks and adepts blended with the ringing of prayer bells on near and distant slopes, accompanied by the raucous croaks of ravens, and the sigh of the wind pouring over the passes, and the flapping of prayer flags, and the distant hush of the river cascading through the far-below gorge.

There the air was a thick and richly textured presence, filled with invisible but nonetheless tactile, olfactory, and audible influences. In the United States, however, the air seemed thin and void of sub-stance or influence. It was not, here, a sensuous medium—the felt matrix of our breath and the breath of the other animals and plants and soils—but was merely an absence, and indeed was constantly re-ferred to in everyday discourse as mere empty space. Hence, in America I found myself lingering near wood fires and even garbage dumps—much to the dismay of my friends—for only such an inten-sity of smells served to remind my body of its immersion in an en-veloping medium, and with this experience of being immersed in a world of influences came a host of body memories from my year among the shamans and village people of rural Asia.

I BEGAN TO FIND OTHER WAYS, AS WELL, OF TAPPING THE VERY DIF-
ferent sensations and perceptions that I had grown accustomed to in
the "undeveloped world," by living for extended periods on native
Indian reservations in the southwestern desert and along the northwestern coast, or by hiking off for weeks at a time into the North
American wilderness. Intermittently, I began to wonder if my culture's assumptions regarding the lack of awareness in other animals
and in the land itself was less a product of careful and judicious reasoning than of a strange inability to clearly perceive other animals—
a real inability to clearly see, or focus upon, anything outside the
realm of human technology, or to hear as meaningful anything other
than human speech. The sad results of our interactions with the rest
of nature were being reported in every newspaper—from the deple-
tion of topsoil due to industrial farming techniques to the fouling of
groundwater by industrial wastes, from the rapid destruction of ancient forests to, worst of all, the ever-accelerating extinction of our
fellow species—and these remarkable and disturbing occurrences, all
readily traceable to the ongoing activity of "civilized" humankind,
did indeed suggest the possibility that there was a perceptual problem in my culture, that modern, "civilized" humanity simply did not
perceive surrounding nature in a clear manner, if we have even been
perceiving it at all.

The experiences that shifted the focus of my research in rural Indonesia and Nepal had shown me that nonhuman nature can be perceived and experienced with far more intensity and nuance than is
generally acknowledged in the West. What was it that made possible
the heightened sensitivity to extrahuman reality, the profound attentiveness to other species and to the Earth that is evidenced in so
many of these cultures, and that had so altered my awareness that
my senses now felt stifled and starved by the patterns of my own culture? Or, reversing the question, what had made possible the absence
of this attentiveness in the modern West? For Western culture, too,
has its indigenous origins. If the relative attunement to environing
nature exhibited by native cultures is linked to a more primordial,
participatory mode of perception, how had Western civilization
come to be so exempt from this sensory reciprocity? How, that is,
have we become so deaf and so blind to the vital existence of other

species, and to the animate landscapes they inhabit, that we now so casually bring about their destruction?

To be sure, our obliviousness to nonhuman nature is today held in place by ways of speaking that simply deny intelligence to other species and to nature in general, as well as by the very structures of our civilized existence—by the incessant drone of motors that shut out the voices of birds and of the winds; by electric lights that eclipse not only the stars but the night itself; by air "conditioners" that hide the seasons; by offices, automobiles, and shopping malls that finally obviate any need to step outside the purely human world at all. We consciously encounter nonhuman nature only as it has been circumscribed by our civilization and its technologies: through our domesticated pets, on the television, or at the zoo (or, at best, in carefully managed "nature preserves"). The plants and animals we consume are neither gathered nor hunted—they are bred and harvested in huge, mechanized farms. "Nature," it would seem, has become simply a stock of "resources" for human civilization, and so we can hardly be surprised that our civilized eyes and ears are somewhat oblivious to the existence of perspectives that are not human at all, or that a person either entering into or returning to the West from a nonindustrial culture would feel startled and confused by the felt absence of nonhuman powers.

Still, the current commodification of "nature" by civilization tells us little or nothing of the perceptual shift that made possible this reduction of the animal (and the earth) to an object, little of the process whereby our senses first relinquished the power of the Other, the vision that for so long had motivated our most sacred rituals, our dances, and our prayers.

But can we even hope to catch a glimpse of this process, which has given rise to so many of the habits and linguistic prejudices that now structure our very thinking? Certainly not if we gaze toward that origin from within the midst of the very civilization it engendered. But perhaps we may make our stand along the *edge* of that civilization, like a magician, or like a person who, having lived among another tribe, can no longer wholly return to his own. He lingers half within and half outside of his community, open as well, then, to the shifting voices and flapping forms that crawl and hover beyond the mirrored walls of the city. And even there, moving along those walls, he may hope to find the precise clues to the mystery of how those walls were erected, and how a simple boundary became a barrier, only if the moment is timely—only, that is, if the margin he frequents is a temporal as well as a spatial edge, and the temporal structure that it bounds is about to dissolve, or metamorphose, into something else.

Philosophy on the Way to Ecology

A TECHNICAL INTRODUCTION TO THE INQUIRY

PART I:
EDMUND HUSSERL AND PHENOMENOLOGY

I
T IS NATURAL THAT WE TURN TO THE TRADITION OF PHENOM-
enology in order to understand the strange difference between
the experienced world, or worlds, of indigenous, vernacular
cultures and the world of modern European and North American
civilization. For phenomenology is the Western philosophical tradition that has most forcefully called into question the modern assumption of a single, wholly determinable, objective reality.

This assumption has its source in René Descartes's well-known
separation of the thinking mind, or subject, from the material world

of things, or objects. Actually, Galileo had already asserted that only those properties of matter that are directly amenable to mathematical measurement (such as size, shape, and weight) are real; the other, more "subjective" qualities such as sound, taste, and color are merely illusory impressions, since the "book of nature" is written in the language of mathematics alone. In his words:

> This grand book the universe . . . is written in the language of mathematics, and its characters are triangles, circles, and other geometric figures without which it is humanly impossible to understand a single word of it; without these, one wanders about in a dark labyrinth.[1]

Yet it was only after the publication of Descartes's *Meditations,* in 1641, that material reality came to be commonly spoken of as a strictly mechanical realm, as a determinate structure whose laws of operation could be discerned only via mathematical analysis. By apparently purging material reality of subjective experience, Galileo cleared the ground and Descartes laid the foundation for the construction of the objective or "disinterested" sciences, which by their feverish and forceful investigations have yielded so much of the knowledge and so many of the technologies that have today become commonplace in the West. The chemical table of the elements, automobiles, smallpox vaccines, "close-up" images of the outer planets—so much that we have come to assume and depend upon has emerged from the bold experimentalization of the world by the objective sciences.

Yet these sciences consistently overlook our ordinary, everyday experience of the world around us. Our direct experience is necessarily subjective, necessarily relative to our own position or place in the midst of things, to our particular desires, tastes, and concerns. The everyday world in which we hunger and make love is hardly the mathematically determined "object" toward which the sciences direct themselves. Despite all the mechanical artifacts that now surround us, the world in which we find ourselves before we set out to calculate and measure it is not an inert or mechanical object but a living field, an open and dynamic landscape subject to its own moods and metamorphoses.

My life and the world's life are deeply intertwined; when I wake up one morning to find that a week-long illness has subsided and that my strength has returned, the world, when I step outside, fairly sparkles with energy and activity: swallows are swooping by in vivid flight; waves of heat rise from the newly paved road smelling strongly of tar; the old red barn across the field juts into the sky at an intense angle. Likewise, when a haze descends upon the valley in which I dwell, it descends upon my awareness as well, muddling my thoughts, making my muscles yearn for sleep. The world and I reciprocate one another. The landscape as I directly experience it is hardly a determinate object; it is an ambiguous realm that responds to my emotions and calls forth feelings from me in turn. Even the most detached scientist must begin and end her study in this indeterminate field of experience, where shifts of climate or mood may alter his experiment or her interpretation of "the data": the scientist, too, must take time off from his measurements and analyses to eat, to defecate, to converse with friends, to interact straightforwardly with a familiar world that is never explicitly thematized and defined. Indeed, it is precisely from his experience in this preconceptual and hence ambiguous world that an individual is first drawn to become a scientist, to adopt the ways of speaking and seeing that are acknowledged as appropriate by the scientific community, to affect the proper disinterested or objective attitude with regard to a certain range of natural events. The scientist does not randomly choose a specific discipline or specialty, but is drawn to a particular field by a complex of subjective experiences and encounters, many of which unfold far from the laboratory and its rarefied atmosphere. Further, the scientist never completely succeeds in making himself into a pure spectator of the world, for he cannot cease to live in the world as a human among other humans, or as a creature among other creatures, and his scientific concepts and theories necessarily borrow aspects of their character and texture from his untheorized, spontaneously lived experience.

Indeed, the ostensibly "value-free" results of our culture's investigations into biology, physics, and chemistry ultimately come to display themselves in the open and uncertain field of everyday life, whether embedded in social policies with which we must come to terms or embodied in new technologies with which we all must grapple. Thus, the living world—this ambiguous realm that we experience in anger and joy, in grief and in love—is both the soil in which all our sciences are rooted and the rich humus into which their results ultimately return, whether as nutrients or as poisons. Our spontaneous experience of the world, charged with subjective, emotional, and intuitive content, remains the vital and dark ground of all our objectivity.

And yet this ground goes largely unnoticed or unacknowledged in scientific culture. In a society that accords priority to that which is predictable and places a premium on certainty, our spontaneous, preconceptual experience, when acknowledged at all, is referred to as "merely subjective." The fluid realm of direct experience has come to be seen as a secondary, derivative dimension, a mere consequence of events unfolding in the "realer" world of quantifiable and measurable scientific "facts." It is a curious inversion of the actual, demonstrable state of affairs. Subatomic quanta are now taken to be more primordial and "real" than the world we experience with our unaided senses. The living, feeling, and thinking organism is assumed to derive, somehow, from the mechanical body whose reflexes and "systems" have been measured and mapped, the living person now an epiphenomenon of the anatomized corpse. That it takes living, sensing subjects, complete with their enigmatic emotions and unpredictable passions, to conceive of those subatomic fields, or to dissect and anatomize the body, is readily overlooked, or brushed aside as inconsequential.

Nevertheless, the ambiguity of experience is already a part of any phenomenon that draws our attention. For whatever we perceive is necessarily entwined with our own subjectivity, already blended with the dynamism of life and sentience. The living pulse of subjective experience cannot finally be stripped from the things that we study (in order to expose the pure unadulterated "objects") without the things themselves losing all existence for us. Such conundrums are commonly consigned to psychology, to that science that studies subjective awareness and perception. And so perhaps by turning to psychology we can expect to find a recognition and avowal of the pre-objective dimension that permeates and sustains every reality that we know, and hence an understanding of the manner in which subjective experience both supports and sets limits to the positive sciences.

In psychology, however, we discover nothing of the sort. Instead, we find a discipline that is itself modeled on the positivism of the "hard" sciences, a science wherein the psyche has itself been reified into an "object," a thing to be studied like any other thing in the determinate, objective world. Much of cognitive science strives to model the computational processes that ostensibly underlie mental experience. While for Galileo and Descartes perceptual qualities like color and taste were illusory, unreal properties because of their ambiguous and indeterminate character, mathematical indices have at last been found for *these* qualities as well, or rather such qualities are now studied only to the extent that they can be rendered, by whatever process of translation, into *quantities*. Here as elsewhere, the everyday world—the world of our direct, spontaneous experience—is still assumed to derive from an impersonal, objective dimension of pure "facts" that we glimpse only through our instruments and equations.

IT WAS HIS FRUSTRATION WITH SUCH ASSUMPTIONS, AND WITH THE early discipline of psychology—which, far from directing attention toward the fluid region of direct experience, was already at the start of the twentieth century solidifying the "mind" into another "object" in the mathematized and mechanical universe—that led Edmund Husserl to inaugurate the philosophical discipline of phenomenology. Phenomenology, as he articulated it in the early 1900s, would turn toward "the things themselves," toward the world as it is experienced in its felt immediacy. Unlike the mathematics-based sciences, phenomenology would seek not to explain the world, but to describe as closely as possible the way the world makes itself evident to awareness, the way things first arise in our direct, sensorial experience.[2] By thus returning to the taken-for-granted realm of subjective experience, not to explain it but simply to pay attention to its rhythms and textures, not to capture or control it but simply to become familiar with its diverse modes of appearance—and ultimately to give voice to its enigmatic and ever-shifting patterns—phenomenology would articulate the ground of the other sciences. It was Husserl's hope that phenomenology, as a rigorous "science of experience," would establish the other sciences at last upon a firm footing—not, perhaps, as solid as the fixed and finished "object" upon which those sciences *pretend* to stand, but the only basis possible for a knowledge that necessarily emerges from our lived experience of the things around us. In the words of the French phenomenologist Maurice Merleau-Ponty:

> All my knowledge of the world, even my scientific knowledge, is gained from my own particular point of view, or from some experience of the world without which the symbols of science would be meaningless. The whole universe of science is built upon the world as directly experienced, and if we want to subject science itself to rigorous scrutiny and arrive at a precise assessment of its meaning and scope, we must begin by reawakening the basic experience of the world, of which science is the second-order expression. . . . To return to things themselves is to return to that world which precedes knowledge, of which knowledge always *speaks,* and in relation to which every scientific schematization is an abstract and derivative sign-language, as is geography in relation to the countryside in which we have learnt beforehand what a forest, a prairie or a river is.[3]

Intersubjectivity

In the early stages of his project, Husserl spoke of the world of experience (the "phenomenal" world) as a thoroughly subjective realm. In order to explore this realm philosophically, he insisted that it be viewed as a wholly mental dimension, an immaterial field of appearances. That which experiences this dimension—the experiencing self, or subject—was similarly described by Husserl as a pure consciousness, a "transcendental" mind or ego.

Perhaps by designating subjective reality as a nonmaterial, transcendental realm, Husserl hoped to isolate this qualitative dimension from the apparently mechanical world of material "facts" that was then being constructed by the objective sciences (and thus to protect this realm from being colonized by those technological methods of inquiry). Yet his insistence upon the mental character of phenomenal reality led critics to attack Husserl's method as being inherently solipsistic—an approach that seals the philosopher inside his own solitary experience, rendering him ultimately unable to recognize anyone or anything outside of his own mind.

Husserl struggled long and hard to answer this important criticism. How does our subjective experience enable us to recogize the reality of other selves, other experiencing beings? The solution seemed to implicate the body—one's own as well as that of the other—as a singularly important structure within the phenomenal field. The body is that mysterious and multifaceted phenomenon that seems always to accompany one's awareness, and indeed to be the very location of one's awareness within the field of appearances. Yet the phenomenal field also contains many *other* bodies, other forms that move and gesture in a fashion similar to one's own. While one's own body is experienced, as it were, only from within, these other bodies are experienced from outside; one can vary one's distance from these bodies and can move around them, while this is impossible in relation to one's own body.

Despite this difference, Husserl discerned that there was an inescapable affinity, or affiliation, between these other bodies and one's own. The gestures and expressions of these other bodies, viewed from without, echo and resonate one's own bodily movements and gestures, experienced from within. By an associative "empathy," the embodied subject comes to recognize these other bodies as other centers of experience, other subjects.[4]

In this manner, carefully describing the ways in which the subjective field of experience, mediated by the body, opens onto other subjectivities—other selves besides one's own self—Husserl sought to counter the charge of solipsism that had been directed against his phenomenology. The field of appearances, while still a thoroughly subjective realm, was now seen to be inhabited by *multiple* subjectivities; the phenomenal field was no longer the isolate haunt of a solitary ego, but a collective landscape, constituted by other experiencing subjects as well as by oneself.

There remain, however, many phenomena in the experiential field that are not collective or commonly shared. When daydreaming, for example, my attention is carried by phenomena whose

contours and movements I am able to alter at will, a whole phantas-
magoria of images that nevertheless lack the solidity of bodies. Such
forms offer very little resistance to my gaze. They are not, that is,
held in place by gazes other than my own—these are entirely *my* images, *my* phantasies and fears, *my* dreamings. And so I am brought,
like Husserl, to recognize at least two regions of the experiential or
phenomenal field: one of phenomena that unfold entirely for me—
images that arise, as it were, on this side of my body—and another
region of phenomena that are, evidently, responded to and experienced by other embodied subjects as well as by myself. These latter
phenomena are still subjective—they appear to me within a field of
experience colored by my mood and my current concerns—and yet I
cannot alter or dissipate them at will, for they seem to be buttressed
by many involvements besides my own. That tree bending in the
wind, this cliff wall, the cloud drifting overhead: these are not
merely subjective; they are *intersubjective* phenomena—phenomena
experienced by a multiplicity of sensing subjects.

❧

HUSSERL'S NOTION OF *INTERSUBJECTIVITY* SUGGESTED A REMARK-
able new interpretation of the so-called "objective world." For the
conventional contrast between "subjective" and "objective" realities
could now be reframed as a contrast within the subjective field of experience itself—as the felt contrast between subjective and intersubjective phenomena.

The sciences are commonly thought to aim at clear knowledge of
an objective world utterly independent of awareness or subjectivity.
Considered experientially, however, the scientific method enables
the achievement of greater intersubjectivity, greater knowledge of
that which is or can be experienced by many different selves or subjects. The striving for objectivity is thus understood, phenomenologically, as a striving to achieve greater consensus, greater
agreement or consonance among a plurality of subjects, rather than
as an attempt to avoid subjectivity altogether. The pure "objective
reality" commonly assumed by modern science, far from being the
concrete basis underlying all experience, was, according to Husserl,
a theoretical construction, an unwarranted idealization of intersubjective experience.[5]

The "real world" in which we find ourselves, then—the very world our sciences strive to fathom—is not a sheer "object," not a fixed and finished "datum" from which all subjects and subjective qualities could be pared away, but is rather an intertwined matrix of sensations and perceptions, a collective field of experience lived through from many different angles. The mutual inscription of others in my experience, and (as I must assume) of myself in their experiences, effects the interweaving of our individual phenomenal fields into a single, ever-shifting fabric, a single phenomenal world or "reality."

And yet, as we know from our everyday experience, the phenomenal world is remarkably stable and solid; we are able to count on it in so many ways, and we take for granted much of its structure and character. This experienced solidity is precisely sustained by the continual encounter with others, with other embodied subjects, other centers of experience. The encounter with other perceivers continually assures me that there is more to any thing, or to the world, than I myself can perceive at any moment. Besides that which I directly see of a particular oak tree or building, I know or intuit that there are also those facets of the oak or building that are visible to the other perceivers that I see. I sense that that tree is much more than what I directly see of it, since it is also what the others whom I see perceive of it; I sense that as a perceivable presence it already existed before I came to look at it, and indeed that it will not dissipate when I turn away from it, since it remains an experience for others—not just for other persons, but (as we shall see later in this chapter) for other sentient organisms, for the birds that nest in its branches and for the insects that move along its bark, and even, finally, for the sensitive cells and tissues of the oak itself, quietly drinking sunlight through its leaves. It is this informing of my perceptions by the evident perceptions and sensations of other bodily entities that establishes, for me, the relative solidity and stability of the world.

The Life-world

Although Husserl at first wrote of the nonmaterial, mental character of experienced reality, his growing recognition of intersubjective experience, and of the body's importance for such experience, ultimately led him to recognize a more primary, corporeal dimension, midway between the transcendental "consciousness" of his earlier analyses and the utterly objective "matter" assumed by the natural sciences. This was the intersubjective world of life, the *Lebenswelt,* or "life-world."

The life-world is the world of our immediately lived experience, *as* we live it, prior to all our thoughts about it. It is that which is present to us in our everyday tasks and enjoyments—reality as it engages us before being analyzed by our theories and our science. The life-world is the world that we count on without necessarily paying it much attention, the world of the clouds overhead and the ground underfoot, of getting out of bed and preparing food and turning on the tap for water. Easily overlooked, this primordial world is always already there when we begin to reflect or philosophize. It is not a private, but a collective, dimension—the common field of our lives and the other lives with which ours are entwined—and yet it is profoundly ambiguous and indeterminate, since our experience of this field is always relative to our situation within it. The life-world is thus the world as we organically experience it in its enigmatic multiplicity and open-endedness, prior to conceptually freezing it into a static space of "facts"—prior, indeed, to conceptualizing it in any complete fashion. All of our concepts and representations, scientific and otherwise, necessarily draw nourishment from this indeterminate realm, as the physicist analyzing data is still nourished by the air that she is breathing, by the feel of the chair that supports her and the light flooding in through the window, without her being particularly conscious of these participations.

The life-world is thus peripherally present in any thought or activity we undertake. Yet whenever we attempt to *explain* this world conceptually, we seem to forget our active participation within it. Striving to represent the world, we inevitably forfeit its direct presence. It was Husserl's genius to realize that the assumption of objectivity had led to an almost total eclipse of the life-world in the modern era, to a nearly complete forgetting of this living dimension in which all of our endeavors are rooted. In their striving to attain a finished blueprint of the world, the sciences had become frightfully estranged from our direct human experience. Their many specialized and technical discourses had lost any obvious relevance to the sensuous world of our ordinary engagements. The consequent impoverishment of language, the loss of a common discourse tuned to the qualitative nuances of living experience, was leading, Husserl felt, to a clear crisis in European civilization. Oblivious to the quality-laden life-world upon which they themselves depend for their own meaning and existence, the Western sciences, and the technologies that accompany them, were beginning to blindly overrun the experiential world—even, in their errancy, threatening to obliterate the world-of-life entirely.[6]

IT SHOULD BE EVIDENT THAT THE LIFE-WORLD MAY BE QUITE different for different cultures. The world that a people experiences and comes to count on is deeply influenced by the ways they live and engage that world. The members of any given culture necessarily inhabit an experienced world very different from that of another culture with a very different language and way of life. Even the scientifically disclosed "objective universe" of contemporary Western civilization cannot genuinely be separated from the particular institutions, technologies, and ways of life endemic to this society since the seventeenth century.

If the worlds experienced by humans are so diverse, how much more diverse, still, must be the life-worlds of other animals—of wolves, or owls, or a community of bees! And yet, despite this multiplicity, it would seem that there are basic structures of the life-world that are shared, elements that are common to different cultures and even, we may suspect, to different species. Husserl's writings seem to suggest that the life-world has various layers, that underneath the layer of the diverse cultural life-worlds there reposes a deeper, more unitary life-world, always already there beneath all our cultural acquisitions, a vast and continually overlooked dimension of experience that nevertheless supports and sustains all our diverse and discontinuous worldviews.

Husserl sheds light on this most primordial, most deeply intersubjective dimension of the life-world in a series of notes written in 1934. The notes describe a set of phenomenological investigations into the contemporary understanding of *space*. Underneath the modern, scientific conception of space as a mathematically infinite and homogenous void, Husserl discloses the experienced spatiality of the *earth* itself. The encompassing earth, he suggests, provides the most immediate, bodily awareness of space, from which all later *conceptions* of space are derived.[7] While according to contemporary physics the earth is but one celestial body among many others "in" space, phenomenologically considered *all* bodies (including our own) are first located relative to the ground of the earth, whereas the earth itself is not "in" space, since it is earth that, from the first, *provides* space. To our most immediate sensorial experience, "bodies are given as having the sense of being earthly bodies, and space is given as having the sense of being earth-space."[8] Further, while contemporary science maintains that "in reality" the earth is in motion (around its own axis, and around the sun), Husserl maintains that the very concepts of "motion" and "rest" derive all their meaning from our primary, bodily experience of being in motion or at rest relative to the "absolute" rest of the "earth-basis."

Husserl's notes on these matters were found in an envelope on which he had written a few summary words: *"Overthrow of the Copernican Theory* . . . The original ark, earth, does not move."[9] Such a remarkable assertion illustrates well the radical nature of Husserl's thought. He suggests in these notes that there is a profound instability in the scientific worldview, resulting from the continual clash between our scientific convictions and our spontaneous experience. After the investigations of Copernicus, Kepler, and Galileo, the sun came to be conceived as the center of the phenomenal world. Yet this conception simply did not agree with our spontaneous sensory *perception,* which remained the experience of a radiant orb traversing the sky of a stable earth. A profound schism was thus brought about between our intellectual convictions and the most basic conviction of our senses, between our mental *concepts* and our bodily *percepts.* (Descartes's philosophical disjunction of

the mind from the body was surely prompted by this already existing state of affairs—it was necessary, for the maintenance of the new,
Copernican worldview, that the rational intellect hold itself apart
from the experiencing body.) Nevertheless, our very words have
continued to betray the intellect and to prevent the clean ascendancy
of the Copernican system: we still say "the sun rises" and "the sun
sets" whether we are farmers or physicists. It is in this sense, writing
from the perspective of the experiencing body, that Husserl is able to
claim that *earth,* "the original ark," *does not move.*

Finally, Husserl seems to suggest that the earth lies at the heart of
our notions of time as well as of space. He writes of the earth as our
"primitive home" and our "primitive history." Every unique cultural history is but an episode in this larger story; every culturally
constructed notion of time presupposes our deep history as carnal
beings present to a single earth.[10]

The earth is thus, for Husserl, the secret depth of the life-world.
It is the most unfathomable region of experience, an enigma that exceeds the structurations of any particular culture or language. In his
words, the earth is the encompassing "ark of the world," the common "root basis" of all relative life-worlds. Husserl's late insights
into the importance of the earth for all human cognition were, as we
shall see, to have profound implications for the subsequent unfolding of phenomenological philosophy.

✦

EDMUND HUSSERL'S WORK WAS IN NO SENSE A REJECTION OF SCI-
ence. It was a plea that science, for its own integrity and meaning-
fulness, must acknowledge that it is rooted in the same world that we
all engage in our everyday lives and with our unaided senses—that,
for all its technological refinements, quantitative science remains an
expression of, and hence must be guided by, the qualitative world
of our common experience. The true task of phenomenology, as
Husserl saw it at the end of his career, lay in the careful demonstration of the manner in which every theoretical and scientific practice
grows out of and remains supported by the forgotten ground of our
directly felt and lived experience, and has value and meaning only in
reference to this primordial and open realm.

Originally an attempt to certify theoretical awareness by placing it on a firm footing, Husserl's project culminated in the still ongoing attempt to rejuvenate the full-blooded world of our sensorial experience, and, consequently, in the dawning recognition of Earth as the forgotten basis of all our awareness.

I now turn to the work of the phenomenologist Maurice Merleau-Ponty, in order to show how Husserl's legacy was taken up and transformed in a manner that endowed this philosophy with a particular power and relevance for the ecological questions that now confront us.

PART II: MAURICE MERLEAU-PONTY AND THE PARTICIPATORY NATURE OF PERCEPTION

Maurice Merleau-Ponty set out to radicalize Husserl's phenomenology, both by clarifying the inconsistencies lodged in this philosophy by Husserl's own ambivalences, and further, by disclosing a more eloquent way of speaking, a style of language which, by virtue of its fluidity, its carnal resonance, and its careful avoidance of abstract terms, might itself draw us into the sensuous depths of the life-world.

The Mindful Life of the Body

We have seen, for instance, that the physical body came to play an increasingly important role in Husserl's philosophy. Only by acknowledging the embodied nature of the experiencing self was Husserl able to avoid the pitfalls of solipsism. It is as visible, animate bodies that other selves or subjects make themselves evident in my subjective experience, and it is only as a body that I am visible and sensible to others. The body is precisely my insertion in the common, or intersubjective, field of experience.

Nevertheless, the body remained a mere appearance, albeit a

unique and pivotal one, in Husserl's thought. The body was, to be sure, the very locus of the experiencing subject, or self, in the phenomenal world—in the manifold of appearances—but the self was still affirmed, by Husserl, as a transcendental ego, ultimately separable from the phenomena (including the body) that it posits and ponders. Despite his growing recognition of the living body's centrality in all experience, and despite his disclosure of the thoroughly incarnate, intersubjective realm of our preconceptual life, Husserl was unable to drop the transcendental, idealist aspirations of his early philosophy.

It is precisely this lingering assumption of a self-subsistent, disembodied, transcendental ego that Merleau-Ponty rejects. If this body is my very presence in the world, if it is the body that alone enables me to enter into relations with other presences, if without these eyes, this voice, or these hands I would be unable to see, to taste, and to touch things, or to be touched by them—if without this body, in other words, there would be no possibility of experience—then the body itself is the true subject of experience. Merleau-Ponty begins, then, by identifying the subject—the experiencing "self"—with the bodily organism.

It is indeed a radical move. Most of us are accustomed to consider the self, our innermost essence, as something incorporeal. Yet consider: Without this body, without this tongue or these ears, you could neither speak nor hear another's voice. Nor could you have anything to speak about, or even to reflect on, or to think, since without any contact, any encounter, without any glimmer of sensory experience, there could be nothing to question or to know. The living body is thus the very possibility of contact, not just with others but with oneself—the very possibility of reflection, of thought, of knowledge. The common notion of the experiencing self, or mind, as an immaterial phantom ultimately independent of the body can only be a mirage: Merleau-Ponty invites us to recognize, at the heart of even our most abstract cogitations, the sensuous and sentient life of the body itself.

This breathing body, as it experiences and inhabits the world, is very different from that objectified body diagrammed in physiology textbooks, with its separable "systems" (the circulatory system, the digestive system, the respiratory system, etc.) laid bare on each page.

The body I here speak of is very different from the body we have been taught to see and even to feel, very different, finally, from that complex machine whose broken parts or stuck systems are diagnosed by our medical doctors and "repaired" by our medical technologies. Underneath the anatomized and mechanical body that we have learned to conceive, prior indeed to all our conceptions, dwells the body as it actually experiences things, this poised and animate power that initiates all our projects and suffers all our passions.

The living, attentive body—which Merleau-Ponty called the "body subject"—is this very being that, pondering a moment ago, suddenly took up this pen and scribbled these thoughts. It is the very power I have to look and to see things, or to turn away and look elsewhere, the ability to cry and to laugh, or to howl at night with the wolves, to find and gather food whether in a forest or a market, the power to walk upon the ground and to imbibe the swirling air. Yet "I" do not deploy these powers like a commander piloting a ship, for I am, in my depths, indistinguishable from them, as my sadness is indistinguishable from a certain heaviness of my bodily limbs, or as my delight is only artificially separable from the widening of my eyes, from the bounce in my step and the heightened sensitivity of my skin. Indeed, facial expressions, gestures, and spontaneous utterances like sighs and cries seem to immediately incarnate feelings, moods, and desires without "my" being able to say which came first—the corporeal gesture or its purportedly "immaterial" counterpart.

To acknowledge that "I am this body" is not to reduce the mystery of my yearnings and fluid thoughts to a set of mechanisms, or my "self" to a determinate robot. Rather it is to affirm the uncanniness of this physical form. It is not to lock up awareness within the density of a closed and bounded object, for as we shall see, the boundaries of a living body are open and indeterminate; more like membranes than barriers, they define a surface of metamorphosis and exchange. The breathing, sensing body draws its sustenance and its very substance from the soils, plants, and elements that surround it; it continually contributes itself, in turn, to the air, to the composting earth, to the nourishment of insects and oak trees and squirrels, ceaselessly spreading out of itself as well as breathing the world into itself, so that it is very difficult to discern, at any moment, precisely where this living body begins and where it ends. Considered phenomenologically—that is, as we actually experience and *live* it—the body is a creative, shape-shifting entity. Certainly, it has its finite character and style, its unique textures and temperaments that distinguish it from other bodies; yet these mortal limits in no way close me off from the things around me or render my relations to them wholly predictable and determinate. On the contrary, my finite bodily presence alone is what enables me to freely engage the things around me, to choose to affiliate with certain persons or places, to insinuate myself in other lives. Far from restricting my access to things and to the world, the body is my very means of entering into relation with all things.

To be sure, by disclosing the body itself as the very subject of awareness, Merleau-Ponty demolishes any hope that philosophy might eventually provide a complete picture of reality (for any such total account of "what is" requires a mind or consciousness that stands somehow *outside* of existence, whether to compile the account or, finally, to receive and comprehend it). Yet by this same move he opens, at last, the possibility of a truly authentic phenomenology, a philosophy which would strive, not to explain the world as if from outside, but to give voice to the world from our experienced situation *within* it, recalling us to our participation in the here-and-now, rejuvenating our sense of wonder at the fathomless things, events and powers that surround us on every hand.[11]

ULTIMATELY, TO ACKNOWLEDGE THE LIFE OF THE BODY, AND TO affirm our solidarity with this physical form, is to acknowledge our existence as one of the earth's animals, and so to remember and rejuvenate the organic basis of our thoughts and our intelligence. According to the central current of the Western philosophical tradition, from its source in ancient Athens up until the present moment, human beings alone are possessed of an incorporeal intellect, a "rational soul" or mind which, by virtue of its affinity with an eternal or divine dimension outside the bodily world, sets us radically apart from, or above, all other forms of life. In Aristotle's writings, for instance, while plants are endowed with a *vegetal soul* (which enables nourishment, growth, and reproduction), and while animals possess, in addition to the vegetal soul, an *animal soul* (which provides sensation and locomotion), these souls remain inseparable from the earthly world of generation and decay. Humans, however, possess along with these other souls a *rational soul,* or intellect, which alone provides access to the less corruptible spheres and has affinities with the divine "Unmoved Mover" himself. In Descartes's hands, two thousand years later, this hierarchical continuum of living forms, commonly called "the Great Chain of Being," was polarized into a thorough dichotomy between mechanical, unthinking matter (including all minerals, plants, and animals, as well as the human body) and pure, thinking mind (the exclusive province of humans and God). Since humans alone are a mixture of extended matter and thinking mind, we alone are able to feel and to experience our body's mechanical sensations. Meanwhile, all other organisms, consisting solely of extended matter, are in truth nothing more than automatons, incapable of actual experience, unable to feel pleasure or suffer pain. Hence, we humans need have no scruples about manipulating, exploiting, or experimenting upon other animals in any manner we see fit.

Curiously, such arguments for human specialness have regularly been utilized by human groups to justify the exploitation not just of other organisms, but of other *humans* as well (other nations, other races, or simply the "other" sex); armed with such arguments, one had only to demonstrate that these others were not *fully* human, or were "closer to the animals," in order to establish one's right of dominion. According to Aristotle, for example, women are deficient in the rational soul, and hence "the relation of male to female is naturally that of the superior to the inferior—of the ruling to the ruled."[12] Such justifications for social exploitation draw their force from the prior hierarchicalization of the natural landscape, from that hierarchical ordering that locates "humans," by virtue of our incorporeal intellect, above and apart from all other, "merely corporeal," entities.

Such hierarchies are wrecked by any phenomenology that takes seriously our immediate sensory experience. For our senses disclose to us a wild-flowering proliferation of entities and elements, in which humans are thoroughly immersed. While this diversity of sensuous forms certainly displays some sort of reckless order, we find ourselves in the midst of, rather than on top of, this order. We may cast our gaze downward to watch the field mice and the insects that creep along the bending grasses, or to glimpse the snakes that slither into hollows deep underfoot, yet, at the same moment, hawks soaring on great winds gaze down upon *our* endeavors. Melodious feathered beings flit like phantoms among the high branches of the trees, while other animate powers, known only by their traces, move within the hidden depths of the forest. In the waters that surge in waves against the distant edge of the land, still stranger powers, multihued and silent, move in crowds among alien forests of coral and stone. . . . Does the human intellect, or "reason," really spring us free from our inherence in the depths of this wild proliferation of forms? *Or on the contrary, is the human intellect rooted in, and secretly borne by, our forgotten contact with the multiple nonhuman shapes that surround us?*

The Body's Silent Conversation with Things

For Merleau-Ponty, all of the creativity and free-ranging mobility that we have come to associate with the human intellect is, in truth, an elaboration, or recapitulation, of a profound creativity already underway at the most immediate level of sensory perception. The sensing body is not a programmed machine but an active and open form, continually improvising its relation to things and to the world. The body's actions and engagements are never wholly determinate, since they must ceaselessly adjust themselves to a world and a terrain that is itself continually shifting. If the body were truly a set of closed or predetermined mechanisms, it could never come into gen-uine contact with anything outside of itself, could never perceive anything really new, could never be genuinely startled or surprised. All of its experiences, and all its responses, would already have been anticipated from the beginning, already programmed, as it were, into the machine. But could we even, then, call them experiences? For is not experience, or more precisely, *perception,* the constant thwarting of such closure?

Consider a spider weaving its web, for instance, and the assumption still held by many scientists that the behavior of such a diminutive creature is thoroughly "programmed in its genes." Certainly, the spider has received a rich genetic inheritance from its parents and its predecessors. Whatever "instructions," however, are enfolded within the living genome, they can hardly predict the specifics of the microterrain within which the spider may find itself at any particular moment. They could hardly have determined in advance the exact distances between the cave wall and the branch that the spider is now employing as an anchorage point for her current web, or the exact strength of the monsoon rains that make web-spinning a bit more difficult on this evening. And so the genome could not explicitly have commanded the order of every flexion and extension of her various limbs as she weaves this web into its place. However complex are the inherited "programs," patterns, or predispositions, they must still be adapted to the immediate situation in which the spider finds itself. However determinate one's genetic inheritance, it must still, as it were, be woven into the present, an activity that necessarily involves both a receptivity to the specific shapes and textures of that present and a spontaneous creativity in adjusting oneself (and one's inheritance) to those contours. It is this open activity, this dynamic blend of receptivity and creativity by which every animate organism necessarily orients itself to the world (and orients the world around itself), that we speak of by the term "perception."

BUT LET US NOW PONDER THE EVENT OF PERCEPTION AS WE OURselves experience and live it. The human body with its various predilections is, to be sure, our *own* inheritance, our own rootedness in an evolutionary history and a particular ancestry. Yet it is also our insertion in a world that exceeds our grasp in every direction, our means of contact with things and lives that are still unfolding, open and indeterminate, all around us. Indeed, from the perspective of my bodily senses, there is no thing that appears as a completely determinate or finished object. Each thing, each entity that my body sees, presents some face or facet of itself to my gaze while withholding other aspects from view.

The clay bowl resting on the table in front of me meets my eyes with its curved and grainy surface. Yet I can only see one side of that surface—the other side of the bowl is invisible, hidden by the side that faces me. In order to view that other side, I must pick up the bowl and turn it around in my hands, or else walk around the wooden table. Yet, having done so, I can no longer see the first side of the bowl. Surely I know that it still exists; I can even *feel* the presence of that aspect which the bowl now presents to the lamp on the far side of the table. Yet I myself am simply unable to see the whole of this bowl all at once.

Moreover, while examining its outer surface I have caught only a glimpse of the smooth and finely glazed *inside* of the bowl. When I stand up to look down into that interior, which gleams with curved reflections from the skylight overhead, I can no longer see the unglazed outer surface. This earthen vessel thus reveals aspects of its presence to me only by withholding other aspects of itself for further exploration. There can be no question of ever totally exhausting the presence of the bowl with my perception; its very existence as a bowl ensures that there are dimensions wholly inaccessible to me—most obviously the patterns hidden *between* its glazed and unglazed surfaces, the interior density of its clay body. If I break it into pieces, in hopes of discovering these interior patterns or the delicate structure of its molecular dimensions, I will have destroyed its integrity as a bowl; far from coming to know it completely, I will simply have wrecked any possibility of coming to know it further, having traded the relation between myself and the bowl for a relation to a collection of fragments.

Even a single facet of this bowl resists being plumbed by my gaze once and for all. For, like myself, the bowl is a temporal being, an entity shifting and changing in time, although the rhythm of its changes may be far slower than my own. Each time that I return to gaze at the outward surface of the bowl, my eyes and my mood have shifted, however slightly; informed by my previous encounters with the bowl, my senses now more attuned to its substance, I continually discover new and unexpected aspects. But this is in part because the bowl has changed as well, as a result perhaps of shifts in the light pouring through the window, of dust and of wear—as a result, even, of my own earlier explorations. When I look now at its unglazed outer surface, where before I had seen a homogeneous expanse of bright grey, I now see various faint smudges, some of them ancient and some of them recent—the record of the many hands that have held it through the seasons. Each spot invites me to peer at it more closely, to distinguish that smudge from the others, to try to discern which are the traces of my own hands, and which are of hands larger, or more delicate, and which may be the trace even of those hands that first threw this fine and useful bowl on some potter's wheel years ago.

As this bowl awaits the further involvement of my eyes and my hands, so also every other object in this room invites the participation of my senses—the wooden dresser with its stuffed drawers, the plants on the windowsill quietly turning toward the sun, the individual glasses and dishes stashed above the old sink with its hidden and clattering pipes, and the ancient pinewood table that I now write upon, its coffee stains and countless knife scratches cutting across the curving grain of the wood, and those pens and pencils that beckon to my fingers, and the books that call to me from the shelves, one always asking to be read more deeply, another chanting to me of my childhood, another merely waiting, coldly it seems, to be returned to the library. Like the bowl, each presence presents some facet that catches my eye while the rest of it lies hidden behind the horizon of my current position, each one inviting me to focus my senses upon it, to let the other objects fall into the background as I enter into its particular depth. When my body thus responds to the mute solicitation of another being, that being responds in turn, disclosing to my senses some new aspect or dimension that in turn invites further exploration. By this process my sensing body gradually attunes itself to the style of this other presence—to the *way* of this stone, or tree, or table—as the other seems to adjust itself to my own style and sensitivity. In this manner the simplest thing may become a world for me, as, conversely, the thing or being comes to take its place more deeply in *my* world.

Perception, in Merleau-Ponty's work, is precisely this reciprocity, the ongoing interchange between my body and the entities that surround it. It is a sort of silent conversation that I carry on with things, a continuous dialogue that unfolds far below my verbal awareness—and often, even, *independent* of my verbal awareness, as when my hand readily navigates the space between these scribed pages and the coffee cup across the table without my having to think about it, or when my legs, hiking, continually attune and adjust themselves to the varying steepness of the mountain slopes behind this house without my verbal consciousness needing to direct those adjustments. Whenever I quiet the persistent chatter of words within my head, I find this silent or wordless dance always already going on— this improvised duet between my animal body and the fluid, breathing landscape that it inhabits.

The Animateness of the Perceptual World

Where does perception originate? I cannot say truthfully that my perception of a particular wildflower, with its color and its fragrance, is determined or "caused" entirely by the flower—since other persons may experience a somewhat different fragrance, as even I, in a different moment or mood, may see the color differently, and indeed since any bumblebee that alights on that blossom will surely have a very different perception of it than I do. But neither can I say truthfully that my perception is "caused" solely by myself—by my physiological or neural organization—or that it exists entirely "in my head." For without the actual existence of this other entity, of this flower rooted not in my brain but in the soil of the earth, there would be no fragrant and colorful perception at all, neither for myself nor for any others, whether human or insect.

Neither the perceiver nor the perceived, then, is wholly passive in the event of perception:

[M]y gaze pairs off with colour, and my hand with hardness and softness, and in this transaction between the subject of sensation and the sensible it cannot be held that one acts while the other suffers the action, or that one confers significance on the other. Apart from the probing of my eye or my hand, and before my body synchronizes with it, the sensible is nothing but a vague beckoning.[13]

There is thus a solicitation of my body by the sensible, and a questioning of the sensible by my body, a reciprocal encroachment:

> . . . [a sensible quality, like the color blue,] which is on the point of being felt sets a kind of muddled problem for my body to solve. I must find the attitude which will provide it with the means of becoming determinate, of showing up as blue; I must find the reply to a question which is obscurely expressed. And yet I do so only when I am invited by it; my attitude is never sufficient to make me really see blue or really touch a hard surface. The sensible gives back to me what I lent to it, but this is only what I took from it in the first place. As I contemplate the blue of the sky . . . I abandon myself to it and plunge into this mystery, it 'thinks itself within me,' I am the sky itself as it is drawn together and unified, and as it begins to exist for itself; my consciousness is saturated with this limitless blue. . . .[14]

In the act of perception, in other words, I enter into a sympathetic relation with the perceived, which is possible only because neither my body nor the sensible exists outside the flux of time, and so each has its own dynamism, its own pulsation and style. Perception, in this sense, is an attunement or synchronization between my own rhythms and the rhythms of the things themselves, their own tones and textures:

> . . . in so far as my hand knows hardness and softness, and my gaze knows the moon's light, it is as a certain way of linking up with the phenomenon and communicating with it. Hardness and softness, roughness and smoothness, moonlight and sunlight, present themselves in our recollection not pre-eminently as sensory contents but as certain kinds of symbioses, certain ways the outside has of invading us and certain ways we have of meeting this invasion. . . .[15]

In this ceaseless dance between the carnal subject and its world, at one moment the body leads, at another the things. In one luminous passage, which suggests the profound intimacy of the body's preconceptual relation to the sensible things or powers that surround it, Merleau-Ponty writes of perception in terms of an almost magical invocation enacted by the body, and the body's subsequent "possession" by the perceived:

> The relations of sentient to sensible are comparable with those of the sleeper to his slumber: sleep suddenly comes when a certain voluntary attitude suddenly receives from outside the confirmation for which it was waiting. I am breathing deeply and slowly in order to summon sleep, and suddenly it is as if my mouth were connected to some great lung outside myself which alternately calls forth and forces back my breath. A certain rhythm of respiration, which a moment ago I voluntarily maintained, now becomes my very being, and sleep, until now aimed at . . . , suddenly becomes my situation. In the same way I give ear, or look, in the expectation of a sensation, and suddenly the sensible takes possession of my ear or my gaze, and I surrender a part of my body, even my whole body, to this particular manner of vibrating and filling space known as blue or red. . . .[16]

What are we to make of these strange ways of speaking? In these and other passages throughout Merleau-Ponty's major work, *Phenomenology of Perception,* the sensible thing, commonly considered by our philosophical tradition to be passive and inert, is consistently described in the active voice: the sensible "beckons to me," "sets a problem for my body to solve," "responds" to my summons and "takes possession of my senses," and even "thinks itself within me." The sensible world, in other words, is described as active, animate, and, in some curious manner, alive: it is not I, when asleep, who breathes, but "some great lung outside myself which alternately calls forth and forces back my breath"; a color is "a manner of vibrating and filling space"; a thing is an "entity," an "Other" which at one moment "holds itself aloof from us" and at another moment actively "expresses itself" directly to our senses, so that we may ultimately describe perception as a mutual interaction, an intercourse, "a coition, so to speak, of my body with things."[17]

Are such animistic turns of phrase to be attributed simply to some sort of poetic license that Merleau-Ponty has introduced into his philosophy? Are they evidence, that is, merely of an idiosyncratic style of writing, as some critics have asserted? I think not. Merleau-Ponty writes of the perceived things as entities, of sensible qualities as powers, and of the sensible itself as a field of animate presences, in order to acknowledge and underscore their active, dynamic contribution to perceptual experience. To describe the animate life of particular things is simply the most precise and parsimonious way to articulate the things *as we spontaneously experience them,* prior to all our conceptualizations and definitions.

Our most immediate experience of things, according to Merleau-Ponty, is necessarily an experience of reciprocal encounter—of tension, communication, and commingling. From within the depths of this encounter, we know the thing or phenomenon only as our interlocutor—as a dynamic presence that confronts us and draws us into relation. We conceptually immobilize or objectify the phenomenon only by mentally absenting ourselves from this relation, by forgetting or repressing our sensuous involvement. To define another being as an inert or passive object is to deny its ability to actively engage us and to provoke our senses; *we thus block our perceptual reciprocity with that being.* By linguistically defining the surrounding world as a determinate set of objects, we cut our conscious, speaking selves off from the spontaneous life of our sensing bodies.

If, on the other hand, we wish to describe a particular phenomenon without repressing our direct experience, then we cannot avoid speaking of the phenomenon as an active, animate entity with which we find ourselves engaged. It is for this reason that Merleau-Ponty so consistently uses the active voice to describe things, qualities, and even the enveloping world itself. To the sensing body, *no* thing presents itself as utterly passive or inert. *Only by affirming the animateness of perceived things do we allow our words to emerge directly from the depths of our ongoing reciprocity with the world.*

Perception as Participation

If we wish to choose a single term to characterize the event of perception, as it is disclosed by phenomenological attention, we may borrow the term "participation," used by the early French anthropologist Lucien Lévy-Bruhl. The brilliant forerunner of today's "cognitive" and "symbolic" schools of anthropology, Lévy-Bruhl used the word "participation" to characterize the animistic logic of indigenous, oral peoples—for whom ostensibly "inanimate" objects like stones or mountains are often thought to be alive, for whom certain names, spoken aloud, may be felt to influence at a distance the things or beings that they name, for whom particular plants, particular animals, particular places and persons and powers may all be felt to *participate* in one another's existence, influencing each other and being influenced in turn.[18]

For Lévy-Bruhl participation was thus a perceived relation between diverse phenomena; Merleau-Ponty's work, however, suggests that participation is a defining attribute of perception itself. By asserting that perception, phenomenologically considered, is inherently participatory, we mean that perception always involves, at its most intimate level, the experience of an active interplay, or coupling, between the perceiving body and that which it perceives. Prior to all our verbal reflections, at the level of our spontaneous, sensorial engagement with the world around us, we are *all* animists.

SOME INSIGHT INTO THE PARTICIPATORY NATURE OF PERCEPTION may be gleaned by considering the craft of the sleight-of-hand magician. For the conjuror depends upon this active participation between the body and the world for the creation of his magic. Working, for instance, with a silver dollar, he uses his sleights to enhance the animation of the object, generating ambiguous gaps and lacunae in the visible trajectory of the coin. The spectators' eyes, already drawn by the coin's fluid dance across the magician's fingers, spontaneously fill in those gaps with impossible events, and it is this spontaneous involvement of the spectators' own senses that enables the coin to vanish and reappear, or to pass through the magician's hand.

After flourishing a silver dollar in my right hand, for example, spinning it a few times to catch the audience's attention, I may suddenly hide that coin behind the hand, clipping it between two fingers so that it is no longer visible to their gaze. If, an instant later, I reach into the air on the other side of my body with my left hand, and bring into view *another* silver dollar that had been clipped behind *that* hand, the audience will commonly perceive something quite wondrous. They will *not* perceive that one coin has been momentarily hidden while a wholly different coin, in another place, has been brought out of hiding, although this would surely be the most obvious and rational interpretation. Rather, they will perceive that a single coin, having vanished from my right hand, has traveled invisibly through the air and reappeared in my left hand! For the perceiving body does not calculate logical probabilities; it gregariously participates in the activity of the world, lending its imagination to things in order to see them more fully. The invisible journey of the coin is contributed, quite spontaneously, by the promiscuous creativity of the senses. The magician induces us to assist in the metamorphosis of his objects, and then startles us with what we ourselves have created!

From the magician's, or the phenomenologist's, perspective, that which we call *imagination* is from the first an attribute of the senses themselves; imagination is not a separate mental faculty (as we so often assume) but is rather the way the senses themselves have of throwing themselves beyond what is immediately given, in order to make tentative contact with the other sides of things that we do not sense directly, with the hidden or invisible aspects of the sensible. And yet such sensory anticipations and projections are not arbitrary; they regularly respond to suggestions offered by the sensible itself. The magician, for instance, may make the magic palpable for the audience by following the invisible coin's journey with the focus of his own eyes, and by imaginatively "feeling" the coin depart from the one hand and arrive in the palm of the other; the audience's senses, responding to subtle shifts in the magician's body as well as to the coin, will then find the effect irresistible. In other words, it is when the magician lets *himself* be captured by the magic that his audience will be most willing to join him.

Of course, there are those few who simply will not see any magic, either at a performance or in the world at large; armored with count-less explanations and analyses, they "see" only how the trick must have been accomplished. Commonly, they will claim to have "caught sight of the wires," or to have seen me clandestinely "throw the coin into the other hand" although I myself have done no such thing. En-couraged by a cultural discourse that disdains the unpredictable and puts a premium on detached objectivity, such persons attempt to halt the participation of their senses in the phenomenon. Yet they can do so only by imaginatively projecting other phenomena (wires, or threads, or mirrors), or by looking away.

In truth, since the act of perception is always open-ended and un-finished, we are never wholly locked into any particular instance of participation. As the spectator can turn away from the magician's magic, we are always somewhat free to break our participation with any particular phenomenon. It is thus that, caught up in contempla-tion of a blade of grass, I may nevertheless shift my attention to the grove of trees nearby, or my focus may suddenly be usurped by a fly that lands upon my nose. Similarly, we may readily break our fasci-nation with a television commercial in order to notice how it plays upon our emotions and our desires. But we suspend this participa-tion only on behalf of other participations already going on—with the other persons in the room, with the hard and uncomfortable chair on which we sit, with our own thoughts and analyses. We al-ways retain the ability to alter or suspend any particular instance of participation. Yet we can never suspend the flux of participation itself.

Synaesthesia—The Fusion of the Senses

Until now we have spoken of perception in primarily visual terms. Yet perception involves touching as well, and hearing and smelling and tasting. By the term "perception" we mean the concerted activ-ity of *all* the body's senses as they function and flourish together. In-deed, if I attend closely to my nonverbal experience of the shifting landscape that surrounds me, I must acknowledge that the so-called separate senses are thoroughly blended with one another, and it is only after the fact that I am able to step back and isolate the specific contributions of my eyes, my ears, and my skin. As soon as I attempt to distinguish the share of any one sense from that of the others, I inevitably sever the full participation of my sensing body with the sensuous terrain.

When, for instance, I perceive the wind surging through the branches of an aspen tree, I am unable, at first, to distinguish the sight of those trembling leaves from their delicate whispering. My muscles, too, feel the torsion as those branches bend, ever so slightly, in the surge, and this imbues the encounter with a certain tactile tension. The encounter is influenced, as well, by the fresh smell of the autumn wind, and even by the taste of an apple that still lingers on my tongue.

Yet already, in this brief attempt to acknowledge the contribution of the various senses, I have had to remove myself from that "primary layer of sense experience that precedes its division among the separate senses."[19] Although contemporary neuroscientists study "synaesthesia"—the overlap and blending of the senses—as though it were a rare or pathological experience to which only certain persons are prone (those who report "seeing sounds," "hearing colors," and the like), our primordial, preconceptual experience, as Merleau-Ponty makes evident, is *inherently* synaesthetic. The intertwining of sensory modalities seems unusual to us only to the extent that we have become estranged from our direct experience (and hence from our primordial contact with the entities and elements that surround us):

> . . . Synaesthetic perception is the rule, and we are unaware of it only because scientific knowledge shifts the center of gravity of experience, so that we have unlearned how to see, hear, and generally speaking, feel, in order to deduce, from our bodily organization and the world as the *physicist* conceives it, what we are to see, hear, and feel.[20]

Nevertheless, we still speak of "cool" or "warm" colors, of "loud" clothing, of "hard" or "brittle" sounds. The speaking body readily transposes qualities from one sensory domain into another, according to a logic we easily understand but cannot easily explain.

Many Westerners become conscious of this overlapping of the senses only when their allegiance to the presumably impartial, analytic logic of their culture temporarily breaks down. Merleau-Ponty discusses the effect upon European researchers of mescaline, the psychoactive component of the peyote cactus, a plant traditionally used in ceremonial practice by indigenous tribes in Mexico and North America:

> The influence of mescalin, by weakening the attitude of impartiality and surrendering the subject to his vitality, should [if we are correct] favor forms of synaesthetic experience. And indeed, under mescalin, the sound of a flute gives a bluish-green colour, [and] the tick of a metronome, in darkness, is translated as grey patches, the spatial intervals between them corresponding to the intervals of time between the ticks, the size of the patch to the loudness of the tick, and its height to the pitch of the sound. A subject under mescalin finds a piece of iron, strikes the window-sill with it and exclaims: "This is magic"; the trees are growing greener. . . . Seen in the perspective of the objective [Cartesian] world, with its opaque qualities, the phenomenon of synaesthetic experience is paradoxical. . . .[21]

Seen, however, from the perspective of the life-world—from the perspective, that is, of our pretheoretical awareness—such experiences are recognized as amplifications or intensifications of quite ordinary phenomena that are always going on.

This is not to deny that the senses are distinct modalities. It is to assert that they are divergent modalities of a single and unitary living body, that they are complementary powers evolved in complex interdependence with one another. Each sense is a unique modality of this body's existence, yet in the activity of perception these divergent modalities necessarily intercommunicate and overlap. It is thus that a raven soaring in the distance is not, for me, a mere visual image; as I follow it with my eyes, I inevitably feel the stretch and flex of its wings with my own muscles, and its sudden swoop toward the nearby trees is a visceral as well as a visual experience for me.

The raven's loud, guttural cry, as it swerves overhead, is not circumscribed within a strictly audible field—it echoes *through* the visible, immediately animating the visible landscape with the reckless style or mood proper to that jet black shape. My various senses, diverging as they do from a single, coherent body, coherently *converge,* as well, in the perceived thing, just as the separate perspectives of my two eyes converge upon the raven and convene there into a single focus. My senses connect up with each other in the things I perceive, or rather each perceived thing gathers my senses together in a coherent way, and it is this that enables me to experience the thing itself as a center of forces, as another nexus of experience, as an Other.

Hence, just as we have described perception as a dynamic participation between my body and things, so we now discern, within the act of perception, a participation between the various sensory systems of the body itself. Indeed, these events are not separable, for the intertwining of my body with the things it perceives is effected only through the interweaving of my senses, and vice versa. The relative divergence of my bodily senses (eyes in the front of the head, ears toward the back, etc.) and their curious bifurcation (not one but *two* eyes, one on each side, and similarly two ears, two nostrils, etc.), indicates that this body is a form destined to the world; it ensures that my body is a sort of open circuit that completes itself only in things, in others, in the encompassing earth.

The Recuperation of the Sensuous Is the Rediscovery of the Earth

In the autumn of 1985, a strong hurricane ripped across suburban Long Island, where I was then living as a student. For several days afterward much of the populace was without electricity; power lines were down, telephone lines broken, and the roads were strewn with toppled trees. People had to walk to their jobs, and to whatever shops were still open. We began encountering each other on the streets, "in person" instead of by telephone. In the absence of automobiles and their loud engines, the rhythms of crickets and birdsong became clearly audible. Flocks were migrating south for the winter, and many of us found ourselves simply listening, with new and childlike curiosity, to the ripples of song in the still-standing trees and the fields. And at night the sky was studded with stars! Many children, their eyes no longer blocked by the glare of houselights and street-lamps, saw the Milky Way for the first time, and were astonished. For those few days and nights our town became a community aware of its place in an encompassing cosmos. Even our noses seemed to come awake, the fresh smells from the ocean somehow more vibrant and salty. The breakdown of our technologies had forced a return to our senses, and hence to the natural landscape in which those senses are so profoundly embedded. We suddenly found ourselves inhabiting a sensuous world that had been waiting, for years, at the very fringe of our awareness, an intimate terrain infused by birdsong, salt spray, and the light of stars.

✦

AS WE REACQUAINT OURSELVES WITH OUR BREATHING BODIES, then the perceived world itself begins to shift and transform. When we begin to consciously frequent the wordless dimension of our sensory participations, certain phenomena that have habitually commanded our focus begin to lose their distinctive fascination and to slip toward the background, while hitherto unnoticed or overlooked presences begin to stand forth from the periphery and to engage our awareness. The countless human artifacts with which we are commonly involved—the asphalt roads, chain-link fences, telephone wires, buildings, lightbulbs, ballpoint pens, automobiles, street signs, plastic containers, newspapers, radios, television screens—all begin to exhibit a common style, and so to lose some of their distinctiveness; meanwhile, organic entities—crows, squirrels, the trees and wild weeds that surround our house, humming insects, streambeds, clouds and rainfalls—all these begin to display a new vitality, each coaxing the breathing body into a unique dance. Even boulders and rocks seem to speak their own uncanny languages of gesture and shadow, inviting the body and its bones into silent communication. In contact with the native forms of the earth, one's senses are slowly energized and awakened, combining and recombining in ever-shifting patterns.

For these other shapes and species have coevolved, like ourselves, with the rest of the shifting earth; their rhythms and forms are composed of layers upon layers of earlier rhythms, and in engaging them our senses are led into an inexhaustible depth that echoes that of our own flesh. The patterns on the stream's surface as it ripples over the rocks, or on the bark of an elm tree, or in a cluster of weeds, are all composed of repetitive figures that *never exactly repeat themselves,* of iterated shapes to which our senses may attune themselves even while the gradual drift and metamorphosis of those shapes draws our awareness in unexpected and unpredictable directions.

In contrast, the mass-produced artifacts of civilization, from milk cartons to washing machines to computers, draw our senses into a dance that endlessly reiterates itself *without variation.* To the sensing body these artifacts are, like all phenomena, animate and even alive, but their life is profoundly constrained by the specific "functions" for which they were built. Once our bodies master these functions, the machine-made objects commonly teach our senses nothing further; they are unable to surprise us, and so we must continually acquire *new* built objects, new technologies, the latest model of this or that if we wish to stimulate ourselves.

Of course, our human-made artifacts inevitably retain an element of more-than-human otherness. This unknowability, this otherness, resides most often in the materials from which the object is made. The tree trunk of the telephone pole, the clay of the bricks from which the building is fashioned, the smooth metal alloy of the car door we lean against—all these still carry, like our bodies, the textures and rhythms of a pattern that we ourselves did not devise, and their quiet dynamism responds directly to our senses. Too often, however, this dynamism is stifled within mass-produced structures closed off from the rest of the earth, imprisoned within technologies that plunder the living land. The superstraight lines and right angles of our office architecture, for instance, make our animal senses wither even as they support the abstract intellect; the wild, earth-born nature of the materials—the woods, clays, metals, and stones that went into the building—are readily forgotten behind the abstract and calculable form.[22]

It is thus that so much of our built environment, and so many of the artifacts that populate it, seem sadly superfluous and dull when we identify with our bodies and taste the world with our animal senses. (Of course, this is not to say that these artifacts are innocuous: many of them are exceedingly loud, even blaring, for what they lack in variation and nuance they must make up in clamorous insistence, monopolizing the perceptual field.) Whenever we assume the position and poise of the human animal—Merleau-Ponty's body-subject—then the entire material world itself seems to come awake and to speak, yet organic, earth-born entities speak far more eloquently than the rest. Like suburbanites after a hurricane, we find ourselves alive in a living field of powers far more expressive and diverse than the strictly human sphere to which we are accustomed.

𝓌

SO THE RECUPERATION OF THE INCARNATE, SENSORIAL DIMENSION of experience brings with it a recuperation of the living landscape in which we are corporeally embedded. As we return to our senses, we gradually discover our sensory perceptions to be simply our part of a vast, interpenetrating webwork of perceptions and sensations borne by countless other bodies—supported, that is, not just by ourselves, but by icy streams tumbling down granitic slopes, by owl wings and lichens, and by the unseen, imperturbable wind.

This intertwined web of experience is, of course, the "life-world" to which Husserl alluded in his final writings, yet now the life-world has been disclosed as a profoundly *carnal* field, as this very dimension of smells and tastes and chirping rhythms warmed by the sun and shivering with seeds. It is, indeed, nothing other than the biosphere—the matrix of earthly life in which we ourselves are embedded. Yet this is not the biosphere as it is conceived by an abstract and objectifying science, not that complex assemblage of planetary mechanisms presumably being mapped and measured by our remote-sensing satellites; it is, rather, the biosphere as it is experienced and *lived from within* by the intelligent body—by the attentive human animal who is entirely a part of the world that he, or she, experiences.

Matter as Flesh

In his final work, *The Visible and the Invisible* (a work interrupted by his sudden death in 1961), Merleau-Ponty was striving for a new way of speaking that would express this consanguinity of the human animal and the world it inhabits. Here he writes less about "the body" (which in his earlier work had signified primarily the *human* body) and begins to write instead of the collective "Flesh," which signifies both *our* flesh and "the flesh of the world."[23] By "the Flesh" Merleau-Ponty means to indicate an elemental power that has had no name in the entire history of Western philosophy. The Flesh is the mysterious tissue or matrix that underlies and gives rise to both the perceiver and the perceived as interdependent aspects of its own spontaneous activity. It is the reciprocal presence of the sentient in the sensible and of the sensible in the sentient, a mystery of which we have always, at least tacitly, been aware, since we have never been able to affirm one of these phenomena, the perceivable world or the perceiving self, without implicitly affirming the existence of the other. We are unable even to *imagine* a sensible landscape that would not at the same time be sensed (since in imagining any landscape we inevitably envisage it from a particular perspective, and thus implicate our own senses, and indeed our own sentience, in that landscape), and are similarly unable to fully imagine a sensing self, or sentience, that would not be situated in some field of sensed phenomena.

Nevertheless, conventional scientific discourse privileges the sensible field in abstraction from sensory experience, and commonly maintains that subjective experience is "caused" by an objectifiable set of processes in the mechanically determined field of the sensible. Meanwhile, New Age spiritualism regularly privileges pure sentience, or subjectivity, in abstraction from sensible matter, and often maintains that material reality is itself an illusory effect caused by an immaterial mind or spirit. Although commonly seen as opposed world-views, both of these positions assume a qualitative difference between the sentient and the sensed; by prioritizing one or the other, both of these views perpetuate the distinction between human "subjects" and natural "objects," and hence neither threatens the common conception of sensible nature as a purely passive dimension suitable for human manipulation and use. While both of these views are unstable, each bolsters the other; by bouncing from one to the other—from scientific determinism to spiritual idealism and back again—contemporary discourse easily avoids the possibility that both the perceiving being and the perceived being are *of the same stuff,* that the perceiver and the perceived are interdependent and in some sense even reversible aspects of a common animate element, or Flesh, that is *at once both sensible and sensitive.*

We readily experience this paradox in relation to other persons; this stranger who stands before me and is an object for my gaze suddenly opens his mouth and speaks to me, forcing me to acknowledge that he is a sentient subject like myself, and that I, too, am an object for his gaze. Each of us, in relation to the other, is both subject and object, sensible and sentient. Why, then, might this not also be the case in relation to another, nonhuman entity—a mountain lion, for instance, that I unexpectedly encounter in the northern forest? Indeed, such a meeting brings home to me even more forcefully that I am not just a sentient subject but also a sensible object, even an *edible* object, in the eyes (and nose) of the other. Even an ant crawling along my arm, visible to my eyes and tactile to my skin, displays at the same time its own sentience, responding immediately to my movements, even to the chemical changes of my mood. In relation to the ant I feel myself as a dense and material object, as capricious in my actions as the undulating earth itself. Finally, then, why might not this "reversibility" of subject and object extend to every entity that I experience? Once I acknowledge that my own sentience, or subjectivity, does not preclude my visible, tactile, objective existence for others, I find myself forced to acknowledge that *any* visible, tangible form that meets my gaze may also be an experiencing subject, sensitive and responsive to the beings around it, and to me.

Touching and Being Touched: The Reciprocity of the Sensuous

In order to demonstrate, empirically, his notion of the Flesh, Merleau-Ponty provides what may be the most direct illustration of that which we have termed "participation." He calls attention to the obvious but easily overlooked fact that my hand is able to touch things only because my hand is itself a touchable thing, and thus is entirely a part of the tactile world that it explores. Similarly, the eyes, with which I see things, are themselves visible. With their gleaming surfaces, their colors and hues, they are included *within* the visible field that they see—they are themselves part of the visible, like the bark of a cedar, or a piece of sandstone, or the blue sky.

To touch the coarse skin of a tree is thus, at the same time, to experience one's own tactility, to feel oneself touched *by* the tree. And to see the world is also, at the same time, to experience oneself as visible, to feel oneself *seen*. Clearly, a wholly immaterial mind could neither see things nor touch things—indeed, could not experience anything at all. *We* can experience things—can touch, hear, and taste things—only because, as bodies, we are ourselves included in the sensible field, and have our own textures, sounds, and tastes. We can perceive things at all only because we ourselves are entirely a part of the sensible world that we perceive! We might as well say that we are organs of this world, flesh of its flesh, and that the world is perceiving itself *through* us.

Walking in a forest, we peer into its green and shadowed depths, listening to the silence of the leaves, tasting the cool and fragrant air. Yet such is the transitivity of perception, the reversibility of the flesh, that we may suddenly feel that the trees are looking at us—we feel ourselves exposed, watched, observed from all sides. If we dwell in this forest for many months, or years, then our experience may shift yet again—we may come to feel that we are a part of this forest, consanguineous with it, and that our experience of the forest is nothing other than the forest experiencing itself.

Such are the exchanges and metamorphoses that arise from the simple fact that our sentient bodies are entirely continuous with the vast body of the land, that "the presence of the world is precisely the presence of its flesh to my flesh."[24]

⚘

MERLEAU-PONTY'S NOTION OF THE FLESH OF THE WORLD, ALONG with his related discoveries regarding the reciprocity of perception, bring his work into startling consonance with the worldviews of many indigenous, oral cultures. According to cultural anthropologist Richard Nelson, in his exhaustive study of the ecology of the Koyukon Indians of north central Alaska:

> [t]raditional Koyukon people live in a world that watches, in a forest of eyes. A person moving through nature—however wild, remote, even desolate the place may be—is never truly alone. The surroundings are aware, sensate, personified. They feel. They can be offended. And they must, at every moment, be treated with the proper respect.[25]

Such a mode of experience, which seems so strange and confused to our civilized ways of thinking, becomes understandable as soon as we acknowledge, underneath our conventional assumptions, the reciprocal nature of direct perception—the fact that to touch is also to feel oneself being touched, that to see is also to feel oneself seen. Nelson's description suggests, as well, that such perceptual reciprocity, when consciously acknowledged, may profoundly influence one's behavior. If the surroundings are experienced as sensate, attentive, and watchful, then I must take care that my actions are mindful and respectful, even when I am far from other humans, lest I offend the watchful land itself.

It may be that the new "environmental ethic" toward which so many environmental philosophers aspire—an ethic that would lead us to respect and heed not only the lives of our fellow humans but also the life and well-being of the rest of nature—will come into existence not primarily through the logical elucidation of new philosophical principles and legislative strictures, but through a renewed attentiveness to this perceptual dimension that underlies all our logics, through a rejuvenation of our carnal, sensorial empathy with the living land that sustains us.

Such a recuperation is, perhaps, already underway. Many individuals today experience a profound anguish that only deepens with each report of more ancient forests cleared, of new oil spills, of the ever-accelerating loss of species. It is an anguish that seems to come from the earth itself, from this vast Flesh in which our own sentient flesh is embedded. In the words of a Koyukon elder: "The country knows. If you do wrong things to it, the whole country knows. It feels what's happening to it."[26]

⚹

THE INFLUENCE OF A KIND OF PERCEPTUAL RECIPROCITY UPON oneself and one's actions is evident as well in these words spoken by Old Torlino, a Navajo elder, before telling part of the creation story:

I am ashamed before the earth;
I am ashamed before the heavens;
I am ashamed before the dawn;
I am ashamed before the evening twilight;
I am ashamed before the blue sky;
I am ashamed before the sun.
I am ashamed before that standing within me which speaks with me.
Some of these things are always looking at me.
I am never out of sight.
Therefore I must tell the truth.
I hold my word tight to my breast.[27]

The final lines of this prayer/incantation call our attention to speaking itself as a form of behavior that can be mindful or callous, truthful or dishonest, in the face of a sentient cosmos. Spoken words here are real presences, entities that may be cherished—"held tight to my breast"—or flung carelessly into the world. These phrases from the Navajo, like the Koyukon words before them, provide evidence not only of a different way of seeing, but also of a way of speaking very different from that to which so many of us are accustomed. The practice of language among indigenous peoples would seem to carry a very different significance than it does in the modern West. Enacted primarily in song, prayer, and story, among oral peoples language functions not simply to dialogue with other humans but also to converse with the more-than-human cosmos, to renew reciprocity with the surrounding powers of earth and sky, to invoke kinship even with those entities which, to the civilized mind, are utterly insentient and inert. Hence, a Lakota medicine person may address a stone as "Tunkashila"—"Grandfather." Likewise, among the Omaha, a rock may be addressed with the respect and reverence that one pays to an ancient elder:

> unmoved
> from time without
> end
> you rest
> there in the midst of the paths
> in the midst of the winds
> you rest
> covered with the droppings of birds
> grass growing from your feet
> your head decked with the down of birds
> you rest
> in the midst of the winds
> you wait
> Aged one.[28]

Here words do not speak *about* the world; rather they speak *to* the world, and to the expressive presences that, with us, inhabit the world. In multiple and diverse ways, taking (as we shall see) a unique form in each indigenous culture, spoken language seems to give voice to, and thus to enhance and accentuate, the sensorial affinity between humans and the environing earth.

This would appear, at least at first, to be in direct contradiction to the character of linguistic discourse in the "developed" or "civilized" world, where language functions largely to *deny* reciprocity with nature—by defining the rest of nature as inert, mechanical, and determinate—and where, in consequence, our sensorial participation with the land around us must remain mute, inchoate, and in most cases wholly unconscious. In indigenous, oral cultures, in other words, language seems to encourage and augment the participatory life of the senses, while in Western civilization language seems to deny or deaden that life, promoting a massive distrust of sensorial experience while valorizing an abstract realm of ideas hidden behind or beyond the sensory appearances.

How can we account for this divergence? In what manner can we make sense of this difference in the character of language, and in the relation between language and perception? Before attempting a precise answer to this question, we must come to a clearer understanding of just what is meant, in this context, by "language."

The Flesh of Language

The rain surrounded the cabin . . . with a whole world of meaning, of secrecy, of rumor. Think of it: all that speech pouring down, selling nothing, judging nobody, drenching the thick mulch of dead leaves, soaking the trees, filling the gullies and crannies of the wood with water, washing out the places where men have stripped the hillside. . . . Nobody started it, nobody is going to stop it. It will talk as long as it wants, the rain. As long as it talks I am going to listen.

—THOMAS MERTON

EVERY ATTEMPT TO DEFINITIVELY SAY *WHAT LANGUAGE IS* is subject to a curious limitation. For the only medium with which we can define language is language itself. We are therefore unable to circumscribe the whole of language within our definition. It may be best, then, to leave language undefined, and to thus acknowledge its open-endedness, its mysteriousness. Nevertheless, by paying attention to this mystery we may develop a conscious familiarity with it, a sense of its texture, its habits, its sources of sustenance.

Merleau-Ponty, as we have seen, spent much of his life demonstrating that the event of perception unfolds as a reciprocal exchange between the living body and the animate world that surrounds it. He showed, as well, that this exchange, for all its openness and indeterminacy, is nevertheless highly articulate. (Although it confounds the causal logic that we attempt to impose upon it, perceptual experience has its own coherent structure; it seems to embody an open-ended logos that we enact from within rather than the abstract logic we deploy from without.) The disclosure that preverbal perception is already an exchange, and the recognition that this exchange has its own coherence and articulation, together suggested that perception, this ongoing reciprocity, is the very soil and support of that more conscious exchange we call language.

Already in the *Phenomenology of Perception,* Merleau-Ponty had begun to work out a notion of human language as a profoundly carnal phenomenon, rooted in our sensorial experience of each other and of the world. In a famous chapter entitled "The Body as Expression, and Speech," he wrote at length of the gestural genesis of language, the way that communicative meaning is first incarnate in the gestures by which the body spontaneously expresses feelings and responds to changes in its affective environment. The gesture is spontaneous and immediate. It is not an arbitrary sign that we mentally attach to a particular emotion or feeling; rather, the gesture *is* the bodying-forth of that emotion into the world, it *is* that feeling of delight or of anguish in its tangible, visible aspect. When we encounter such a spontaneous gesture, we do not first see it as a blank behavior, which we then mentally associate with a particular content or significance; rather, the bodily gesture speaks directly to our own body, and is thereby understood without any interior reflection:

> Faced with an angry or threatening gesture, I have no need, in order to understand it, to [mentally] recall the feelings which I myself experienced when I used these gestures on my own account. . . . I do not see anger or a threatening attitude as a psychic fact hidden behind the gesture, I read anger in it. The gesture *does not make me think of anger,* it is anger itself.[1]

Active, living speech is just such a gesture, a vocal gesticulation wherein the meaning is inseparable from the sound, the shape, and the rhythm of the words. Communicative meaning is always, in its depths, affective; it remains rooted in the sensual dimension of experience, born of the body's native capacity to resonate with other bodies and with the landscape as a whole. Linguistic meaning is not some ideal and bodiless essence that we arbitrarily assign to a physical sound or word and then toss out into the "external" world. Rather, meaning sprouts in the very depths of the sensory world, in the heat of meeting, encounter, participation.

We do not, as children, first enter into language by consciously studying the formalities of syntax and grammar or by memorizing the dictionary definitions of words, but rather by actively making sounds—by crying in pain and laughing in joy, by squealing and babbling and playfully mimicking the surrounding soundscape, gradually entering through such mimicry into the specific melodies of the local language, our resonant bodies slowly coming to echo the inflections and accents common to our locale and community.

We thus learn our native language not mentally but bodily. We appropriate new words and phrases first through their expressive tonality and texture, through the way they feel in the mouth or roll off the tongue, and it is this direct, felt significance—the *taste* of a word or phrase, the way it influences or modulates the body—that provides the fertile, polyvalent source for all the more refined and rarefied meanings which that term may come to have for us.

> . . . the meaning of words must be finally induced by the words themselves, or more exactly, their conceptual meaning must be formed by a kind of subtraction from a *gestural meaning,* which is immanent in speech.[2]

Language, then, cannot be genuinely studied or understood in isolation from the sensuous reverberation and resonance of active speech. James M. Edie attempts to summarize this aspect of Merleau-Ponty's thought in this manner:

> . . . Merleau-Ponty's first point is that words, even when they finally achieve the ability to carry referential and, eventually, conceptual levels of meaning, never completely lose that primitive, strictly phonemic, level of 'affective' meaning which is not translatable into their conceptual definitions. There is, he argues, an affective tonality, a mode of conveying meaning beneath the level

of thought, beneath the level of the words themselves . . . which
is contained in the words *just insofar as they are patterned sounds,*
as just the sounds which this particular historical language
uniquely uses, and which are much more like a melody—a
'singing of the world'—than fully translatable, conceptual
thought. Merleau-Ponty is almost alone among philosophers of
language in his sensitivity to this level of meaning. . . .[3]

Edie here emphasizes Merleau-Ponty's originality with regard to
language, and asserts that Merleau-Ponty gave special attention to
"what no philosopher from Plato on down ever had any interest in"
(namely, the gestural significance of spoken sounds). Yet this assertion is true only if one holds a very restricted view of the philosophical tradition. The expressive, gestural basis of language had already
been emphasized in the first half of the eighteenth century by the
Italian philosopher Giambattista Vico (1668–1744), who in his *New
Science* wrote of language as arising from expressive gestures, and
suggested that the earliest and most basic words had taken shape
from expletives uttered in startled response to powerful natural
events, or from the frightened, stuttering mimesis of such events—
like the crack and rumble of thunder across the sky.[4] Shortly thereafter, in France, Jean-Jacques Rousseau (1712–1778) wrote of
gestures and spontaneous expressions of feeling as the earliest
forms of language, while in Germany, Johann Gottfried Herder
(1744–1803) argued that language originates in our sensuous receptivity to the sounds and shapes of the natural environment.[5]

In his embodied philosophy of language, then, Merleau-Ponty is
the heir of a long-standing, if somewhat heretical, lineage. Linguistic meaning, for him, is rooted in the felt experience induced by specific sounds and sound-shapes as they echo and contrast with one
another, each language a kind of song, a particular way of "singing
the world."

Toward an Ecology of Language

The more prevalent view of language, at least since the scientific revolution, and still assumed in some manner by most linguists today, considers any language to be a set of arbitrary but conventionally agreed upon words, or "signs," linked by a purely formal system of syntactic and grammatical rules. Language, in this view, is rather like a *code;* it is a way of *representing* actual things and events in the perceived world, but it has no internal, nonarbitrary connections to that world, and hence is readily separable from it.

If we agree with Merleau-Ponty's assertion that active speech is the generative core of all language, how can we possibly account for the overwhelming prevalence of a view that considers language to be an ideal or formal system readily detachable from the material act of speaking? Merleau-Ponty suggests that such a view of language could arise only at a time when the fresh creation of meaning has become a rare occurrence, a time when people commonly speak in conventional, ready-made ways "which demand from us no real effort of expression and . . . demand from our listeners no real effort of comprehension"—at a time, in short, when meaning has become impoverished.[6]

Yet there is another, more overt reason for the dominance of the idea that language is an arbitrary, or strictly conventional, set of signs. As we noted earlier, European philosophy has consistently occupied itself with the question of human specialness. Ever since Aristotle, philosophers have been concerned to demonstrate, in the most convincing manner possible, that human beings are significantly different from all other forms of life. It was not enough to demonstrate that human beings were unique, for each species is evidently unique in its way; rather, it was necessary to show that the human form was *uniquely* unique, that our noble gifts set us definitively apart from, and above, the rest of the animate world. Such demonstrations were, we may suspect, needed to justify the increasing manipulation and exploitation of nonhuman nature by, and for, (civilized) humankind. The necessity for such philosophical justification became especially urgent in the wake of the scientific revolution, when our capacity to manipulate other organisms increased a hundredfold. Descartes's radical separation of the immaterial human mind from the wholly mechanical world of nature did much to fill this need, providing a splendid rationalization for the vivisection experiments that soon began to proliferate, as well as for the steady plundering and despoilment of nonhuman nature in the New World and the other European colonies.

But in the latter half of the nineteenth century, the publication of Darwin's *Origin of Species* and *The Descent of Man* introduced a profound tension into the anthropocentric trajectory of European philosophy and science. If humans are animals evolved like other animals, if in truth we are descended by "natural selection" from primates, if indeed fish are our distant ancestors and mice are our cousins, then our own traits and capacities must be, to some degree, continuous with those found in the rest of the earthly environment.

Most scientists, however, while accepting Darwin's theories, were reluctant to relinquish the assumption of human specialness—the assumption that alone justifies so many of the cultural and research practices to which we have now become accustomed. In earlier centuries we could ascribe our superiority to the dispensation of God, who had "created" us as his representatives on earth, or who had bequeathed to humans alone the divine capacity for awareness and intelligence. After Darwin, however, we no longer had such easy recourse to extraworldly dispensation; it became necessary to find new, more naturalistic evidence for the superiority of humankind.

In our own time it is *language,* conceived as an exclusively human property, that is most often used to demonstrate the excellence of humankind relative to all other species. Other animals have been shown to build complex dwellings, even to use tools. But language, it is widely asserted, remains the special provenance of the human species. To be sure, most other animals manage to communicate with each other, often employing a repertoire of gestures, from "marking" territory with chemical secretions, to the facial expressions of many mammal species, to the host of rattles, cries, howls, and growls that sound across the fields and forests—to say nothing of the complex melodic songs employed, most obviously by birds, as well as by various marine-dwelling mammals like orcas and humpback whales. One of the founding events of the science of ethology, earlier in this century, was the discovery of the intricate "waggle-dance" whereby individual bees communicate the precise direction and distance of a newfound food source to the rest of the hive. Yet each of these communicative arrays—these "dances," "songs," and gestures, both vocal and visual—may be said to remain within the sphere of felt, bodily expression. The meanings here, it is assumed, are tied to the expressive nature of the gestures themselves, and to the direct sensations induced by these movements—to the immediacy of instinct and bodily urge.

In everyday human discourse, on the other hand, we readily locate a dimension of significance beyond the merely expressive power of the words, a layer of abstract meanings fixed solely, it would seem, by convention. Thus, the term "Wow!" may at first be a simple expression of wonder, but it may also come to designate, if we so choose, a particular type of hairdo, or a shade of blue, or a specific tactic to be used when debating with fishermen. It is this second layer of agreed-upon meanings that is identified with "language in the proper sense" by most philosophers and scientists since the Enlightenment. Only by isolating this secondary layer of conventional meanings from the felt significance carried by the tone, rhythm, and resonance of spoken expressions can we conceive of language as a code—as a determinate and mappable structure composed of arbitrary signs linked by purely formal rules. And only thus, by conceiving language as a purely abstract phenomenon, can we claim it as an exclusively human attribute. Only by overlooking the sensuous, evocative dimension of human discourse, and attending solely to the denotative and conventional aspect of verbal communication, can we hold ourselves apart from, and outside of, the rest of animate nature.

If Merleau-Ponty is right, however, then the denotative, conventional dimension of language can never be truly severed from the sensorial dimension of direct, affective meaning. If we are not, in truth, immaterial minds merely housed in earthly bodies, but are from the first material, corporeal beings, then it is the sensuous, gestural significance of spoken sounds—their direct bodily resonance—that makes verbal communication possible at all. It is this expressive potency—the soundful influence of spoken words upon the sensing body—that supports all the more abstract and conventional meanings that we assign to those words.[7] Although we may be oblivious to the gestural, somatic dimension of language, having repressed it in favor of strict dictionary definitions and the abstract precision of specialized terminologies, this dimension remains subtly operative in all our speaking and writing—if, that is, our words have any significance whatsoever. For meaning, as we have said, remains rooted in the sensory life of the body—it cannot be completely cut off from the soil of direct, perceptual experience without withering and dying.[8]

Yet to affirm that linguistic meaning is primarily expressive, gestural, and poetic, and that conventional and denotative meanings are inherently secondary and derivative, is to renounce the claim that "language" is an exclusively human property. If language is always, in its depths, physically and sensorially resonant, then it can never be definitively separated from the evident expressiveness of birdsong, or the evocative howl of a wolf late at night. The chorus of frogs gurgling in unison at the edge of a pond, the snarl of a wildcat as it springs upon its prey, or the distant honking of Canadian geese veeing south for the winter, all reverberate with affective, gestural significance, the same significance that vibrates through our own conversations and soliloquies, moving us at times to tears, or to anger, or to intellectual insights we could never have anticipated. Language as a bodily phenomenon accrues to *all* expressive bodies, not just to the human. Our own speaking, then, does not set us outside of the animate landscape but—whether or not we are aware of it—inscribes us more fully in its chattering, whispering, soundful depths.

If, for instance, one comes upon two human friends unexpectedly meeting for the first time in many months, and one chances to hear their initial words of surprise, greeting, and pleasure, one may readily notice, if one pays close enough attention, a tonal, melodic layer of communication beneath the explicit denotative meaning of the words—a rippling rise and fall of the voices in a sort of musical duet, rather like two birds singing to each other. Each voice, each side of the duet, mimes a bit of the other's melody while adding its own inflection and style, and then is echoed by the other in turn—the two singing bodies thus tuning and attuning to one another, rediscovering a common register, *remembering* each other. It requires only a slight shift in focus to realize that this melodic singing is carrying the bulk of communication in this encounter, and that the explicit meanings of the actual words ride on the surface of this depth like waves on the surface of the sea.

It is by a complementary shift of attention that one may suddenly come to hear the familiar song of a blackbird or a thrush in a surprisingly new manner—not just as a pleasant melody repeated mechanically, as on a tape player in the background, but as active, meaningful speech. Suddenly, subtle variations in the tone and rhythm of that whistling phrase seem laden with expressive intention, and the two birds singing to each other across the field appear for the first time as attentive, conscious beings, earnestly engaged in the same world that we ourselves engage, yet from an astonishingly different angle and perspective.

Moreover, if we allow that spoken meaning remains rooted in gesture and bodily expressiveness, we will be unable to restrict our renewed experience of language solely to animals. As we have already recognized, in the untamed world of direct sensory experience *no* phenomenon presents itself as utterly passive or inert. To the sensing body *all* phenomena are animate, actively soliciting the participation of our senses, or else withdrawing from our focus and repelling our involvement. Things disclose themselves to our immediate perception as vectors, as styles of unfolding—not as finished chunks of matter given once and for all, but as dynamic ways of engaging the senses and modulating the body. Each thing, each phenomenon, has the power to reach us and to influence us. Every phenomenon, in other words, is potentially expressive. At the end of his chapter "The Body as Expression, and Speech," Merleau-Ponty writes:

> It is the body which points out, and which speaks. . . . This disclosure [of the body's immanent expressiveness] . . . extends, as we shall see, to the whole sensible world, and our gaze, prompted by the experience of our own body, will discover in all other "objects" the miracle of expression.[9]

Thus, at the most primordial level of sensuous, bodily experience, we find ourselves in an expressive, gesturing landscape, in a world that *speaks*.

We regularly talk of howling winds, and of chattering brooks. Yet these are more than mere metaphors. Our own languages are continually nourished by these other voices—by the roar of waterfalls and the thrumming of crickets. It is not by chance that, when hiking in the mountains, the English terms we spontaneously use to describe the surging waters of the nearby river are words like "rush," "splash," "gush," "wash." For the sound that unites all these words is that which the water itself chants as it flows between the banks. If language is not a purely mental phenomenon but a sensuous, bodily activity born of carnal reciprocity and participation, then our discourse has surely been influenced by many gestures, sounds, and rhythms besides those of our single species. Indeed, if human language arises from the perceptual interplay between the body and the world, then this language "belongs" to the animate landscape as much as it "belongs" to ourselves.

IN 1945, MERLEAU-PONTY BEGAN READING THE WORK OF THE SWISS linguist Ferdinand de Saussure (1857–1913), whose posthumously published *Course in General Linguistics* signaled the emergence of scientific linguistics in the twentieth century.[10] Merleau-Ponty was intrigued by Saussure's theoretical distinction between *la langue*—language considered as a system of terminological, syntactic, and semantic rules, and *la parole*—the concrete act of speech itself.

Language considered as a formal system of rules and conventions is that aspect of language which, alone, is susceptible to objective, scientific study. By isolating this aspect of language, Saussure effectively cleared the way for the rigorous, scientific analysis of language systems. Yet the proper way to understand the relation *between* the formal structure of language and the expressive act of speaking (between *la langue* and *la parole*) remained enigmatic, and it was this enigma that most fascinated Merleau-Ponty.

For Saussure, *la langue*—language considered as a purely structural system—was not a mechanical structure that could readily be taken apart into its separable components, but more an organic, living system, each of whose parts is internally related to all the others. Saussure described the structure of any language as a thoroughly interdependent matrix, a webwork wherein each term has meaning only by virtue of its relation to other terms within the system. In English, for instance, the sounded word "red" draws its precise meaning from its situation in a network of like-sounding terms, including, for instance, "read," "rod," "reed," and "raid," and in a whole complex of color terms, such as "orange," "yellow," "purple," "brown"; as well as from its participation in a still wider nexus of related terms like "blood," "rose," "sunset," "fire," "blush," "angry," "hot," each of which holds significance only in relation to a constellation of still other words, expanding thus outward to every term within the language. By describing any particular language as a *system of differences,* Saussure indicated that meaning is found not in the words themselves but in the intervals, the contrasts, the participations *between* the terms. As Merleau-Ponty states:

> What we have learned from Saussure is that, taken singly, signs do not signify anything, and that each one of them does not so much express a meaning as mark a divergence of meaning between itself and other signs.[11]

This does not mean that it is necessary to know, explicitly, the whole of a language in order to speak it. Rather, the weblike nature of language ensures that the whole of the system is implicitly present in every sentence, in every phrase. In order to learn a community's language, suggests Merleau-Ponty, it is necessary simply to begin speaking, to enter the language with one's body, to begin to move within it. The language in its entirety is invoked by the child in his first attempts at speech. "[Then] the whole of the spoken language surrounding the child snaps him up like a whirlwind, tempts him by its internal articulations. . . ."[12]

The enigma that is language, constituted as much by silence as by sounds, is not an inert or static structure, but an evolving bodily field. It is like a vast, living fabric continually being woven by those who speak. Merleau-Ponty here distinguishes sharply between genuine, expressive speech and speech that merely repeats established formulas. The latter is hardly "speech" at all; it does not really carry meaning in the weave of its words but relies solely upon the memory of meanings that once lived there. It does not alter the already existing structures of the language, but rather treats the language as a finished institution. Nevertheless, those preexisting structures must at some moment have been created, and this can only have been effected by active, expressive speech. Indeed, all truly meaningful speech is inherently creative, using established words in ways they have never quite been used before, and thus altering, ever so slightly, the whole webwork of the language. Wild, living speech takes up, from within, the interconnected matrix of the language and *gestures* with it, subjecting the whole structure to a "coherent deformation."

At the heart of any language, then, is the poetic productivity of expressive speech. A living language is continually being made and remade, woven out of the silence by those who speak. . . . And this silence is that of our wordless participations, of our perceptual immersion in the depths of an animate, expressive world.

Thus, Saussure's distinction between the structure of language and the activity of speech is ultimately undermined by Merleau-Ponty, the two dimensions blended back together into a single, ever-evolving matrix. While individual speech acts are surely guided by the structured lattice of the language, that lattice is nothing other than the sedimented result of all previous acts of speech, and will itself be altered by the very expressive activity it now guides. Language is not a fixed or ideal form, but an evolving medium we collectively inhabit, a vast topological matrix in which the speaking bodies are generative sites, vortices where the matrix itself is continually being spun out of the silence of sensorial experience.

What Merleau-Ponty retains from Saussure is Saussure's notion of any language as an interdependent, weblike system of relations. But since our expressive, speaking bodies are for Merleau-Ponty necessary parts of this system—since the web of language is for him a carnal medium woven in the depths of our perceptual participation with the things and beings around us—Merleau-Ponty comes in his final writings to affirm that it is first the sensuous, perceptual world that is relational and weblike in character, and hence that the organic, interconnected structure of any language is an extension or echo of the deeply interconnected matrix of sensorial reality itself.[13] Ultimately, it is not human language that is primary, but rather the sensuous, perceptual life-world, whose wild, participatory logic ramifies and elaborates itself in language.

Since the mid-nineteenth century, the study of our earthly environment has increasingly yielded a view of nature as a realm of complexly interwoven relationships, a field of subtle interdependencies from which, in John Muir's words, no single phenomenon can be picked out without "finding it hitched to everything else." The character of an individual fruit tree simply cannot be understood without reference to the others of its species, to the insects that fertilize it and to the animals that consume its fruit and so disperse its seeds. Yet a single one of those animals can hardly be comprehended without learning of the *other* plants or animals that it eats throughout the year, and of the predators that prey upon *it*—without, in other words, acknowledging the host of other organisms upon which that animal depends, and which depend upon it. We have at last come to realize that neither the soils, the oceans, nor the atmosphere can be comprehended without taking into account the participation of innumerable organisms, from the lichens that crumble rocks, and the bacterial entities that decompose organic detritus, to all the respiring plants and animals exchanging vital gases with the air. The notion of earthly nature as a densely interconnected organic network— a "biospheric web" wherein each entity draws its specific character from its relations, direct and indirect, to all the others—has today become commonplace, and it converges neatly with Merleau-Ponty's late description of sensuous reality, "the Flesh," as an intertwined, and actively intertwining, lattice of mutually dependent phenomena, both sensorial and sentient, of which our own sensing bodies are a part.

It is this dynamic, interconnected reality that provokes and sustains all our speaking, lending something of its structure to all our various languages. The enigmatic nature of language echoes and "prolongs unto the invisible" the wild, interpenetrating, interdependent nature of the sensible landscape itself.

Ultimately, then, it is not the human body alone but rather the whole of the sensuous world that provides the deep structure of language. As we ourselves dwell and move within language, so, ultimately, do the other animals and animate things of the world; if we do not notice them there, it is only because language has forgotten its expressive depths. "Language is a life, is our life and the life of the things. . . ."[14] It is no more true that *we* speak than that the things, and the animate world itself, *speak within us:*

That the things have us and that it is not we who have the things. . . . That it is being that speaks within us and not we who speak of being.[15]

From such reflections we may begin to suspect that the complexity of human language is related to the complexity of the earthly ecology—not to any complexity of our species considered apart from that matrix. Language, writes Merleau-Ponty, "is the very voice of the trees, the waves, and the forests."[16]

As technological civilization diminishes the biotic diversity of the earth, language itself is diminished. As there are fewer and fewer songbirds in the air, due to the destruction of their forests and wetlands, human speech loses more and more of its evocative power. For when we no longer hear the voices of warbler and wren, our own speaking can no longer be nourished by their cadences. As the splashing speech of the rivers is silenced by more and more dams, as we drive more and more of the land's wild voices into the oblivion of extinction, our own languages become increasingly impoverished and weightless, progressively emptied of their earthly resonance.[17]

Word Magic

Merleau-Ponty's work on language is admittedly fragmentary and unfinished, cut short by his sudden death. Yet it provides the most extensive investigation we have, as yet, into the living *experience* of language—the way the expressive medium discloses itself to us when we do not pretend to stand outside it, but rather accept our inherence *within* it, as speaking animals. When we attend to our experience not as intangible minds but as sounding, speaking bodies, we begin to sense that we are heard, even listened to, by the numerous other bodies that surround us. Our sensing bodies respond to the eloquence of certain buildings and boulders, to the articulate motions of dragonflies. We find ourselves alive in a listening, speaking world.

Here (as we saw earlier with regard to perception) Merleau-Ponty's work resonates, and brings us close to, the spoken beliefs of many indigenous, oral peoples.

In such indigenous cultures the solidarity between language and the animate landscape is palpable and evident. According to Ogotemmêli, an elder of the Dogon tribe of Mali, spoken language was originally a swirling garment of vapour and breath worn by the encompassing earth itself. Later this undulating garment was stolen by the jackal, an animal whose movements, ever since, have disclosed the prophetic speech of the world to seers and diviners.[18] Many tribes, like the Swampy Cree of Manitoba, hold that they were given spoken language by the animals,[19] For the Inuit (Eskimo), as for numerous other peoples, humans and animals all originally spoke the same language. According to Nalungiaq, an Inuit woman interviewed by ethnologist Knud Rasmussen early in the twentieth century:

> *In the very earliest time*
> *when both people and animals lived on earth,*
> *a person could become an animal if he wanted to*
> *and an animal could become a human being.*
> *Sometimes they were people*
> *and sometimes animals*
> *and there was no difference.*
> *All spoke the same language.*
> *That was the time when words were like magic.*
> *The human mind had mysterious powers.*
> *A word spoken by chance*
> *might have strange consequences.*
> *It would suddenly come alive*
> *and what people wanted to happen could happen—*
> *all you had to do was say it.*
> *Nobody could explain this:*
> *That's the way it was.[20]*

Despite this originary language common to both people and animals, the various animals and other natural forms today speak their own unique dialects. But nevertheless *all speak,* all have the power of language. Moreover, traces of the primordial common language remain, and just as a human may suddenly understand the subtle gestures of a deer, or the guttural speech of a raven, so the other entities hear, and may understand, our own talking.

> Owls often make it difficult to speak Cree with them. They can cause stuttering, and when stuttering is going on they are attracted to it. It is said that stuttering is laughable to owls. Yet this can work to the Cree's advantage as well, for if you think an owl is causing trouble in your village, then go stutter in the woods. There's a good chance an owl will arrive. Then you can confront this owl, question it, argue with it, perhaps solve the problem.[21]

Most indigenous hunting peoples carefully avoid speaking about the hunt beforehand, or referring directly to the species that they are hunting, lest they offend the listening animals themselves. After the kill, however, they will speak directly to the dying animal, praising it, promising respect, and thanking it for offering itself to them.[22]

Yet it is those who are recognized as shamans, or medicine persons, who most fully remember the primordial sacred language, and who are thus able to slip, at will, out of the purely human discourse in order to converse directly with the other powers. As Mircea Eliade writes:

> The existence of a specific secret language has been verified among the Lapps, the Ostyak, the Chukchee, the Yakut, and the Tungus. During his trance the Tungus shaman is believed to understand the language of all nature. . . .
>
> Very often this secret language is actually the "animal language" or originates in animal cries. In South America the neophyte must learn, during his initiation period, to imitate the voices of animals. The same is true of North America. The Pomo and the Menomini shamans, among others, imitate bird songs. During séances among the Yakut, the Yukagir, the Chukchee, the Goldi, the Eskimo, and others, wild animal cries and bird calls are heard. . . .
>
> Many words used during the séance have their origin in the cries of birds or other animals. . . . "Magic" and "song"—espe-

cially song like that of birds—are frequently expressed by the same term. The Germanic word for magic formula is *galdr,* derived from the verb *galan,* "to sing," a term applied especially to bird calls.[23]

We will later explore at length specific instances of this affinity between language and the animate landscape as it is embodied not only in myths and magical practices but in the everyday discourse of several contemporary indigenous tribes. Here it is enough to mention that Merleau-Ponty's view of language as a thoroughly incarnate medium, of speech as rhythm and expressive gesture, and hence of spoken words and phrases as active sensuous presences afoot in the material landscape (rather than as ideal forms that represent, but are not a part of, the sensuous world)—goes a long way toward helping us understand the primacy of language and word magic in native rituals of transformation, metamorphosis, and healing. *Only if words are felt, bodily presences, like echoes or waterfalls, can we understand the power of spoken language to influence, alter, and transform the perceptual world.* As this is expressed in a Modoc song:

> *I*
> *the song*
> *I walk here*[24]

To neglect this dimension—to overlook the power that words or spoken phrases have to influence the body, and hence to modulate our sensory experience of the world around us—is to render even the most mundane, communicative capacity of language incomprehensible.

❧

WE MAY VERY BRIEFLY SUMMARIZE THE GENERAL RESULTS OF Merleau-Ponty's phenomenological investigations, or at least our own interpretation of those results, as follows: (1) The event of perception, experientially considered, is an inherently interactive, *participatory* event, a reciprocal interplay between the perceiver and the perceived. (2) Perceived things are encountered by the perceiving body as animate, living powers that actively draw us into relation. Our spontaneous, pre-conceptual experience yields no evidence for a dualistic division between animate and "inanimate" phenomena, only for relative distinctions between diverse forms of animateness. (3) The perceptual reciprocity between our sensing bodies and the animate, expressive landscape both engenders and supports our more conscious, linguistic reciprocity with others. The complex interchange that we call "language" is rooted in the non-verbal exchange always already going on between our own flesh and the flesh of the world. (4) Human languages, then, are informed not only by the structures of the human body and the human community, but by the evocative shapes and patterns of the more-than-human terrain. Experientially considered, language is no more the special property of the human organism than it is an expression of the animate earth that enfolds us.

Such, at any rate, are the sort of descriptions at which we arrive when we carefully attend to perception and to language as we directly experience them.

Here, however, this philosophy encounters an impasse that threatens to dissipate its conclusions and to invalidate all its efforts. Specifically, if sensory perception is inherently participatory, and if, as Merleau-Ponty has maintained, perception (broadly considered) is the inescapable source of all experience, how can we possibly account for the apparent absence of participation in the modern world? "What right have I," asks Merleau-Ponty, "to call 'immediate' this original that can be forgotten to such an extent?"[25] If our primordial experience is inherently animistic, if our "immediate" awareness discloses a field of phenomena that are all potentially animate and expressive, how can we ever account for the *loss* of such animateness from the world around us? How can we account for our culture's experience of other animals as senseless automata, or of trees as purely passive fodder for lumber mills? If perception, in its depths, is wholly participatory, how could we ever have broken out of those depths into the inert and determinate world we now commonly perceive?

We may suspect, at first, that the apparent loss of participation has something to do with language. For language, although it is rooted in perception, nevertheless has a profound capacity to turn back upon, and influence, our sensorial experience. While the reciprocity of perception engenders the more explicit reciprocity of speech and language, perception always remains vulnerable to the decisive influence of language, as a mother remains especially sensitive to the actions of her child. It was this influence that led the American linguist Edward Sapir to formulate his hypothesis of linguistic determination, suggesting that one's perception is largely determined by the language that one speaks:

> We see and hear and otherwise experience very largely as we do because the language habits of our community predispose certain choices of interpretation.[26]

Certainly, the perceptual style of any community is both reflected in, and profoundly shaped by, the common language of the community. Yet the influence of language alone can hardly explain the shift from a participatory to a nonparticipatory world. Indeed, if we accept the phenomenological position sketched at length in this chapter, then the turn toward language for a solution can only confront us with a problem analogous to that which meets us with regard to perception. If human discourse is experienced by indigenous, oral peoples to be participant with the speech of birds, of wolves, and even of the wind, how could it ever have become severed from that vaster life? How could we ever have become so *deaf* to these other voices that nonhuman nature now seems to stand mute and dumb, devoid of any meaning besides that which we choose to give it?

If perception, in its depths, is truly participatory, why do we not experience the rest of the world as animate and alive? If our own language is truly dependent upon the existence of other, nonhuman voices, why do we now experience language as an exclusively human property or possession? These two questions are in fact the same query asked from two different angles. Moreover, this query is the very same that arose at the end of the first chapter, the same that I there posed with regard to the felt shift in my own experience of nonhuman nature upon returning to the West from my sojourn in rural Asia. The question, however, is now set in a more methodic context; it is backed up by a whole tradition of philosophical inquiry. It should now be evident, as well, that the question has more than a purely personal relevance. Nonhuman nature seems to have withdrawn from both our speaking and our senses. What event could have precipitated this double withdrawal, constricting our ways of speaking even as it muffled our ears and set a veil before our eyes?

4

Animism and the Alphabet

> Lifting a brush, a burin, a pen, or a stylus
> is like releasing a bite or lifting a claw.
>
> —GARY SNYDER

THE QUESTION REGARDING THE ORIGINS OF THE ECOLOGI-
cal crisis, or of modern civilization's evident disregard for
the needs of the natural world, has already provoked various responses from philosophers. There are those who suggest that
a generally exploitative relation to the rest of nature is part and par-
cel of being human, and hence that the human species has from the
start been at war with other organisms and the earth. Others, however, have come to recognize that long-established indigenous cultures often display a remarkable solidarity with the lands that they
inhabit, as well as a basic respect, or even reverence, for the other
species that inhabit those lands. Such cultures, much smaller in scale
(and far less centralized) than modern Western civilization, seem to
have maintained a relatively homeostatic or equilibrial relation with

their local ecologies for vast periods of time, deriving their necessary sustenance from the land without seriously disrupting the ability of the earth to replenish itself. The fecundity and flourishing diversity of the North American continent led the earliest European explorers to speak of this terrain as a primeval and unsettled wilderness—yet this continent had been continuously inhabited by human cultures for at least ten thousand years. That indigenous peoples can have gathered, hunted, fished, and settled these lands for such a tremendous span of time without severely degrading the continent's wild integrity readily confounds the notion that humans are innately bound to ravage their earthly surroundings. In a few centuries of European settlement, however, much of the native abundance of this continent has been lost—its broad animal populations decimated, its many-voiced forests overcut and its prairies overgrazed, its rich soils depleted, its tumbling clear waters now undrinkable.

European civilization's neglect of the natural world and its needs has clearly been encouraged by a style of awareness that disparages sensorial reality, denigrating the visible and tangible order of things on behalf of some absolute source assumed to exist entirely beyond, or outside of, the bodily world. Some historians and philosophers have concluded that the Jewish and Christian traditions, with their otherworldly God, are primarily responsible for civilization's negligent attitude toward the environing earth. They cite, as evidence, the Hebraic God's injunction to humankind in Genesis: "Be fertile and increase, fill the earth and master it; and rule the fish of the sea, the birds of the sky, and all the living things that creep on earth."[1]

Other thinkers, however, have turned toward the Greek origins of our philosophical tradition, in the Athens of Socrates and Plato, in their quest for the roots of our nature-disdain. A long line of recent philosophers, stretching from Friedrich Nietzsche down to the present, have attempted to demonstrate that Plato's philosophical derogation of the sensible and changing forms of the world—his claim that these are mere simulacra of eternal and pure ideas existing in a nonsensorial realm beyond the apparent world—contributed profoundly to civilization's distrust of bodily and sensorial experience, and to our consequent estrangement from the earthly world around us.

So the ancient Hebrews, on the one hand, and the ancient Greeks on the other, are variously taken to task for providing the mental context that would foster civilization's mistreatment of nonhuman nature. Each of these two ancient cultures seems to have sown the seeds of our contemporary estrangement—one seeming to establish the spiritual or religious ascendancy of humankind over nature, the other effecting a more philosophical or rational dissociation of the human intellect from the organic world. Long before the historical amalgamation of Hebraic religion and Hellenistic philosophy in the Christian New Testament, these two bodies of belief already shared—or seem to have shared—a similar intellectual distance from the nonhuman environment.

In every other respect these two traditions, each one originating out of its own specific antecedents, and in its own terrain and time, were vastly different. In every other respect, that is, but one: they were both, from the start, profoundly informed by writing. Indeed, they both made use of the strange and potent technology which we have come to call "the alphabet."

*

WRITING, LIKE HUMAN LANGUAGE, IS ENGENDERED NOT ONLY within the human community but between the human community and the animate landscape, born of the interplay and contact between the human and the more-than-human world. The earthly terrain in which we find ourselves, and upon which we depend for all our nourishment, is shot through with suggestive scrawls and traces, from the sinuous calligraphy of rivers winding across the land, inscribing arroyos and canyons into the parched earth of the desert, to the black slash burned by lightning into the trunk of an old elm. The swooping flight of birds is a kind of cursive script written on the wind; it is this script that was studied by the ancient "augurs," who could read therein the course of the future. Leaf-miner insects make strange hieroglyphic tabloids of the leaves they consume. Wolves urinate on specific stumps and stones to mark off their territory. And today you read these printed words as tribal hunters once read the tracks of deer, moose, and bear printed in the soil of the forest floor. Archaeological evidence suggests that for more than a million years the subsistence of humankind has depended upon the acuity of such hunters, upon their ability to read the traces—a bit of scat

here, a broken twig there—of these animal Others. These letters I
print across the page, the scratches and scrawls you now focus upon,
trailing off across the white surface, are hardly different from the
footprints of prey left in the snow. We read these traces with organs
honed over millennia by our tribal ancestors, moving instinctively
from one track to the next, picking up the trail afresh whenever it
leaves off, hunting the *meaning*, which would be the *meeting* with the
Other.[2]

The multiform meanings of the Chinese word for writing, *wen*,
illustrate well this interpenetration of human and nonhuman scripts:

> The word *wen* signifies a conglomeration of marks, the simple
> symbol in writing. It applies to the veins in stones and wood, to
> constellations, represented by the strokes connecting the stars, to
> the tracks of birds and quadrapeds on the ground (Chinese tradi-
> tion would have it that the observation of these tracks suggested
> the invention of writing), to tattoos and even, for example, to the
> designs that decorate the turtle's shell ("The turtle is wise," an
> ancient text says—gifted with magico-religious powers—"for it
> carries designs on its back"). The term *wen* has designated, by ex-
> tension, literature. . . .[3]

Our first writing, clearly, was our own tracks, our footprints, our
handprints in mud or ash pressed upon the rock. Later, perhaps, we
found that by copying the distinctive prints and scratches made by
other animals we could gain a new power; here was a method of
identifying with the other animal, taking on its expressive magic in
order to learn of its whereabouts, to draw it near, to make it appear.
Tracing the impression left by a deer's body in the snow, or trans-
ferring that outline onto the wall of the cave: these are ways of placing oneself in distant contact with the Other, whether to invoke its
influence or to exert one's own. Perhaps by multiplying its images on
the cavern wall we sought to ensure that the deer itself would multi-
ply, be bountiful in the coming season. . . .

All of the early writing systems of our species remain tied to the
mysteries of a more-than-human world. The petroglyphs of pre-
Columbian North America abound with images of prey animals, of
rain clouds and lightning, of eagle and snake, of the paw prints of

bear. On rocks, canyon walls, and caves these figures mingle with human shapes, or shapes part human and part Other (part insect, or owl, or elk.)

Some researchers assert that the picture writing of native North America is not yet "true" writing, even where the pictures are strung together sequentially—as they are, obviously, in many of the rock inscriptions (as well as in the calendrical "winter counts" of the Plains tribes). For there seems, as yet, no strict relation between image and utterance.

In a much more conventionalized pictographic system, like the Egyptian hieroglyphics (which first appeared during the First Dynasty, around 3000 B.C.E. and remained in use until the second century C.E.),[4] stylized images of humans and human implements are still interspersed with those of plants, of various kinds of birds, as well as of serpents, felines, and other animals. Such pictographic systems, which were to be found as well in China as early as the fifteenth century B.C.E., and in Mesoamerica by the middle of the sixth century B.C.E., typically include characters that scholars have come to call "ideograms." An ideogram is often a pictorial character that refers not to the visible entity that it explicitly pictures but to some quality or other phenomenon readily associated with that entity. Thus—to invent a simple example—a stylized image of a jaguar with its feet off the ground might come to signify "speed." For the Chinese, even today, a stylized image of the sun and moon together signifies "brightness"; similarly, the word for "east" is invoked by a stylized image of the sun rising behind a tree.[5]

The efficacy of these pictorially derived systems necessarily entails a shift of sensory participation away from the voices and gestures of the surrounding landscape toward our own human-made images. However, the glyphs which constitute the bulk of these ancient scripts continually remind the reading body of its inherence in a more-than-human field of meanings. As signatures not only of the human form but of other animals, trees, sun, moon, and landforms, they continually refer our senses beyond the strictly human sphere.[6]

Yet even a host of pictograms and related ideograms will not suffice for certain terms that exist in the local discourse. Such terms may refer to phenomena that lack any precise visual association. Consider, for example, the English word "belief." How might we signify this term in a pictographic, or ideographic, manner? An image of a phantasmagorical monster, perhaps, or one of a person in prayer. Yet no such ideogram would communicate the term as readily and precisely as the simple image of a bumblebee, followed by the figure of a leaf. We could, that is, resort to a visual pun, to images of things that have nothing overtly to do with belief but which, when named in sequence, carry the same *sound* as the spoken term "belief" ("bee-leaf"). And indeed, such pictographic puns, or *rebuses,* came to be employed early on by scribes in ancient China and in Mesoamerica as well as in the Middle East, to record certain terms that were especially amorphous or resistant to visual representation. Thus, for instance, the Sumerian word *ti,* which means "life," was written in cuneiform with the pictorial sign for "arrow," which in Sumerian is also called *ti*.[7]

An important step has been taken here. With the rebus, a pictorial sign is used to directly invoke a particular sound of the human voice, rather than the outward reference of that sound. The rebus, with its focus upon the sound of a name rather than the thing named, inaugurated the distant possibility of a *phonetic* script (from the Greek *phonein*: "to sound"), one that would directly transcribe the sound of the speaking voice rather than its outward intent or meaning.[8]

However, many factors impeded the generalization of the rebus principle, and thus prevented the development of a fully phonetic writing system. For example, a largely pictographic script can easily be utilized, for communicative purposes, by persons who speak very different dialects (and hence cannot understand one another's speech). The same image or ideogram, readily understood, would simply invoke a different sound in each dialect. Thus a pictographic script allows for commerce between neighboring and even distant linguistic communities—an advance that would be lost if rebuslike signs alone were employed to transcribe the spoken sounds of one community. (This factor helps explain why China, a vast society comprised of a multitude of distinct dialects, has never developed a fully phonetic script.)[9]

Another factor inhibiting the development of a fully phonetic script was the often elite status of the scribes. Ideographic scripts must make use of a vast number of stylized glyphs or characters, since every term in the language must, at least in principle, have its own written character. (In 1716 a dictionary of Chinese—admittedly an extreme example—listed 40,545 written characters! Today a mere 8,000 characters are in use.)[10] Complete knowledge of the pictographic system, therefore, could only be the province of a few highly trained individuals. Literacy, within such cultures, was in fact the literacy of a caste, or cult, whose sacred knowledge was often held in great esteem by the rest of society. It is unlikely that the scribes would willingly develop innovations that could simplify the new technology and so render literacy more accessible to the rest of the society, for this would surely lessen their own importance and status.

> . . . it is clear that ancient writing was in the hands of a small literate elite, the scribes, who manifested great conservatism in the practice of their craft, and, so far from being interested in its simplification, often chose to demonstrate their virtuosity by a proliferation of signs and values. . . .[11]

Nevertheless, in the ancient Middle East the rebus principle was eventually generalized—probably by scribes working at a distance from the affluent and established centers of civilization—to cover all the common sounds of a given language. Thus, "syllabaries" appeared, wherein every basic sound-syllable of the language had its own conventional notation or written character (often rebuslike in origin). Such writing systems employed far fewer signs than the pictographic scripts from which they were derived, although the number of signs was still very much larger than the alphabetic script we now take for granted.

The innovation which gave rise to the alphabet was itself developed by Semitic scribes around 1500 B.C.E.[12] It consisted in recognizing that almost every syllable of their language was composed of one or more silent consonantal elements plus an element of sounded breath—that which we would today call a vowel. The silent consonants provided, as it were, the bodily framework or shape through which the sounded breath must flow. The original Semitic *aleph-beth,* then, established a character, or letter, for each of the consonants of the language. The vowels, the sounded breath that must be added to the written consonants in order to make them come alive and to speak, had to be chosen by the reader, who would vary the sounded breath according to the written context.

By this innovation, the *aleph-beth* was able to greatly reduce the necessary number of characters for a written script to just twenty-two—a simple set of signs that could be readily practiced and learned in a brief period by anyone who had the chance, even by a young child. The utter simplicity of this technical innovation was such that the early Semitic *aleph-beth,* in which were written down the various stories and histories that were later gathered into the Hebrew Bible, was adopted not only by the Hebrews but by the Phonecians (who presumably carried the new technology across the Mediterranean to Greece), the Aramaeans, the Greeks, the Romans, and indeed eventually gave rise (directly or indirectly) to virtually every alphabet known, including that which I am currently using to scribe these words.

With the advent of the *aleph-beth,* a new distance opens between human culture and the rest of nature. To be sure, pictographic and ideographic writing already involved a displacement of our sensory participation from the depths of the animate environment to the flat surface of our walls, of clay tablets, of the sheet of papyrus. However, as we noted above, the written images themselves often related us back to the other animals and the environing earth. The pictographic glyph or character still referred, implicitly, to the animate phenomenon of which it was the static image; it was that worldly phenomenon, in turn, that provoked from us the sound of its name. *The sensible phenomenon and its spoken name were, in a sense, still participant with one another*—the name a sort of emanation of the sensible entity. With the phonetic *aleph-beth,* however, the written character no longer refers us to any sensible phenomenon out in the world, or even to the name of such a phenomenon (as with the rebus), but solely to a gesture to be made by the human mouth. There is a concerted shift of attention away from any outward or worldly reference of the pictorial image, away from the sensible phenomenon that had previously called forth the spoken utterance, to the shape of the utterance itself, now invoked directly by the written character. *A direct association is established between the pictorial sign and the vocal gesture, for the first time completely bypassing the thing pictured.* The evocative phenomena—the entities imaged—are no longer a necessary part of the equation. Human utterances are now elicited, directly, by human-made signs; *the larger, more-than-human life-world is no longer a part of the semiotic, no longer a necessary part of the system.*

Or is it? When we ponder the early Semitic *aleph-beth,* we readily recognize its pictographic inheritance. *Aleph,* the first letter, is written thus: ▷ *Aleph* is also the ancient Hebrew word for "ox." The shape of the letter, we can see, was that of an ox's head with horns; turned over, it became our own letter *A.*[13] The name of the Semitic letter *mem* is also the Hebrew word for "water"; the letter, which later became our own letter *M,* was drawn as a series of waves: ᙢ . The letter *ayin,* which also means "eye" in Hebrew, was drawn as a simple circle, the picture of an eye; it is this letter, made over into a vowel by the Greek scribes, that eventually became our letter *O.* The Hebrew letter *qoph,* which is also the Hebrew term for "monkey," was drawn as a circle intersected by a long, dangling, tail φ . Our letter *Q* retains a sense of this simple picture.[14]

These are a few examples. By thus comparing the names of the letters with their various shapes, we discern that the letters of the early *aleph-beth* are still implicitly tied to the more-than-human field of phenomena. But these ties to other animals, to natural elements like water and waves, and even to the body itself, are far more tenuous than in the earlier, predominantly nonphonetic scripts. These traces of sensible nature linger in the new script only as vestigial holdovers from the old—they are no longer necessary participants in the transfer of linguistic knowledge. The other animals, the plants, and the natural elements—sun, moon, stars, waves—are beginning to lose their own voices. In the Hebrew Genesis, the animals do not speak their own names to Adam; rather, they are *given* their names by this first man. Language, for the Hebrews, was becoming a purely *human* gift, a human power.

❧

IT WAS ONLY, HOWEVER, WITH THE TRANSFER OF PHONETIC WRITING to Greece, and the consequent transformation of the Semitic *aleph-beth* into the Greek "alphabet," that the progressive abstraction of linguistic meaning from the enveloping life-world reached a type of completion. The Greek scribes took on, with slight modifications, both the shapes of the Semitic letters and their Semitic names. Thus *aleph*—the name of the first letter, and the Hebrew word for "ox"—became *alpha; beth*—the name of the second letter, as well as the word for "house"—became *beta; gimel*—the third letter, and the word for "camel," became *gamma,* etc. But while the Semitic names had older, nongrammatological meanings for those who spoke a Semitic tongue, the Greek versions of those names had no nongrammatological meaning whatsoever for the Greeks. That is, while the Semitic name for the letter was also the name of the sensorial entity commonly imaged by or associated with the letter, the Greek name had no sensorial reference at all.[15] While the Semitic name had served as a reminder of the worldy origin of the letter, the Greek name served only to designate the human-made letter itself. The pictorial (or iconic) significance of many of the Semitic letters, which was memorialized in their spoken names, was now readily lost. The indebtedness of human language to the more-than-human perceptual field, an indebtedness preserved in the names and shapes of the Semitic letters, could now be entirely forgotten.

The Rapper's Rhythm

". . . I'm a lover of learning, and trees and open country won't teach me anything, whereas men in the town do." These words are pronounced by Socrates, the wise and legendary father of Western philosophy, early in the course of the *Phaedrus*—surely one of the most eloquent and lyrical of the Platonic dialogues.[16] Written by Socrates' most illustrious student, Plato, these words inscribe a new and curious assumption at the very beginning of the European philosophical tradition.

It is difficult to reconcile Socrates' assertion—that trees and the untamed country have nothing to teach—with the Greece that we have come to know through Homer's epic ballads. In the Homeric songs the natural landscape itself bears the omens and signs that instruct human beings in their endeavors; the gods speak directly through the patterns of clouds, waves, and the flight of birds. Zeus rouses storms, sends thunderclaps, dispatches eagles to swoop low over the heads of men, disrupting their gatherings. Athena herself may take the shape of a seahawk, or may stir a wind to fill a ship's sails. Proteus, "the ancient of the salt sea, who serves under Poseidon," can readily transform into any beast, or into a flaming fire, or into water itself. Indeed, the gods seem indistinguishable at times from the natural elements that display their power: Poseidon, "the blue-maned god who makes the islands tremble," is the very life and fury of the sea itself; Helios, "lord of high noon," is not distinct from the sun (the fiery sun here a willful intelligence able even to father children: Circe, the sorceress, is his daughter). Even "fair Dawn, with her spreading fingertips of rose," is a living power. Human events and emotions are not yet distinct from the shifting moods of the animate earth—an army's sense of relief is made palpable in a description of thick clouds dispersing from the land; Nestor's anguish is likened to the darkening of the sea before a gale; the inward release of Penelope's feelings on listening to news of her husband is described as the thawing of the high mountain snows by the warm spring winds, melting the frozen water into streams that cascade down the slopes—as though the natural landscape was the proper home of those emotions, or as though a common psyche moved between humans and clouds and trees. When Odysseus, half-drowned by Poseidon's wrath and nearly dashed to pieces on the rocky coast of Phaiákia, spies the mouth of a calm river between the cliffs, he prays directly to the spirit of that river to have mercy and offer him shelter—and straightaway the tide shifts, and the river draws him into safety. Here, then, is a land that is everywhere alive and awake, animated by a multitude of capricious but willful forces, at times vengeful and at other times tender, yet always in some sense responsive to human situations. The diverse forms of the earth still speak and offer guidance to humankind, albeit in gestures that we cannot always directly understand.[17]

This participatory and animate earth contrasts vividly with the dismissive view of nature espoused by Socrates in the *Phaedrus*. To make sense of this contrast, it is necessary to realize that the Homeric epics, probably written down in the seventh century B.C.E., are essentially orally evolved creations, oral poems that had been sung and resung, shifting and complexifying, long before they were written down and thus frozen in the precise form in which we now know them.[18] The Platonic dialogues, on the other hand, written in the first half of the fourth century B.C.E., are thoroughly lettered constructions, composed in a literate context by a manifestly literate author. And indeed they inscribe for the first time many of the mental patterns or thought styles that today we of literate culture take for granted.

The Greek alphabet was first invented—or, rather, adapted from the Semitic *aleph-beth*—several centuries before Plato, probably during the eighth century B.C.E.[19] The new technology did not spread rapidly through Greece; rather, it encountered remarkable resistance in the form of a highly developed and ritualized oral culture.[20] That is, the traditions of prealphabetic Greece were actively preserved in numerous oral stories regularly recited and passed along from generation to generation by the Greek bards, or "rhapsodes." The chanted tales carried within their nested narratives much of the accumulated knowledge of the culture. Since they were not written down, they were never wholly fixed, but would shift incrementally with each telling to fit the circumstances or needs of a particular audience, gradually incorporating new practical knowledge while letting that which was obsolete fall away. The sung stories, along with the numerous ceremonies to which they were linked, were in a sense the living encyclopedias of the culture—carrying and preserving the collected knowledge and established customs of the community—and they themselves were preserved through constant repetition and ritual reenactment. There was thus little overt need for the new technology of reading and writing. According to literary historian Eric Havelock, for the first two or three centuries after its appearance in Greece, "[t]he alphabet was an interloper, lacking social standing and achieved use. The elite of society were all reciters and performers."[21]

The alphabet, after all, had not here developed gradually, as it had across the Mediterranean, out of a series of earlier scripts, and there was thus no already existing context of related inscriptions and scribal practices for it to latch onto. Moreover, the oral techniques for preserving and transmitting knowledge, and the sensorial habits associated with those techniques, were, as we shall see, largely incompatible with the sensorial patterns demanded by alphabetic literacy.

In a culture as thoroughly and complexly oral as Greek culture in this period, the alphabet could take root only by allying itself, at first, with the oral tradition. Thus, the first large written texts to appear in Greece—namely, the *Iliad* and the *Odyssey*—are, paradoxially, "oral texts." That is, they are not written compositions, as had long been supposed, but rather alphabetic transcriptions of orally chanted poems. Homer, as an oral bard, or rhapsode (from the Greek *rhapsoidein,* which meant "to stitch song together"), improvised the precise form of the poems by "stitching together" an oral tapestry from a vast fund of memorized epithets and formulaic phrases, embellishing and elaborating a cycle of stories that had already been variously improvised or "stitched together" by earlier bards since the Trojan War itself.[22]

We owe our recognition of the oral nature of the Homeric epics to the pioneering research undertaken by the Harvard classicist Milman Parry and his assistant Albert Lord, in the 1930s.[23] Parry had noticed the existence of certain stock phrases—such as "the wine-dark sea," "there spoke clever Odysseus," or "when Dawn spread out her fingertips of rose"—that are continually repeated throughout the poems. Careful study revealed that the poems were composed almost entirely of such expressions (in the twenty-seven thousand hexameters there are twenty-nine thousand repetitions of phrases with two or more words).[24] Moreover, Homer's choice of one particular epithet or formula rather than another seemed at times to be governed less by the exact meaning of the phrase than by the metrical exigencies of the line; the bard apparently called upon one specific formula after another in order to fit the driving meter of the chant, in a trance of rhythmic improvisation. This is not at all to minimize Homer's genius, but simply to indicate that his poetic brilliance was performative as much as creative—less the genius of an author writing a great novel than that of an inspired and eloquent rap artist.

The reliance of the Homeric texts upon repeated verbal formulas and stock epithets—this massive dependence upon that which we today refer to, disparagingly, as "clichés"—offered Parry and subsequent researchers a first insight into the very different world of a

European culture without writing. In a literate society, like our own, any verbal discovery or realization can be preserved simply by being written down. Whenever we wish to know how to accomplish a certain task, we need only find the book wherein that knowledge is inscribed. When we wish to ponder a particular historical encounter, we simply locate the text wherein that encounter is recorded. Oral cultures, however, lacking the fixed and permanent record that we have come to count on, can preserve verbal knowledge only by constantly repeating it. Practical knowledge must be embedded in spoken formulas that can be easily recalled—in prayers and proverbs, in continually recited legends and mythic stories. The rhythmic nature of many such spoken formulas is a function of their mnemonic value; such pulsed phrases are much easier for the pulsing, breathing body to assimilate and later recall than the strictly prosaic statements that appear only after the advent of literacy. (For example, the phrase "an apple a day keeps the doctor away" is vastly easier to remember than the phrase "one should always eat fruit in order to stay healthy"). The discourse of nonwriting cultures is, of necessity, largely comprised of such formulaic and rhythmic phrases, which readily spring to the tongue in appropriate situations.[25]

Parry's insights regarding the orally composed nature of the Homeric epics remained somewhat speculative until he was able to neet and observe representatives of an actual bardic tradition still in existence in Eastern Europe. In the 1930s, Parry and his student Albert Lord traveled to Serbia, where they befriended a number of nonliterate Slavic singers whose craft was still rooted in the ancient oral traditions of the Balkans. These singers (or *guslars*) chanted their long stories—for which there existed no written texts—in coffeehouses and at weddings, accompanying themselves on a simple stringed instrument called a *gusla*. Parry and Lord recorded many of these epic songs on early phonographic disks,[26] and so were later able to compare the metrical structure of these chanted stories with the structure and phrasing of the Homeric poems. The parallels were clear and remarkable.[27]

> When one hears the Southern Slavs sing their tales he has the overwhelming feeling that, in some way, he is hearing Homer. This is no mere sentimental feeling that comes from his seeing a

way of life and a cast of thought that are strange to him. . . . When the hearer looks closely to see why he should seem to be hearing Homer he finds precise reasons: he is ever hearing the same ideas that Homer expresses, and is hearing them expressed in phrases which are rhythmically the same, and which are grouped in the same order.[28]

Parry carefully documented these strong parallels, and after his early death his research into oral modes of composition was carried on by Albert Lord. Among other things, Lord's research indicated that learning to read and write thoroughly disabled the oral poet, ruining his capacity for oral improvisation.[29]

WHEN THE HOMERIC EPICS WERE RECORDED IN WRITING, THEN THE art of the rhapsodes began to lose its preservative and instructive function. The knowledge embedded in the epic stories and myths was now captured for the first time in a visible and fixed form, which could be returned to, examined, and even questioned. Indeed, it was only then, under the slowly spreading influence of alphabetic technology, that "language" was beginning to separate itself from the animate flux of the world, and so becoming a ponderable presence in its own right.

It is only as language is written down that it becomes possible to think about it. The acoustic medium, being incapable of visualization, did not achieve recognition as a phenomenon wholly separable from the person who used it. But in the alphabetized document the medium became objectified. There it was, reproduced perfectly in the alphabet . . . no longer just a function of "me" the speaker but a document with an independent existence.[30]

The scribe, or author, could now begin to dialogue with his own visible inscriptions, viewing and responding to his own words even as he wrote them down. *A new power of reflexivity was thus coming into existence, borne by the relation between the scribe and his scripted text*. We can witness the gradual spread of this new power in the written fragments of the pre-Socratic philosophers of the sixth and fifth centuries B.C.E. These thinkers are still under the sway of the oral-poetic mode of discourse—their teachings are commonly couched in an aphoristic or poetic form, and their attention is still turned toward the sensuous terrain that surrounds them. Nevertheless, they seem to stand at a new distance from the natural order, their thoughts inhabiting a different mode of temporality from the flux of nature, which they now question and strive to understand. The written fragments of Heraclitus or of Empedocles give evidence of a radically new, literate reflection combined with a more traditional, oral preoccupation with a sensuous nature still felt to be mysteriously animate and alive, filled with immanent powers. In the words of the pre-Socratic philosopher Thales, "all things are full of gods."[31]

It was not until the early fourth century B.C.E. that such numinous powers, or gods, were largely expelled from the natural surroundings. For it was only at this time that alphabetic literacy became a collective reality in Greece. Indeed, it was only during Plato's lifetime (428–348 B.C.E.) that the alphabet was incorporated within Athenian life to the extent that we might truthfully speak of Athenian Greece as a "literate" culture:

> Plato, in the early fourth century B.C., stands on the threshold between the oral and written cultures of Greece. The earliest epigraphic and iconographic indications of young boys being taught to write date from Plato's childhood. In his day, people had already been reciting Homer from the text for centuries. But the art of writing was still primarily a handicraft. . . . In the fifth century B.C., craftsmen began to acquire the art of carving or engraving letters of the alphabet. But writing was still not a part of recognized instruction: the most a person was expected to be able to write and spell was his own name. . . .[32]

Plato was teaching, then, precisely at the moment when the new technology of reading and writing was shedding its specialized "craft" status and finally spreading, by means of the Greek curriculum, into the culture at large. The significance of this conjunction has not been well recognized by Western philosophers, all of whom stand—to a greater or lesser extent—within Plato's lineage. Plato, or rather the association between the literate Plato and his mostly non-literate teacher Socrates (469?–399 B.C.E.), may be recognized as the hinge on which the sensuous, mimetic, profoundly embodied style of consciousness proper to orality gave way to the more detached, abstract mode of thinking engendered by alphabetic literacy. Indeed, it was Plato who carefully developed and brought to term the collective thought-structures appropriate to the new technology.

An Eternity of Unchanging Ideas

Although Socrates himself may have been able to write little more than his own name, he made brilliant use of the new reflexive capacity introduced by the alphabet. Eric Havelock has suggested that the famed "Socratic dialectic"—which, in its simplest form, consisted in asking a speaker to explain what he has said—was primarily a method for disrupting the mimetic thought patterns of oral culture. The speaker's original statement, if it concerned important matters of morality and social custom, would necessarily have been a memorized formula, a poetic or proverbial phrase, which presented a vivid example of the matter being discussed. By asking the speaker to explain himself or to repeat his statement in different terms, Socrates forced his interlocutors to separate themselves, for the first time, from their own words—to separate themselves, that is, from the phrases and formulas that had become habitual through the constant repetition of traditional teaching stories. Prior to this moment, spoken discourse was inseparable from the endlessly repeated stories, legends, and myths that provided many of the spoken phrases one needed in one's daily actions and interactions. To speak was to live within a storied universe, and thus to feel one's closeness to those protagonists and ancestral heroes whose words often seemed to speak through one's own mouth. Such, as we have said, is the way culture preserves itself in the absence of written records. But Socrates interrupted all this. By continually asking his interlocutors to repeat and explain what they had said in other words, by getting them thus to listen to and ponder their own speaking, Socrates

stunned his listeners out of the mnemonic trance demanded by orality, and hence out of the sensuous, storied realm to which they were
accustomed. Small wonder that some Athenians complained that
Socrates' conversation had the numbing effect of a stingray's electric shock.

Prior to the spread of writing, ethical qualities like "virtue," "justice," and "temperance" were thoroughly entwined with the specific
situations in which those qualities were exhibited. The terms for
such qualities were oral utterances called forth by particular social
situations; they had no apparent existence independent of those situations. As utterances, they slipped back into the silence immediately after they were spoken; they had no permanent presence to the
senses. "Justice" and "temperance" were thus experienced as living
occurrences, as *events*. Arising in specific situations, they were inseparable from the particular persons or actions that momentarily embodied them.

Yet as soon as such utterances were recorded in writing, they acquired an autonomy and a permanence hitherto unknown. Once
written down, "virtue" was seen to have an unchanging, visible form
independent of the speaker—and independent as well of the corporeal situations and individuals that exhibited it.

Socrates clearly aligned his method with this shift in the perceptual field. Whenever, in Plato's dialogues, Socrates asks his interlocutor to give an account of what "virtue," or "justice," or
"courage" actually is, questioning them regarding the real meaning
of the qualitative terms they unthinkingly employ in their speaking,
they confidently reply by recounting particular instances of the
quality under consideration, enumerating specific examples of "justice," yet never defining "justice" itself. When Socrates invites Meno
to say what "virtue" is, Meno readily enumerates so many different
instances or embodiments of virtue that Socrates retorts sardon-
ically: "I seem to be in luck. I only asked you for one thing, virtue,
but you have given me a whole swarm of virtues."[33] In keeping with
older, oral modes of discourse, Socrates' fellow Athenians cannot
abstract these spoken qualities from the lived situations that seem to
exemplify these terms and call them forth. Socrates, however, has
little interest in these multiple embodiments of "virtue," except in
so far as they all partake of some common, unchanging element,

which he would like to abstract and ponder on its own. In every case Socrates attempts to induce a reflection upon the quality as it exists in itself, independent of particular circumstances. The specific embodiments of "justice" that we may encounter in the material world are necessarily variable and fleeting; genuine knowledge, claims Socrates, must be of what is eternal and unchanging.

Socrates, then, is clearly convinced that there is a fixed, unchanging essence of "justice" that unites all the just instances, as there is an eternal essence of "virtue," of "beauty," of "goodness," "courage," and all the rest. Yet Socrates' conviction would not be possible without the alphabet. For only when a qualitative term is written down does it become ponderable as a fixed form independent of both the speakers and of situations.[34]

Not all writing systems foster this thorough abstraction of a spoken quality from its embeddedness in corporeal situations. The ideographic script of China, as we have seen, still retains pictorial ties to the phenomenal world of sensory experience. Thus, the Chinese ideograph for "red" is itself a juxtaposition of lived examples; it is composed of abbreviated pictorial images of a rose, a cherry, iron rust, and a flamingo. And indeed, according to some observers, if one asks a cultured person in China to explain a general quality like "red," or "loyalty," or "happiness," she will likely reply by describing various instances or examples of that quality, much like Socrates' interlocutors.[35] It was not writing per se, but phonetic writing, and the Greek alphabet in particular, that enabled the abstraction of previously ephemeral qualities like "goodness" and "justice" from their inherence in situations, promoting them to a new realm independent of the flux of ordinary experience. For the Greek alphabet had effectively severed all ties between the written letters and the sensible world from which they were derived; it was the first writing system able to render almost any human utterance in a fixed and lasting form.

While Socrates focused his teaching on the moral qualities, his disciple Plato recognized that not just ephemeral qualities but *all* general terms, from "table" to "cloud," could now be pondered as eternal, unchanging forms. In retrospect, we can see that the alphabet had indeed granted a new autonomy and permanence to all such terms. Besides the various meandering rivers, for instance, that one could view, or wade through, in the sensible world, there was also the singular notion "river," which now had its own visibility; "river" itself could now be pondered apart from all those material rivers that were liable to change their course or to dry up from one season to the next. For Plato, as for his teacher, genuine knowledge must be of what is unchanging and eternal—there can be no "true" knowledge of a particular river, but only of the pure Idea (or *eidos*) "river." That Plato often used the Greek term *eidos* (which meant "visible shape or form") to refer to such unchanging essences is itself, I believe, an indication of the affinity between these eternal essences and the unchanging, visible shapes of the alphabet.

For the letters of the alphabet, like the Platonic Ideas, do not exist in the world of ordinary vision. The letters, and the written words that they present, are not subject to the flux of growth and decay, to the perturbations and cyclical changes common to other visible things; they seem to hover, as it were, in another, strangely timeless dimension. Further, the letters defer and dissimulate their common visibility, each one dissolving into sound even as we look at it, trading our eyes for our ears, so that we seem not to be *seeing* so much as *hearing* something. Alphabetic writing deflects our attention from its visible aspect, effectively vanishing behind the current of human speech that it provokes.[36]

As we have already seen, the process of learning to read and to write with the alphabet engenders a new, profoundly reflexive, sense of self. The capacity to view and even to dialogue with one's own words after writing them down, or even in the process of writing them down, enables a new sense of autonomy and independence from others, and even from the sensuous surroundings that had earlier been one's constant interlocutor. The fact that one's scripted words can be returned to and pondered at any time that one chooses, regardless of when, or in what situation, they were first recorded, grants a timeless quality to this new reflective self, a sense of the relative independence of one's verbal, speaking self from the breathing body with its shifting needs. The literate self cannot help but feel its own transcendence and timelessness relative to the fleeting world of corporeal experience.

This new, seemingly autonomous, reflective awareness is called, by Socrates, the *psychê,* a term he thus twists from its earlier,

Homeric significance as the invisible breath that animates the living body and that remains, as kind of wraith or ghost, after the body's death. (The term *psychê* was derived from an older Greek term, *psychein,* which meant "to breathe" or "to blow".) For Plato, as for Socrates, the *psychê* is now that aspect of oneself that is refined and strengthened by turning away from the ordinary sensory world in order to contemplate the intelligible Ideas, the pure and eternal forms that, alone, truly exist. The Socratic-Platonic *psychê,* in other words, is none other than the literate intellect, that part of the self that is born and strengthened in relation to the written letters.[37]

PLATO HIMSELF EFFECTS A POWERFUL CRITIQUE OF THE INFLUENCE of writing in the *Phaedrus,* that dialogue from which I quoted earlier in this chapter. In the course of that dialogue, Socrates relates to the young Phaedrus a curious legend regarding the Egyptian king Thamus. According to this story, Thamus was approached directly by the god Thoth—the divine inventor of geometry, mathematics, astronomy, and writing—who offers writing as a gift to the king so that Thamus may offer it, in turn, to the Egyptian people. But Thamus, after considering both the beneficent and the baneful aspects of the god's inventions, concludes that his people will be much better off *without* writing, and so he refuses the gift. Against Thoth's claim that writing will make people wiser and improve their memory, the king asserts that the very opposite is the case:

> If men learn this, it will implant forgetfulness in their souls; they will cease to exercise memory because they rely on that which is written, calling things to remembrance no longer from within themselves, but by means of external marks.[38]

Moreover—according to the king—spoken teachings, once written down, easily find their way into the hands of those who will misunderstand those teachings while nevertheless thinking that they understand them. Thus, the written letters bring not wisdom but only "the conceit of wisdom," making men seem to know much when in fact they know little.[39]

Plato's Socrates clearly agrees with the king's judgment, and it is evident that Plato wishes the reader to take these criticisms of writing quite seriously. Later in the same dialogue we read that "a written discourse on any subject is bound to contain much that is fanciful," and that in any case "nothing that has ever been written whether in verse or prose merits much serious attention."[40] Certainly, it is strange to read such strong remarks against writing from a thinker whose numerous written texts are among the most widely distributed and worshipfully read in the Western world. Here is Plato, from whom virtually all Western philosophers draw their literary ancestry, disparaging writing as nothing more than a pastime! What are we to make of these statements?

Such doubts about the alphabet, and such assertions regarding its potentially debilitating effects, must have been legion in Athens just before or during the time that Plato was writing. It is remarkable that Plato held to such criticisms despite the fact that he was an inveterate participant in the alphabetic universe. Given his multiple and diverse writings, which constitute what is probably the first large corpus of prose by a single author in the history of the alphabet, it seems clear that Plato did not intend his own criticisms to dissuade his students and readers from writing, or from reading him further. Rather, it is as though he meant to build into the very body of his writings a caution that they not be given too much weight. Not because he was uncertain about the genuine and serious worth of his philosophy, but simply because he had strong reservations about the written word and its ability to convey the full meaning of a philosophy that was as much a practice—involving direct, personal interaction and instruction—as it was a set of static formulations and reflections. Writing, according to Socrates, can at best serve as a *reminder* to a reader who already knows those things that have been written.[41] It is possible that Plato wrote his various dialogues to serve just such a restricted function; to act as reminders, for the students of his academy, of the methods and insights that they first learned in direct, face-to-face dialogue with their teacher.

Nevertheless Plato, despite his cautions, did not recognize the extent to which the very content of his teaching—with its dependence upon the twin notions of a purely rational *psychê* and a realm of eternal, unchanging Ideas—was already deeply under the influence of alphabetic writing. In the early fourth century B.C.E., when literacy was gradually spreading throughout Athenian society, it was certainly possible to witness the impact that writing was having upon the dissemination of particular teachings. An astute observer might discern as well the debilitating effects of writing upon the collective practice of memory, as what had previously been accomplished through the memorized repetition of ritual poems, songs, and stories was transferred to an external and fixed artifact. But it was hardly possible to discern the pervasive influence of letters upon patterns of perception and contemplation in general. Similarly, today we are simply unable to discern with any clarity the manner in which our own perceptions and thoughts are being shifted by our sensory involvement with electronic technologies, since any thinking that seeks to discern such a shift is itself subject to the very effect that it strives to thematize. Nevertheless, we may be sure that the shapes of our consciousness *are* shifting in tandem with the technologies that engage our senses—much as we can now begin to discern, in retrospect, how the distinctive shape of Western philosophy was born of the meeting between the human senses and the alphabet in ancient Greece.

Of Tongues in Trees

Socrates' critique of writing, in the *Phaedrus,* is occasioned by a written text carried by the young Phaedrus at the very beginning of the dialogue, when Socrates encounters him on his way out of the city. Phaedrus has just heard a friend of his, Lysias, declaiming a newly written speech on the topic of love; impressed by Lysias's speech, Phaedrus has obtained a copy of the speech and is going for a walk outside the city walls to ponder the text at his leisure. Socrates, always eager for philosophical discourse, agrees to accompany Phaedrus into the open country where they may together consider Lysias's text and discuss its merits. It is summer; the two men walk along the Ilissus River, wade across it, then settle on the grass in the shade of a tall, spreading plane tree. Socrates compliments Phaedrus for leading them to this pleasant glen, and Phaedrus replies, with some incredulity, that Socrates seems wholly a stranger to the country, like one who had hardly ever set foot outside the city walls. It is then that Socrates explains himself: "You must forgive me, dear friend. I'm a lover of learning, and trees and open country won't teach me anything, whereas men in the town do."[42]

We have already seen how peculiar this statement seems in relation to the world of the Homeric poems. How much more bizarre Socrates' words would seem to the members of an oral society still less exposed to the influence of literate traders than was Homeric Greece—to a culture, in other words, whose gods were not yet as anthropomorphic as even frothy-haired Poseidon and eruptive Hephaestus. The claim that "trees and open country won't teach anything" would have scant coherence within an indigenous hunting community, for the simple reason that such communities necessarily take their most profound teachings or instructions directly from the more-than-human earth. Whether among the Plains Indians of North America, the bushmen of the Kalahari Desert, or the Pintupi of the Australian outback, the elders and "persons of high degree" within such hunting communities continually defer to the animate powers of the surrounding landscape—to those nonhuman powers from which they themselves draw their deepest inspiration.

When a young person within such a culture is chosen, by whatever circumstance, to become a seer or shaman for the community, he or she may be trained by an elder seer within the tribe. Yet the most learned and powerful shaman will be one who has first learned his or her skills directly from the land itself—from a specific animal or plant, from a river or a storm—during a prolonged sojourn out beyond the boundaries of the human society. Indeed, among many of the tribes once indigenous to North America, a boy could gain the insight necessary to enter the society of grown men only by undertaking a solitary quest for vision—only by rendering himself vulnerable to the wild forces of the land and, if need be, crying to those forces for a vision.[43] The initiatory "Walkabout" undertaken by Aboriginal Australians is again just such an act whereby oral peoples turn toward the more-than-human earth for the teachings that must vitalize and sustain the human community.

In indigenous, oral cultures, nature itself is articulate; it *speaks*. The human voice in an oral culture is always to some extent participant with the voices of wolves, wind, and waves—participant, that is, with the encompassing discourse of an animate earth. There is no element of the landscape that is definitively void of expressive resonance and power: any movement may be a gesture, any sound may be a voice, a meaningful utterance.

Socrates' claim that trees have nothing to teach is a vivid indicator of the extent to which the human senses in Athens had already withdrawn from direct participation with the natural landscape. To directly perceive any phenomenon is to enter into relation with it, to feel oneself in a living interaction with another being. To define the phenomenon as an inert object, to deny the ability of a tree to inform and even instruct one's awareness, is to have turned one's senses away from that phenomenon. It is to ponder the tree from outside of its world, or, rather, from outside of the world in which both oneself and the tree are active participants.

Yet even here Plato seems to waver and vacillate. Indeed, just as the *Phaedrus* is the prime locus of Plato's apparent ambivalence with regard to his own practice of writing, so it is also the locus of a profound ambivalence with regard to nature, or to the expressive power of the natural world. Although the dialogue opens with Socrates' disparagement of trees and the open countryside, it is significant that the dialogue itself takes place in the midst of that very countryside. Unlike the other Platonic dialogues, the *Phaedrus* alone occurs outside the walls of the city, out beyond the laws and formalities that enclose and isolate the human community from the more-than-human earth. Socrates and Phaedrus have themselves embarked, as it were, on a kind of vision quest, stepping outside the city norms in order to test their citified knowledge against the older knowings embedded in the land. Plato is here, in a sense, putting philosophy itself to the test, by opening and exposing it to the nonhuman powers that for so long had compelled the awe and attention of humankind. In direct contrast to *The Republic,* in which Plato vilifies the ancient gods and effectively banishes the oral poets and storytellers from the utopian city that he envisions, in the *Phaedrus,* Plato brings philosophy itself outside the city, there to confront and come to terms with the older, oral ways of knowing which, although they may be banished from the city, nevertheless still dwell in the surrounding countryside. It is only outside the city walls that Plato will allow himself to question and critique the practice of writing to which he (and all later philosophy) is indissolubly tied. And it is only outside those walls that he will allow himself to fully acknowledge and offer respect to the oral, animistic universe that is on the wane.

Thus, shortly after his assertion that trees can teach him nothing, Socrates allows himself to be goaded into making an impromptu speech by an oath that Phaedrus swears upon the spirit of the very tree beneath which they sit![44] Trees, it would seem, still retain a modicum of efficacious power. Later in the dialogue Socrates himself will remind Phaedrus that, according to tradition, "the first prophetic utterances came from an oak tree."[45]

Not just trees but animals, too, have—in the *Phaedrus*—magical powers. Socrates initiates the discussion of writing by speculating that the cicadas chirping and "conversing with one another" in the tree overhead are probably observing the two of them as well; he maintains that the cicadas will intercede with the Muses on their behalf if he and Phaedrus continue to converse on philosophical matters.[46] And he proceeds to recount a story that describes how the cicadas, who were originally persons, were transformed into their present form:

> The story is that once upon a time these creatures were men— men of an age before there were any Muses—and that when the latter came into the world, and music made its appearance, some of the people of those days were so thrilled with pleasure that they went on singing and quite forgot to eat and drink until they actually died without noticing it. From them in due course sprang the race of cicadas, to which the Muses have granted the boon of needing no sustenance right from their birth, but of singing from the very first, without food or drink, until the day of their death, after which they go and report to the Muses how they severally are paid honor among mankind and by whom. . . .[47]

Any student of indigenous, oral cultures will hear a ring of familiarity in this tale. The story of the cicadas is identical in its character to the stories of the "Distant Time" told today by the Koyukon Indians of Alaska, identical to stories from that mysterious realm "long ago, in the future" which are told by the Inuit (or eastern Eskimo), or to the "Dreamtime" stories told by Aboriginal Australians. We may recall, in this context, these Inuit words quoted toward the end of the last chapter: "In the very earliest time, when both people and animals lived on earth, a person could become an animal if he wanted to, and an animal could become a human being. . . ." Here is a typical Distant Time story told by the Koyukon:

> When the burbot [ling cod] was human, he decided to leave the land and become a water animal. So he started down the bank, taking a piece of bear fat with him. But the other animal people wanted him to stay and tried to hold him back, stretching him all out of shape in the process. This is why the burbot has such a long, stretched-out body, and why its liver is rich and oily like the bear fat its ancestor carried to the water long ago.[48]

Like all oral stories of the Distant Time or Dreamtime, Socrates' myth of the cicadas is a functional myth; it serves to explain certain observed characteristics of the cicadas, like their endless humming and buzzing, and their apparent lack of any need for nourishment ("when music appeared, some of the people of those days were so thrilled with pleasure that they went on singing, and quite forgot to eat and drink"). Anthropologists have tended to view such stories from the Dreamtime or Distant Time as confused attempts at causal explanation by the primitive mind. Here, however, in the light of our discussion regarding orality and literacy, such stories can be seen to serve a far more practical function.

Without a versatile writing system, there is simply no way to preserve, in any fixed, external medium, the accumulated knowledge regarding particular plants (including where to find them, which parts of them are edible, which poisonous, how they are best prepared, what ailments they may cure or exacerbate), and regarding specific animals (how to recognize them, what they eat, how best to track or hunt them), or even regarding the land itself (how best to orient oneself in the surrounding terrain, what landforms to avoid, where to find water or fuel). Such practical knowledge must be preserved, then, in spoken formulations that can be easily remembered, modified when new facts are learned, and retold from generation to generation. Yet not all verbal formulations are amenable to simple recall—most verbal forms that we are conversant with today are dependent upon a context of writing. To us, for instance, a simple mental list of the known characteristics of a particular plant or animal would seem the easiest and most obvious formulation. Yet such lists have no value in an oral culture; without a visible counterpart that can be brought to mind and scanned by the mind's eye, spoken lists cannot be readily recalled and repeated.[49] Without writing, knowledge of the diverse properties of particular animals, plants, and places can be preserved only by being woven into *stories*, into vital tales wherein the specific characteristics of the plant are made evident through a narrated series of events and interactions. Stories, like rhymed poems or songs, readily incorporate themselves into our felt experience; the shifts of action echo and resonate our own encounters—in hearing or telling the story we vicariously *live* it, and the travails of its characters embed themselves into our own flesh. The sensuous, breathing body is, as we have seen, a dynamic, ever-unfolding form, more a process than a fixed or unchanging object. As such, it cannot readily appropriate inert "facts" or "data" (static nuggets of "information" abstracted from the lived situations in which they arise). Yet the living body can easily assimilate other dynamic or eventful processes, like the unfolding of a story, appropriating each episode or event as a variation of its own unfolding.

And the more lively the story—the more vital or stirring the encounters within it—the more readily it will be in-corporated.[50] Oral memorization calls for lively, dynamic, often violent, characters and encounters. If the story carries knowledge about a particular plant or natural element, then that entity will often be cast, like all of the other characters, in a fully animate form, capable of personlike adventures and experiences, susceptible to the kinds of setbacks or difficulties that we know from our own lives. In this manner the character or personality of a medicinal plant will be easily remembered, its poisonous attributes will be readily avoided, and the precise steps in its preparation will be evident from the sequence of events in the very legend that one chants while preparing it. One has only to recite the appropriate story, from the Distant Time, about a particular plant, animal, or element in order to recall the accumulated cultural knowledge regarding that entity and its relation to the human community.

In this light, that which we literates misconstrue as a naïve attempt at causal explanation may be recognized as a sophisticated mnemonic method whereby precise knowledge is preserved and passed along from generation to generation. The only causality proper to such stories is a kind of cyclical causality alien to modern thought, according to which persons may influence events in the enveloping natural order and yet are themselves continually under the influence of those very events. By invoking a dimension or a time when all entities were in human form, or when humans were in the shape of other animals and plants, these stories affirm human kinship with the multiple forms of the surrounding terrain. They thus indicate the respectful, mutual relations that must be maintained with natural phenomena, the reciprocity that must be practiced in relation to other animals, plants, and the land itself, in order to ensure one's own health and to preserve the well-being of the human community.

This facet of respectful consideration, and its attendant circular causality, is also present in Socrates' tale of the cicadas. By relating the tale to Phaedrus, Socrates indicates, although not without a sense of irony, the respect that is properly due to such insects, who might confer a boon upon the two of them in return. Later, indeed, Socrates will attribute his own loquacious eloquence in this dialogue to the inspiration of the cicadas, "those mouthpieces of the Muses."[51]

It seems clear that in the *Phaedrus,* Plato accords much more consideration to the oral-poetic universe, with its surplus of irrational, sensuous, and animistic powers, than he does in other dialogues. The *Phaedrus* seems to attempt a reconciliation of the transcendent, bodiless world of eternal Ideas proposed in this and other dialogues with the passionate, feeling-toned world of natural magic that still lingered in the common language of his day. But this conciliatory affirmation of the animistic, sensuous universe is effected only within the context of a more subtle devaluation. This is most obviously evident in the allegory at the heart of the dialogue, wherein Socrates gives his own account of love, or "eros." According to Socrates, the divine madness of love is to be honored and praised, for it is love that can most powerfully awaken the soul from its slumber in the bodily world. The lover's soul is stirred by the sensuous beauty of the beloved into remembering, however faintly, the more pure, genuine beauty of the eternal, bodiless Ideas which it once knew. Thus reminded of its own transcendent nature, the previously dormant soul begins to sprout wings, and soon aspires to rise beyond this world of ceaseless "becoming" toward that changeless eternal realm beyond the stars:

> It is there that true being dwells, without color or shape, that cannot be touched; reason alone, the soul's pilot, can behold it, and all true knowledge is knowledge thereof.[52]

In this dialogue, then, the bodily desire for sensuous contact and communion with other bodies and with the bodily earth is honored, but only as an incitement or spur toward the more genuine union of the reasoning soul with the eternal forms of "justice," "temperance," "virtue," and the like, which—according to Plato—lie beyond the sensory world entirely.

We have seen that this affinity between the reasoning soul or *psyché* and the changeless Ideas is inseparable from the relation between the new, literate intellect and the visible letters of the alphabet (which, although not outside of the sensory world, do present an entirely new and stable order of phenomena, relative to which all other phenomenal forms may come to seem remarkedly fleeting, ambiguous, and derivative). Just as Plato's apparent criticisms of alphabetic writing in the *Phaedrus* take place within the context of a much broader espousal of the detached (or disembodied) reflection that writing engenders, so in the same dialogue his apparent affirmation of oral-animistic modes of experience is accomplished only in the context of a broader disparagement. The erotic, participatory world of the sensing body is conjured forth only to be subordinated to the incorporeal world toward which, according to Plato, it points. The literate intellect here certifies its dominion by claiming the sensuous life of the body-in-nature as its subordinate ally. What was previously a threat to the literate mind's clean ascendance is now disarmed by being given a place within the grand project of transcendence. Hence, even and especially in this most pastoral of dialogues, in which the rational intellect seems almost balanced by the desiring body, and in which trees that "can teach nothing" seem balanced by watchful cicadas, we may still discern the seeds of nature's eventual eclipse behind a world of letters, numbers, and texts.

Synaesthesia and the Encounter with the Other

It is remarkable that none of the major twentieth-century scholars who have directed their attention to the changes wrought by literacy have seriously considered the impact of writing—and, in particular, phonetic writing—upon the human experience of the wider natural world. Their focus has generally centered upon the influence of phonetic writing on the structure and deployment of human language,[53] on patterns of cognition and thought,[54] or upon the internal organization of human societies.[55] Most of the major research, in other words, has focused upon the alphabet's impact on processes either internal to human society or presumably "internal" to the human mind. Yet the limitation of such research—its restriction within the bounds of human social interaction and personal interiority—itself reflects an anthropocentric bias wholly endemic to alphabetic culture. In the absence of phonetic literacy, neither society, nor language, nor even the experience of "thought" or consciousness, can be pondered in isolation from the multiple nonhuman shapes and powers that lend their influence to all our activities (we need think only of our ceaseless involvement with the ground underfoot, with the air that swirls around us, with the plants and animals that we consume, with the daily warmth of the sun and the cyclic pull of the moon). Indeed, in the absence of formal writing systems, human communities come to know themselves primarily as they are reflected back by the animals and the animate landscapes with which they are directly engaged. This epistemological dependence is readily evidenced, on every continent, by the diverse modes of identification commonly categorized under the single term "totemism."

It is exceedingly difficult for us literates to experience anything approaching the vividness and intensity with which surrounding nature spontaneously presents itself to the members of an indigenous, oral community. Yet as we saw in the previous chapters, Merleau-Ponty's careful phenomenology of perceptual experience had begun to disclose, underneath all of our literate abstractions, a deeply participatory relation to things and to the earth, a felt reciprocity curiously analogous to the animistic awareness of indigenous, oral persons. If we wish to better comprehend the remarkable shift in the human experience of nature that was occasioned by the advent and spread of phonetic literacy, we would do well to return to the intimate analysis of sensory perception inaugurated by Merleau-Ponty. For without a clear awareness of what reading and writing amounts to when considered at the level of our most immediate, bodily experience, any "theory" regarding the impact of literacy can only be provisional and speculative.

Although Merleau-Ponty himself never attempted a phenomenology of reading or writing, his recognition of the importance of synaesthesia—the overlap and intertwining of the senses—resulted in a number of experiential analyses directly pertinent to the phenomenon of reading. For reading, as soon as we attend to its sensorial texture, discloses itself as a profoundly synaesthetic encounter. Our eyes converge upon a visible mark, or a series of marks, yet what they find there is a sequence not of images but of sounds, something heard; the visible letters, as we have said, trade our eyes for our ears. Or, rather, the eye and the ear are brought together at the surface of the text—a new linkage has been forged between seeing and hearing which ensures that a phenomenon apprehended by one sense is instantly transposed into the other. Further, we should note that this sensory transposition is mediated by the human mouth and tongue; it is not just any kind of sound that is experienced in the act of reading, but specifically human, vocal sounds—those which issue from the human mouth. It is important to realize that the now common experience of "silent" reading is a late development in the story of the alphabet, emerging only during the Middle Ages, when spaces were first inserted between the words in a written manuscript (along with various forms of punctuation), enabling readers to distinguish the words of a written sentence without necessarily sounding them out audibly. Before this innovation, to read was necessarily to read aloud, or at the very least to mumble quietly; after the twelfth century it became increasingly possible to internalize the sounds, to listen inwardly to phantom words (or the inward echo of words once uttered).[56]

Alphabetic reading, then, proceeds by way of a new synaesthetic collaboration between the eye and the ear, between seeing and hearing. To discern the consequences of this new synaesthesia, we need to examine the centrality of synaesthesia in our perception of others and of the earth.

The experiencing body (as we saw in chapter 2) is not a self-enclosed object, but an open, incomplete entity. This openness is evident in the arrangement of the senses: I have these multiple ways of encountering and exploring the world—listening with my ears, touching with my skin, seeing with my eyes, tasting with my tongue, smelling with my nose—and all of these various powers or pathways continually open outward from the perceiving body, like different paths diverging from a forest. Yet my experience of the world is not fragmented; I do not commonly experience the visible appearance of the world as in any way separable from its audible aspect, or from the myriad textures that offer themselves to my touch. When the local tomcat comes to visit, I do not have distinctive experiences of a visible cat, an audible cat, and an olfactory cat; rather, the tomcat is precisely the place where these separate sensory modalities join and dissolve into one another, blending as well with a certain furry tactility. Thus, my divergent senses meet up with each other in the surrounding world, converging and commingling in the things I perceive. We may think of the sensing body as a kind of open circuit that completes itself only in things, and in the world. The differentiation of my senses, as well as their spontaneous convergence in the world at large, ensures that I am a being destined for relationship: it is primarily through my engagement with what is *not* me that I effect the integration of my senses, and thereby experience my own unity and coherence.[57]

Indeed, the synaesthetic flowing together of different senses into a dynamic and unified experience is already operative within the single system of vision itself. For ordinary vision is a blending of two unique vistas, two perspectives, *two eyes*. Even here, within a single sensory system, we discern an originary openness or divergence—

between, in this case, the two sides of my body, each with its own access to the visible—and it is only via the convergence and meeting of these two perspectives at some point out in front of my body that the visible world becomes present to me in all its depth. The double images common to unfocused vision have only a flimsy reality: if I let my eyes focus upon a shelf across the room, and meanwhile hold my index finger up in front of my face, I find that two images of my finger float before me like insubstantial phantoms and that the shelf, despite its greater distance, is much more substantial and present to my awareness than is my finger. Only when I break my focus upon the shelf and let my eyes reunite at the finger does this appendage with its delicate hairs and gnarly knuckles become fully present.

Ordinary seeing, then, involves the convergence of two views into a single dynamic vision; divergent parts of myself are drawn together by the object, and I thus meet up with myself *over there,* at that tree or that spider upon which I focus. Vision itself, in other words, is already a kind of synaesthesia, a collaboration of different sensory channels or organs.[58]

When we attend carefully to our perceptual experience, we discover that the convergence of the eyes often prompts the added collaboration of the other senses. When, for instance, I gaze through the window toward a blackbird in a nearby bush—my two eyes drawn together by the bird's jerking body as it plucks red berries from the branches—other senses are quite naturally drawn into that same focus. Certain tactile sensations, for instance, may accompany the blackbird's movements, and if I have been watching carefully I may notice, as it squoonches each new berry in its beak, a slightly acidic taste burst within my mouth. Or rather, strangely, I seem to feel this burst of taste over there, in *its* mouth, yet I feel its mouth only with my own.

Similarly, when I watch a stranger learning to ride a bicycle for the first time, my own body, although it is standing solidly on the ground, inadvertently experiences the uncertain equilibrum of the rider, and when that bicycle teeters and falls I feel the harsh impact of the asphalt against my own leg and shoulder. My tactile and proprioceptive senses are, it would seem, caught up over there where my eyes have been focused; the momentary shock and subsequent throbbing in my limbs make me wince. My hearing, as well, had been focused by the crash; the other ambient sounds to which I'd been listening just before (birds, children playing) have no existence for me now, only this stranger's pained breathing as he slowly shoves the bicycle aside and accepts the hand I am offering, pulling himself to his feet. He shakes his head, laughs a bit, then grins—all in a manner that readily communicates to my body that he's okay—and then turns to inspect the bicycle.

The diversity of my sensory systems, and their spontaneous convergence in the things that I encounter, ensures this interpenetration or interweaving between my body and other bodies—this magical participation that permits me, at times, to feel what others feel. The gestures of another being, the rhythm of its voice, and the stiffness or bounce in its spine all gradually draw my senses into a unique relation with one another, into a coherent, if shifting, organization. And the more I linger with this other entity, the more coherent the relation becomes, and hence the more completely I find myself face-to-face with another intelligence, another center of experience.

In the encounter with the cyclist, as in my experience of the blackbird, the visual focus induced and made possible the participation of the other senses. In different situations, other senses may initiate the synaesthesia: our ears, when we are at an orchestral concert; or our nostrils, when a faint whiff of burning leaves suddenly brings images of childhood autumns; our skin, when we are touching or being touched by a lover. Nonetheless, the dynamic conjunction of the eyes has a particularly ubiquitous magic, opening a quivering depth in whatever we focus upon, ceaselessly inviting the other senses into a concentrated exchange with stones, squirrels, parked cars, persons, snow-capped peaks, clouds, and termite-ridden logs. This power—the synaesthetic magnetism of the visual focus—will prove crucial for our understanding of literacy and its perceptual effects.

The most important chapter of Merleau-Ponty's last, unfinished work is entitled "The Intertwining—The Chiasm." The word "chiasm," derived from an ancient Greek term meaning "crisscross," is in common use today only in the field of neurobiology: the "optic chiasm" is that anatomical region, between the right and left hemispheres of the brain, where neuronal fibers from the right eye and the left eye cross and interweave. As there is a chiasm between the two eyes, whose different perspectives continually conjoin into a single vision, so—according to Merleau-Ponty—there is a chiasm between the various sense modalities, such that they continually couple and collaborate with one another. Finally, this interplay of the different senses is what enables the chiasm between the body and the earth, the reciprocal participation—between one's own flesh and the encompassing flesh of the world—that we commonly call perception.[59]

Phonetic reading, of course, makes use of a *particular* sensory conjunction—that between seeing and hearing. And indeed, among the various synaesthesias that are common to the human body, the confluence (or chiasm) between seeing and hearing is particularly acute. For vision and hearing are the two "distance" senses of the human organism. In contrast to touch and proprioception (inner-body sensations), and unlike the chemical senses of taste and smell, seeing and hearing regularly place us in contact with things and events unfolding at a substantial distance from our own visible, audible body.

My visual gaze explores the reflective surfaces of things, their outward color and contour. By following the play of light and shadow, the dance of colors, and the gradients of repetitive patterns, the eyes—themselves gleaming surfaces—keep me in contact with the multiple outward facets, or faces, of the things arrayed about me. The ears, meanwhile, are more inward organs; they emerge from the depths of my skull like blossoms or funnels, and their participation tells me less about the outer surface than the interior substance of things. For the audible resonance of beings varies with their material makeup, as the vocal calls of different animals vary with the size and shape of their interior cavities and hollows. I feel their expressive cries resound in my skull or my chest, echoing their sonorous qualities with my own materiality, and thus learn of their inward difference from myself. Looking and listening bring me into contact, respectively, with the outward surfaces and with the interior voluminosity of things, and hence where these senses come together, I experience, over there, the complex interplay of inside and outside that is characteristic of my own self-experience. It is thus at those junctures in the surrounding landscape where my eyes and my ears are drawn together that I most readily feel myself confronted by another power like myself, another life.

If a native hunter is tracking, alone, in the forest, and a whooping cry reaches his ears from the leafy canopy, he will likely halt in his steps, silencing his breathing in order to hear that sound, when it comes again, more precisely. His eyes scan the cacophony of branches overhead with an unfocused gaze, attentive to minute movements on the periphery of the perceptual field. A slight rustle of branches draws his eyes into a more precise focus, his attention now restricted to a small patch of the canopy, yet still open, questioning, listening. When the cry comes again, the eyes, led by the ears, swiftly converge upon the source of that sound, and suddenly a monkey's form becomes evident, half-hidden from the leaves, its tail twirled around a limb, its body poised, watching. As the tribesman's searching eyes are drawn into a common focus with his listening ears, this conjunction, this chiasm, rebounds upon his own tactile and proprioceptive sensations—he feels himself suddenly confronted, caught up in a dynamic exchange with another entity, another carnal intelligence.

Indeed, the synaesthesia between the human eyes and ears is especially concentrated in our relation to other animals, since for a million years these "distance" senses were most tightly coupled at such moments of extreme excitement, when closing in on prey, or when escaping from predators. When backing slowly away from a mother grizzly protecting her cubs, or when watching intently the movements of an aroused rattlenake in order to avoid its numbing strike—these are moments when visual and auditory foci are virtually indistinguishable. For these senses are functioning here as a single, hyperattentive organ; we feel ourselves listening with our eyes and watching with our ears, ready to respond with our whole body to any change in the Other's behavior.

Yet our ears and our eyes are drawn together not only by animals, but by numerous other phenomena within the landscape. And, strangely, *wherever* these two senses converge, we may suddenly feel ourselves in relation with another expressive power, another center of experience. Trees, for instance, can seem to speak to us when they are jostled by the wind. Different forms of foliage lend each tree a distinctive voice, and a person who has lived among them will easily distinguish the various dialects of pine trees from the speech of spruce needles or Douglas fir. Anyone who has walked through cornfields knows the uncanny experience of being scrutinized and spoken to by whispering stalks. Certain rock faces and boulders request from us a kind of auditory attentiveness, and so draw our ears into relation with our eyes as we gaze at them, or with our hands as we touch them—for it is only through a mode of listening that we can begin to sense the interior voluminosity of the boulder, its particular density and depth. There is an expectancy to the ears, a kind of patient receptivity that they lend to the other senses whenever we place ourselves in a mode of listening—whether to a stone, or a river, or an abandoned house. That so many indigenous people allude to the articulate speech of trees or of mountains suggests the ease with which, in an oral culture, one's auditory attention may be joined with the visual focus in order to enter into a living relation with the expressive character of things.

Far from presenting a distortion of their factual relation to the world, the animistic discourse of indigenous, oral peoples is an inevitable counterpart of their immediate, synaesthetic engagement with the land that they inhabit. The animistic proclivity to perceive the angular shape of a boulder (while shadows shift across its surface) as a kind of meaningful gesture, or to enter into felt conversations with clouds and owls—all of this could be brushed aside as imaginary distortion or hallucinatory fantasy if such active participation were not the very structure of perception, if the creative interplay of the senses in the things they encounter was not our sole way of linking ourselves to those things and letting the things weave themselves into our experience. Direct, prereflective perception is inherently synaesthetic, participatory, and animistic, disclosing the things and elements that surround us not as inert objects but as expressive subjects, entities, powers, potencies.

And yet most of us seem, today, very far from such experience. Trees rarely, if ever, speak to us; animals no longer approach us as emissaries from alien zones of intelligence; the sun and the moon no longer draw prayers from us but seem to arc blindly across the sky. How is it that these phenomena *no longer address us,* no longer compel our involvement or reciprocate our attention? If participation is the very structure of perception, how could it ever have been brought to a halt? To freeze the ongoing animation, to block the wild exchange between the senses and the things that engage them, would be tantamount to freezing the body itself, stopping it short in its tracks. And yet our bodies still move, still live, still breathe. If we no longer experience the enveloping earth as expressive and alive, this can only mean that the animating interplay of the senses has been transferred to another medium, another locus of participation.

❧

IT IS THE WRITTEN TEXT THAT PROVIDES THIS NEW LOCUS. FOR TO read is to enter into a profound participation, or chiasm, with the inked marks upon the page. In learning to read we must break the spontaneous participation of our eyes and our ears in the surrounding terrain (where they had ceaselessly converged in the synaesthetic encounter with animals, plants, and streams) in order to recouple those senses upon the flat surface of the page. As a Zuñi elder focuses her eyes upon a cactus and hears the cactus begin to speak, so we focus our eyes upon these printed marks and immediately hear voices. We hear spoken words, witness strange scenes or visions, even experience other lives. As nonhuman animals, plants, and even "inanimate" rivers once spoke to our tribal ancestors, so the "inert" letters on the page now speak to us! *This is a form of animism that we take for granted, but it is animism nonetheless—as mysterious as a talking stone.*

And indeed, it is only when a culture shifts its participation to these printed letters that the stones fall silent. Only as our senses transfer their animating magic to the written word do the trees become mute, the other animals dumb.

But let us be more precise, recalling the distinction between different forms of writing discussed at the start of this chapter. As we saw there, pictographic, ideographic, and even rebuslike writing still makes use of, or depends upon, our sensorial participation with the natural world. As the tracks of moose and bear refer beyond themselves to those entities of whom they are the trace, so the images in early writing systems draw their significance not just from ourselves but from sun, moon, vulture, jaguar, serpent, lightning—from all those sensorial, never strictly human powers, of which the written images were a kind of track or tracing. To be sure, these signs were now inscribed by human hands, not by the hooves of deer or the clawed paws of bear; yet as long as they presented images of paw prints and of clouds , of sun and of serpent , these characters still held us in relation to a more-than-human field of discourse. Only when the written characters lost all explicit reference to visible, natural phenomena did we move into a new order of participation. Only when those images came to be associated, alphabetically, with purely human-made sounds, and even the names of the letters lost all worldly, extrahuman significance, could speech or language come to be experienced as an exclusively human power. For only then did civilization enter into the wholly self-reflexive mode of animism, or magic, that still holds us in its spell:

> We know what the animals do, what are the needs of the beaver, the bear, the salmon, and other creatures, because long ago men married them and acquired this knowledge from their animal wives. Today the priests say we lie, but we know better. The white man has been only a short time in this country and knows very little about the animals; we have lived here thousands of years and were taught long ago by the animals themselves. The white man *writes everything down in a book* so that it will not be forgotten; but our ancestors *married* animals, learned all their ways, and passed on this knowledge from one generation to another.[60]

THAT ALPHABETIC READING AND WRITING WAS ITSELF EXPERI-enced as a form of magic is evident from the reactions of cultures suddenly coming into contact with phonetic writing. Anthropological accounts from entirely different continents report that members of indigenous, oral tribes, after seeing the European reading from a book or from his own notes, came to speak of the written pages as "talking leaves," for the black marks on the flat, leaflike pages seemed to talk directly to the one who knew their secret.

The Hebrew scribes never lost this sense of the letters as living, animate powers. Much of the Kabbalah, the esoteric body of Jewish mysticism, is centered around the conviction that each of the twenty-two letters of the Hebrew *aleph-beth* is a magic gateway or guide into an entire sphere of existence. Indeed, according to some kabbalistic accounts, it was by combining the letters that the Holy One, Blessed Be He, created the ongoing universe. The Jewish kabbalists found that the letters, when meditated upon, would continually reveal new secrets; through the process of *tzeruf,* the magical permutation of the letters, the Jewish scribe could bring himself into sucessively greater states of ecstatic union with the divine. Here, in other words, was an intensely concentrated form of animism—a participation conducted no longer with the sculpted idols and images worshiped by other tribes but solely with the visible letters of the *aleph-beth.*

Perhaps the most succinct evidence for the potent magic of written letters is to be found in the ambiguous meaning of our common English word "spell." As the roman alphabet spread through oral Europe, the Old English word "spell," which had meant simply to recite a story or tale, took on the new double meaning: on the one hand, it now meant to arrange, in the proper order, the written letters that constitute the name of a thing or a person; on the other, it signified a magic formula or charm. Yet these two meanings were not nearly as distinct as they have come to seem to us today. For to assemble the letters that make up the name of a thing, in the correct order, was precisely to effect a magic, to establish a new kind of influence over that entity, to summon it forth! To spell, to correctly arrange the letters to form a name or a phrase, seemed thus at the same time to *cast a spell,* to exert a new and lasting power over the things spelled. Yet we can now realize that to learn to spell was also, and more profoundly, to step under the influence of the written letters ourselves, to cast a spell upon our own senses. It was to exchange the wild and multiplicitous magic of an intelligent natural world for the more concentrated and refined magic of the written word.

❦

THE BULGARIAN SCHOLAR TZVETAN TODOROV HAS WRITTEN AN illuminating study of the Spanish conquest of the Americas, based on extensive study of documents from the first months and years of contact between European culture and the native cultures of the American continent.[61] The lightning-swift conquest of Mexico by Cortéz has remained a puzzle for historians, since Cortéz, leading only a few hundred men, managed to seize the entire kingdom of Montezuma, who commanded *several hundred thousand*. Todorov concludes that Cortéz's astonishing and rapid success was largely a result of the discrepancy between the different forms of participation engaged in by the two societies. The Aztecs, whose writing was highly pictorial, necessarily felt themselves in direct communication with an animate, more-than-human environment. "Everything happens as if, for the Aztecs, [written] signs automatically and necessarily proceed from the world they designate . . ."; the Aztecs are unable to use their spoken words, or their written characters, to hide their true intentions, since these signs belong to the world around them as much as to themselves.[62] To be duplicitous with signs would be, for the Aztecs, to go against the order of nature, against the encompassing speech or logos of an animate world, in which their own tribal discourse was embedded.

The Spaniards, however, suffer no such limitation. Possessed of an *alphabetic* writing system, they experience themselves not in communication with the sensuous forms of the world, but solely with one another. The Aztecs must answer, in their actions as in their speech, to the whole sensuous, natural world that surrounds them; the Spanish need answer only to themselves.

In contact with this potent new magic, with these men who participate solely with their own self-generated signs, whose speech thus seems to float free of the surrounding landscape, and who could therefore be duplicitous and *lie* even in the presence of the sun, the moon, and the forest, the Indians felt their own rapport with those sensuous powers, or gods, beginning to falter:

The testimony of the Indian accounts, which is a description rather than an explanation, asserts that everything happened because the Mayas and the Aztecs lost control of communication. The language of the gods has become unintelligible, or else these gods fell silent. "Understanding is lost, wisdom is lost" [from the Mayan account of the Spanish invasion]. . . . As for the Aztecs,

they describe the beginning of their own end as a silence that
falls: the gods no longer speak to them.[63]

In the face of aggression from this new, entirely self-reflexive
form of magic, the native peoples of the Americas—like those of
Africa and, later, of Australia—felt their own magics wither and become useless, unable to protect them.

In the Landscape
of Language

Tired of all who come with words, words but no language
I went to the snow-covered island.
The wild does not have words.
The unwritten pages spread themselves out in all directions!
I come across the marks of roe-deer's hooves in the snow.
Language, but no words.

TOMAS TRANSTRÖMER

THE FIRST PART OF THIS BOOK RAISED THIS QUESTION: HOW did Western civilization become so estranged from nonhuman nature, so oblivious to the presence of other animals and the earth, that our current lifestyles and activities contribute daily to the destruction of whole ecosystems—whole forests, river valleys, oceans—and to the extinction of countless species? Or, more specifically, how did civilized humankind lose all sense of reciprocity and relationship with the animate natural world, that rapport that so influences (and limits) the activities of most indigenous, tribal peoples? How did civilization break out of, and leave behind, the animistic or participatory mode of experience known to all native, place-based cultures?

In the last chapter, however, we showed that animism was never, in truth, left behind. The participatory proclivity of the senses was simply transferred from the depths of the surrounding life-world to the visible letters of the alphabet. Only by concentrating the synaesthetic magic of the senses upon the written letters could these letters begin to come alive and to speak. "Written words," says Socrates, "seem to talk to you as though they were intelligent. . . ."[1] Indeed, today it is virtually impossible for us to look at a printed word *without* seeing, or rather hearing, what "it says." For our senses are now coupled, synaesthetically, to these printed shapes as profoundly as they were once wedded to cedar trees, ravens, and the moon. As the hills and the bending grasses once spoke to our tribal ancestors, so these written letters and words now speak to us.

We have seen as well that iconic writing systems—those that employ pictographic, ideographic, and/or rebuslike characters—necessarily rely, to some extent, upon our original sensory participation with the enveloping natural field. Only with the emergence of the phonetic alphabet, and its appropriation by the ancient Greeks, did the written images lose all evident ties to the larger field of expressive beings. Each image now came to have a strictly *human* referent: each letter was now associated purely with a gesture or sound of the human mouth. Such images could no longer function as windows opening on to a more-than-human field of powers, but solely as mirrors reflecting the human form back upon itself. The senses that engaged or participated with this new writing found themselves locked within a discourse that had become exclusively human. Only thus, with the advent and spread of phonetic writing, did the rest of nature begin to lose its voice.

The highly anthropocentric (human-centered) mode of experience endemic to alphabetic culture spread throughout Europe in the course of two millennia, receiving a great boost from the calligraphic innovations introduced in the monastic scriptoria (the rooms where monks copied manuscripts) by the English monk Alcuin (732–804) during the reign of Charlemagne, and a major thrust from the invention of movable type by Johann Gutenberg (c. 1394 –1468), in the fifteenth century. The printing press, and the dissemination of uniformly printed texts that it made possible, ushered in the Enlightenment and the profoundly detached view of "nature" that was to prevail in the modern period.[2] In recent centuries the industrial and technological practices made possible by this new distance from the natural world have carried alphabetic awareness throughout the globe, infiltrating even those cultures that had retained iconic, ideographic writing systems.

Nevertheless, there remain, on the edges and even in the midst of this ever-expanding monoculture, small-scale local cultures or communities where the traditional oral, indigenous modes of experience still prevail—cultures that have never fully transferred their sensory participation to the written word. They have not yet closed themselves within an exclusively human field of meanings, and so still dwell within a landscape that is alive, aware, and expressive. To such peoples, that which we term "language" remains as much a property of the animate landscape as of the humans who dwell and speak within that terrain. Indeed, the linguistic discourse of such cultures is commonly bound, in specific and palpable ways, to the expressive earth.

In this chapter, then, we will glance at just a few of the very diverse ways in which the common discourse of an oral culture may open, directly, onto the evocative sounds, shapes, and gestures of the surrounding ecology.

The Language of the Birds

Whenever we of literate culture seek to engage and understand the discourse of oral cultures, we must strive to free ourselves from our habitual impulse to *visualize* any language as a static structure that could be diagrammed, or a set of rules that could be ordered and listed. Without a formal writing system, the language of an oral culture cannot be objectified as a separable entity by those who speak it, and this lack of objectification influences not only the way in which oral cultures experience the field of discursive meanings, but also the very character and structure of that field. In the absence of any written analogue to speech, the sensible, natural environment remains the primary visual counterpart of spoken utterance, the visible accompaniment of all spoken meaning. The land, in other words, is the sensible site or matrix wherein meaning occurs and proliferates. In the absence of writing, we find ourselves situated in the field of discourse as we are embedded in the natural landscape; indeed, the two matrices are not separable. We can no more stabilize the language and render its meanings determinate than we can freeze all motion and metamorphosis within the land.

🌿

IF WE LISTEN, FIRST, TO THE SOUNDS OF AN ORAL LANGUAGE—TO the rhythms, tones, and inflections that play through the speech of an oral culture—we will likely find that these elements are attuned, in multiple and subtle ways, to the contour and scale of the local landscape, to the depth of its valleys or the open stretch of its distances, to the visual rhythms of the local topography. But the human speaking is necessarily tuned, as well, to the various nonhuman calls and cries that animate the local terrain. Such attunement is simply imperative for any culture still dependent upon foraging for its subsistence. Minute alterations in the weather, changes in the migratory patterns of prey animals, a subtle shift in the focus of a predator—sensitivity to such subtleties is a necessary element of all oral, subsistence cultures, and this sensitivity is inevitably reflected not just in the content but in the very shapes and patterns of human discourse.[3]

Hunting, for an indigenous, oral community, entails abilities and sensitivities very different from those associated with hunting in technological civilization. Without guns or gunpowder, a native hunter must often come much closer to his wild prey if he is to take its life. Closer, that is, not just physically but emotionally, empathically entering into proximity with the other animal's ways of sensing and experiencing. The native hunter, in effect, must *apprentice* himself to those animals that he would kill. Through long and careful observation, enhanced at times by ritual identification and mimesis, the hunter gradually develops an instinctive knowledge of the habits of his prey, of its fears and its pleasures, its preferred foods and favored haunts. Nothing is more integral to this practice than learning the communicative signs, gestures, and cries of the local animals. Knowledge of the sounds by which a monkey indicates to the others in its band that it has located a good source of food, or the cries by which a particular bird signals distress, or by which another attracts a mate, enables the hunter to anticipate both the large-scale and small-scale movements of various animals. A familiarity with animal calls and cries provides the hunter, as well, with an expanded set of senses, an awareness of events happening beyond his field of vision, hidden by the forest leaves or obscured by the dark of night. Moreover, the skilled human hunter often can generate and mimic such sounds himself, and it is this that enables him to enter most directly into the society of other animals.

One of the most revealing twentieth-century accounts of a relatively intact indigenous community is that recorded by F. Bruce Lamb from the spoken recollections of the Peruvian doctor Manuel Córdova-Rios.[4] Córdova-Rios was captured in 1907, when he was fifteen years old, by a small tribe of Amahuaca Indians living deep in the Amazonian rain forest (between the headwaters of the Juruá, Purús, Madre de Dios, and Inuya rivers)—probably the remnant of a larger tribe decimated by the incursion of the rubber-tapping industry into the forest. He was carefully trained by the headman of this small tribe to become his successor, and was for six years meticulously tutored in the ways of the hunt, in the medicinal and magical powers of the rain forest plants, and in the traditional preparation and use of extracts from the ayahuasca vine to attain, when necessary, a clairvoyant state of fusion with the enveloping jungle ecosystem.

Curiously, the tribe's language, which remained largely meaningless to Córdova-Rios for six months or more, became understandable to his ears only as his senses became attuned to the subtleties of the rain forest ecology in which the culture was embedded. He did, eventually, become headman of the tribe, yet he fled the rain forest the following year after a series of attempts on his life by a neighboring band.

Córdova-Rios's descriptions of the various hunts in which he participated make vividly evident the extent to which these people's senses were directly coupled to the enveloping forest:

They reacted to the faintest signals of sound and smell, intuitively relating them to all other conditions of the environment

and then interpreting them to achieve the greatest possible capture of game. . . . Many of the best hunters seemed to know by
some special extra sense just where to find the game they sought,
or they had developed some special method of drawing game to
them. Knowing how to imitate and to use the signals the animals
made to communicate between their kind in various situations
helped in locating game and drawing it within sighting range of
an astute hunter.[5]

In the course of Córdova-Rios's account, we read careful descriptions of hunters sequestered in the foliage of high fruit trees luring
partridges toward them with mimicked bird calls signaling the discovery of an abundant food source. We read of one hunter who,
upon hearing a band of monkeys moving through the dense forest
canopy overhead, utters a cry that would be made by a baby monkey
if it had fallen to the ground. This call stops the roving monkeys and
brings them down beneath the thick foliage into the hunter's arrow
range; the hunter shoots two of them to feed his family.[6] Later
Córdova-Rios's native comrades teach him, through imitation, the
principal vocal signals of a species of wild pig that they are hunting.

Through ancestral stories and tales of recent hunts, the hunters
continually exchange knowledge among themselves regarding the
nuanced meanings of particular calls made by various creatures, a
knowledge gleaned from ever-renewed encounters with those animals in the wild. In many instances knowledge of the specific alarm
cries of birds and other animals alert the human hunters to the presence of dangerous predators, like the jaguar, that they themselves
must avoid.

A typical example of such interspecies linguistic savvy is an encounter reported by a man named Raci to the other members of a
hunting expedition, including Córdova-Rios, as the various hunters
lie in their hammocks at night, recounting for each other, in detail,
their individual efforts of the day:

It was time to start back and I had no game. Just as I turned to
come back toward camp a small ground-sleeping tinamou [a type
of jungle partridge] sent out his sad call, close to where I was, and
he was answered by another. You know why their evening call is

so sad? They don't like to sleep alone and at sunset each one wanders around aimlessly calling and calling until an answer comes back from somewhere, and then the two move closer and closer together, guided by the calls. And so they find a sleeping partner. I answered the call and found I was between the two birds. So I backed up between the buttresses of a big tree where the ground could be seen for a good distance in front of me, and I started calling the birds to me. You know that it is dangerous to call the tinamou without the protection of a big tree. The jaguar sometimes comes in answer to the call! The tinamou is also his favorite bird.

One bird was nearby and soon had my arrow in his body. He fluttered his wings and kicked a few turns, but was soon with me at the base of the tree. I broke his leg and put a long streak of his blood under each of my eyes to bring good luck.[7]

Every collective hunting expedition is preceded by careful ritual preparations, during which the hunters eat only certain foods, erasing their human odors by soaking themselves in various herbal baths and immersing themselves in the smoke of burning leaves. The expeditions themselves are accompanied by reverent chants to particular forest spirits. The various practices of the tribe, according to Córdova-Rios, embody clear knowledge of the limits beyond which a species of animal must not be hunted; overhunting of a single type of animal or bird is known to bring poor luck upon the hunter or even upon the whole village. Córdova-Rios, for instance, is taught that if he kills the leader of a band of wild pigs (which leaves the pigs disorganized and all too easy to prey upon until a new leader takes over), he must never again kill a leader of the same band.

Meanwhile Xumu, the tribal headman, oversaw the hunting engagements of the group as a whole. Each of the men was assigned by him to an individual hunting territory, and they all reported daily to Xumu regarding the shifting locations of the various bands of monkeys and wild pigs, of the jaguar and other forest inhabitants. Kept apprised in this manner of systemic events unfolding throughout the forest (to a distance of several days journey in all directions from the village) the headman was able by his instructions to appropriately modulate the hunting activities of the small tribe, continually modifying these activities in response to the living gestures of the forest itself.

Córdova-Rios's narrative provides vivid evidence of the extent to which, in the Amazon rain forest, human and nonhuman life-worlds interpenetrate and inform one another. Analogous forms of interaction may be found in every hunting and foraging culture. For subsistence hunting, once again, entails that the human tribesman enter into a profound sensorial rapport with other animals. And this participation, as Córdova-Rios makes evident, necessarily extends into the vocal dimension, wherein animal cries and communicative calls are pondered, mimicked, and replied to by human hunters, becoming as it were part of the tribal vocabulary. Tribespeople traveling through the forest at some distance from one another, for example, often use mimicked animal cries and bird calls to communicate *among themselves,* as a means of calling out to each other without drawing the attention of certain animals, or of rival human bands that might be lingering in the area. It would be startling if these constantly employed calls, cries, hoots, riffs, and whistles had no influence on the everyday speech of the tribe as a whole. On the contrary, in the absence of any formal writing system that might stabilize the local language and render it impervious to the shifting sounds of the animate landscape, the spoken discourse of oral, foraging peoples remains uniquely responsive to the multiple sounds and rhythms of the nonhuman surroundings, and especially attuned to the vocal gestures and cries of the local animals.

We have learned from Saussure that a human language is structured not so much as a collection of terms, each of which possesses a determinate meaning, but as a complexly ramified web, wherein the knots, or terms, hold their specific place or meaning only by virtue of their direct and indirect relations to all other terms within the language. If such is indeed the case, then even just a few terms or phrases borrowed directly from the vocal speech sounds of other animals would serve to subtly influence all the ratios of the language, rooting the language, as it were, in a particular ecology, a particular terrain. Once again, no indigenous, oral language can be genuinely understood in separation from the more-than-human earth that sustains it, of which the language itself is a kind of internal articulation.

Saussure himself, however, denied the possibility of such intimacy between language and the land; his resolute insistence upon the arbitrariness of the relation between spoken sounds and that which they signify led him to downplay the influence of mimicry, onomatopoeia, and sound symbolism within the life of any language. Nevertheless, more recent research on the echoic and gestural significance of spoken sounds has demonstrated that a subtle sort of onomatopoeia is constantly at work in language: certain meanings inevitably gravitate toward certain sounds, and vice versa.[8] (Every poet is aware of this primordial depth in language, whereby particular sensations are invoked by the sounds themselves, and whereby the shape, rhythm, and texture of particular phrases conjure the expressive character of particular phenomena.)

THE INTERTWINING OF HUMAN SPEECH WITH THE CALLS AND CRIES of the local earth is evident even when we turn away from the tropics toward an oral culture of the far north, like that of the Koyukon Indians of northwestern Alaska. The Koyukon inhabit a vast expanse of wild country extending well north of the Arctic Circle, with camps and villages set along the Yukon and Koyukuk rivers. Their language belongs to the Athapaskan family of languages spoken by native peoples scattered throughout much of northwestern North America and in pockets as far south as Arizona. The ancestors of the Koyukon people may have inhabited Alaska as early as ten thousand years ago,[9] although archaeologists have been unable to date the Athapaskan emergence into North America with any precision. The Koyukon, first encountered by Europeans in the mid-nineteenth century, have in the twentieth century slowly abandoned their traditional pattern of scattered seminomadism, moving into a few settlements built near trading posts or Catholic missions. Yet they still travel widely, using their villages more as home bases from which to journey on foraging expeditions for fish, land animals (for clothing as well as food), berries, and other wild provisions.

According to anthropologist and ethnobiologist Richard Nelson, who has lived and worked closely with the Koyukon people, language to them is as much the province of other animals as it is the domain of humankind. The Koyukon assume that nonhuman animals communicate among themselves, and [that] they understand human behavior and language. They are constantly aware of what people say and do. . . . But animals do not use human language among themselves. They communicate with sounds which are considered their own form of language.[10]

In Koyukon belief, the other animals and the plants once shared a common language with human beings. This was in the Distant Time (*Kk'adonts'idnee*), a time during which all living beings "shared one society and went through dreamlike transmutations from animals or plants to humans, and sometimes back again."[11] We will postpone until the next chapter the question of whether the stories told of the Distant Time by the Koyukon people depict an originary time "long ago" in the past—as they are often interpreted according to the linear-historical view of time first imported into the Koyukon territory by Catholic missionaries—or whether the Distant Time is more coherently understood as a unique dimension or *modality* of time, one that is more integral to the living present than it is to the historical past. In any case, and despite the apparent differentiation of animal and human languages since, or outside of, the Distant Time, the various discourses of humans and animals still overlap and interpenetrate in the everyday experience of Koyukon persons.

Caribou, for instance, are said to "sing through" human beings when in their vicinity, granting the tribespeople songs that certain persons remember upon waking from sleep. When those persons sing these songs later, their success in finding and hunting caribou is ensured.[12] Tribal elders, meanwhile, listen closely to the rippling cries and wails of the loon as a source of inspiration in composing their own songs and chants. When a revered Koyukon elder lay near death, Nelson watched an old woman visiting from another village as she approached the near shore of a lake and began to sing Koyukon "spring songs" to a pair of loons that had been lingering there.

Shortly the loons swam toward her until they rested in the water some fifty yards away, and there they answered her, filling the air with eerie and wonderful voices. When I spoke with her later, she said that loons will often answer spring songs this way. For several days people talked of how beautiful the songs had been that morning.[13]

The lilting cries of the common loon are linguistically meaningful to the Koyukon. According to one man, "Sometimes people will hunt the loon, but me, I don't like to kill it. I like to listen to it all I can and pick up the words it knows."[14] The speech of the rare yellow-billed loon is still more powerful than that of the common loon to the Koyukon: ". . . it says the same words, but its voice is just a little different."[15]

The assumption that nature is all aware, and that the sounds made by animals are at least as meaningful as those made by humans, leads the Koyukon to listen attentively to subtle nuances and variations in the calls of local birds. The Koyukon names for birds are often highly onomatopoeic, so that in speaking their names one is also echoing their cries. The Arctic tern (*k'idagaas'*), the northern phalarope (*tiyee*), the rusty blackbird (*ts'uhutlts'eegga*), the blackpoll warbler (*k'oot'anh*), the slate-colored junco (*k'it'otlt'ahga*)—all have such names. Written transcription, however, cannot convey the remarkable aptness of these names, which when spoken in Koyukon have a lilting, often whistlelike quality. The interpenetration of human and nonhuman utterances is particularly vivid in the case of numerous bird songs that seem to enunciate whole phrases or statements in Koyukon.

> Many bird calls are interpreted as Koyukon words. . . . What is striking about these words is how perfectly they mirror the call's pattern, so that someone [outside the tribe] who knows birdsongs can readily identify the species when the words are spoken in Koyukon. Not only the rhythm comes through, but also some of the tone, the "feel" that goes with it.[16]

As we ponder such correspondences, we come to realize that the sounds and rhythms of the Koyukon language have been deeply nourished by these nonhuman voices.

Hence the whirring, flutelike phrases of the hermit thrush, which sound in the forest thickets at twilight, speak the Koyukon words *sook'eeyis deeyo*—"it is a fine evening." The thrushes also sometimes speak the phrase *nahutl-eeyh*—literally, "a sign of the spirit is perceived." The thrush first uttered these words in the Distant Time, when it sensed a ghost nearby, and even today the call may be heard as a warning.[17]

In fact, many of the phrases spoken by birds are understood by reference to events that happened in the Distant Time, events that contemporary Koyukon persons know of through the innumerable Distant Time stories that are told and retold from one generation to another.

> Once, during the Distant Time, a starving man struggled in deep spring snow, trying to reach a camp called "Ts'eetee Tlot." He was carrying a headband decorated with elongated, ivory-colored dentalium shells that reached the north country through trade from distant places on the coast. It was a hard spring. The man became weaker and weaker, until finally he collapsed in the snow and died. At that moment he was transformed into a white-crowned sparrow, and then he flew on toward his destination. When he reached the camp he sang: *Dzo do'o sik'its'eetee tlot.* "Here is Tse'eetee Tlot, but it is too late." Anyone who listens to a white-crowned sparrow today can still hear these melancholy words. And anyone who looks closely will see the white stripes on its head, remnants of the dentalium shell band he carried to his death long ago.[18]

Another bird commonly seen in the boreal forest is the Bohemian waxwing as it hurries in small flocks from one tree to another, uttering high, wispy trills. The Koyukon call the waxwing *diltsooga*—"he squeaks."

> According to a Distant Time story, the waxwing had a very jealous wife who once dragged him around by the hair, giving him the crest that now adorns his crown and making him cry out until his voice became nothing but a squeak.[19]

Meanwhile, the lesser yellowlegs, a shorebird, sometimes flies straight up, then utters a piercing call as it descends: *"Siyeets, siyeets,*

siyeets," which means "My breath, my breath, my breath" in Koyukon. Sometimes a person will shout back to it—*"Siyeets!"*—hoping
to receive from the bird some indication or omen of how long his or
her life (her span of breath) will be.

Many birds offer such vocal prophesies to the Koyukon. Once,
Nelson's principal Koyukon instructor, along with her grandfather,
heard a grey jay speak in an uncommonly human voice:

> Rain was falling, and the bird sat on a branch overhead, looking
> soggy and disheveled. Suddenly it spoke in clear words, "My
> brother . . . my brother, what is going to happen?" The old man,
> a shaman, was startled by the voice and worried by its message.
> Afterward the rain poured down for nine days, flooding bears
> from their dens and creating general havoc. And then people
> knew what the bird had meant.[20]

However, the preeminent prophet or seer among birds is the great
horned owl, which is called by the Koyukon *nigoodzagha* (small ears)
or *nodneeya* (tells you things). The horned owl dwells in the north
country year-round, rarely seen but often heard, and is sometimes
hunted for food. According to the Koyukon, when the *nodneeya*
speaks to human persons, it utters only what is certain:

> When it is about to speak prophetically, the bird first makes a
> muffled squawking sound—then it hoots in tones and patterns
> that can be interpreted. The most terrifying words it can say are
> "Soon you will cry" (*"Adakk'ut daa'tohtsah"*), meaning that
> someone close to you will die. It may even seal the forecast tightly
> with a name, and not long afterward its omen will be fulfilled.[21]

Once, some years ago, people heard a horned owl clearly intone the
Koyukon words "Black bears will cry." For the next two seasons, the
wild berry crops failed and many bears found it hard to survive.[22]

The owl's augury is not always foreboding. Sometimes it seems to
call repeatedly in Koyukon, "You will eat the belly of something,"
foretelling good luck in one's hunting. It can also predict imminent
storms. According to one Koyukon elder: "When the owl makes a
kind of grunting sound, like this, *Mmmmm . . . Mmmmm,* it means

stormy weather is coming. Owl's call, that's the only weather report we used to have!"[23]

Meanwhile, the robins, when they sing their lilting phrases, are experienced by the Koyukon as making a short speech: *"Dodo Silinh k'oolkkoy ts'eega, tilzoot tilzoot silnee silnee"*—"Down there, my brother-in-law tells me to eat pike entrails." Yet the tribespeople, ever attentive to shifts in the surrounding environment, have noticed that the robin's song is itself shifting. One of them remarked to Nelson: "Even the birds are changing. The robins don't say their song plainly anymore—they only say it halfway, like a kid would when its learning."[24]

Another conspicuous bird in the Koyukon bioregion is the fox sparrow, whose loud and oft-heard call, *"Sitsoo sidziy huldaghudla gheeyits,"* is a sorrowful lament, understood only by reference to a vivid Distant Time story:

> In the Distant Time there was a beautiful woman who lived with her husband and grandmother. Once, when her husband was away, the old woman pretended to search through her grand-daughter's hair for lice but instead she thrust a bone awl into her ear and broke it off, killing her. Then she took her scalp and put it on her own head, disguising herself as the wife. She also put a bone needle into her navel and twisted it to tighten the loose, flabby skin on her belly. Finally she put on the younger woman's clothes; and disguised this way she fooled the husband into thinking she was his wife.
>
> But when she carried game from his canoe she could not move nimbly, so she had to excuse herself by saying that work made her feel stiff. After they went to bed, however, the husband recognized who she was. He remained quiet until the next morning, and then he killed the old woman and dragged her body into the woods, where he also found his wife lying dead.
>
> Then the young woman's body became a little bird that flew into the air, singing: *sitsoo sidziy huldaghudla gheeyits,* "Grandmother poked a bone awl in my ear." Nowadays the fox sparrow still sings this way. . . .[25]

The telling of Distant Time stories is central to the Koyukon way of life. Some of the story cycles are so long that their telling consumes many evenings, even several weeks of evenings.[26] By describing the emergence of the world into its evident form, and by thus articulating the formal relations that exist between the various entities in the enveloping cosmos (including humans and other land animals, birds, fish, the various trees and plants, conspicuous landforms, bodies of water and weather patterns—all of whom, in that time out of time, shared a common society and spoke a common tongue), the Distant Time stories make explicit the proper etiquette that must be maintained by the Koyukon people when dealing with the diverse presences that surround them, the kinships that must be celebrated and the taboos that must be respected if the human community and the land are to support and sustain one another.

Distant Time stories are told only during the late fall and the first half of the long northern winter. Indeed, scholars of native lore have found this to be an almost continentwide rule: throughout North America, at least prior to 1900, native communities listened to their most sacred stories only at night and only during the winter. For the spoken stories themselves carry a magic, a power to influence not only persons but the living land itself; in the dark winter night a story well told may hasten the coming of spring. (Thus, a Koyukon teller may conclude a story with a phrase such as "I thought that winter had just begun, but now I have chewed off part of it.")[27] The dark of winter, when some of the most powerful animals are hibernating, when other animals have gone south and the land itself is sleeping, is also the *safest* time to recount the stories; during the summer, when most of the animals are out and about, the animals and other natural powers may get upset at hearing themselves and their Distant Time exploits referred to so directly.[28]

For since the other animals themselves speak, they can also hear and understand our own talking. We must be careful what we say about animals, especially when they are nearby. The Koyukon people take great care to avoid speaking of certain animals directly, using elaborate circumlocutions so as not to offend them. It is for this reason that at night the red squirrel is never spoken of by its ordinary names, but is referred to by the indirect appellation *dikink k'alyee*—"the one that is on the side of a tree."[29] Women, because they have an excess of spiritual power, must avoid calling the otter by its real name, lest they frighten it, and so refer to the animal only indirectly as *biziya*—"shiny black."[30] The lynx, another profoundly potent animal to the Koyukon, is called by the women *nodooya,* a vague circumlocution that means "something going around."[31] To speak carelessly or to disregard such taboos, which hold for many of the forest animals, would invite bad luck for oneself and one's family.

Such roundabout ways of speaking are particularly important during the hunt, when the slightest disrespect for the hunted animal may ensure failure, not just in the present but in future hunts as well. "Hunting black bears in their dens required many gestures of respect, beginning with the etiquette of speech."[32] Preparing for such an encounter, the hunter cannot speak of his intentions directly, and afterward, even if successful, he must not tell what he has done. Later, in the evening perhaps, he might obliquely tell someone, "I found something in a hole." To speak any more directly would offend the powerful being that he has killed.[33]

As the anthropologist Richard Nelson spends more time with the Koyukon, the efficacy of such spoken etiquette begins to influence even his own solitary experience. At home on the Alaskan coast, preparing for a trip back to Koyukon country, he decides to catch a halibut to bring his native friends. Never even considering that he might not be successful, he mentions to a friend that he will take the whole fish to their village so that they can see what it looks like. But

> [a]s the words came out, I knew Koyukon people would never talk as if catching a fish was a foregone conclusion. That day I spent hours in places where I'd done well all summer, and caught nothing except one quillback and a lingcod so small I didn't have the heart to keep it. When I arrived at the [Koyukon] village and told Sarah Stevens, she shook her head like a mother gently scolding her child. "The most you should say is that you'll *try* to catch a fish, or better yet, don't say anything at all. Otherwise it sounds like you're bragging, and the animals always stay away from people who talk like that."[34]

Of course, it is not only when speaking of other animals that one must be mindful, but also when alluding to the forest trees, to the rivers, even to the winds and the weather. Nelson, stung by the winter cold, reminds himself of the Koyukon elders' advice "about accepting the weather as it comes and avoiding remarks that might offend it. This is especially true of cold, which has great power and is easily provoked to numbing fits of temper."[35]

All things can hear and understand our speaking, for all things are capable of speech. Even the crackling sounds made by the new ice on the lakes are a kind of earthly utterance, laden with meaning:

> In falltime you'll hear the lakes make loud, cracking noises after they freeze. It means they're asking for snow to cover them up, to protect them from the cold. . . .[36]

Such deference in the face of natural elements—the clear sense that the animate terrain is not just speaking to us but also *listening* to us—bears out Merleau-Ponty's thesis of perceptual reciprocity; to listen to the forest is also, primordially, to feel oneself listened to *by* the forest, just as to gaze at the surrounding forest is to feel oneself exposed and visible, to feel oneself watched *by* the forest.

Much as humans communicate not only with audible utterances but with visible movements and gestures, so the land also speaks to the Koyukon through visible gestures and signs. The way a raven flies in the wind, swerving or gliding upside down, may indicate success or failure in the hunt; the movements of other animals may indicate the presence of danger, or the approach of a storm, or that the spring thaw will come early this year. The assumption, common to alphabetic culture, that "reading omens" is a superstitious and utterly irrational activity, prevents us from recognizing the practical importance, for foraging peoples, of such careful attention to the behavior of the natural surroundings. This watching and interpreting of the world's gestures, as if every movement bears a meaning, accords with a worldview that simply has no notion of pure meaninglessness. No event for the Koyukon is ever wholly accident or chance, but neither is any event entirely predetermined. Rather like the trickster, Raven, who first gave it its current form, the sensuous world is a spontaneous, playful, and dangerous mystery in which we participate, an animate and articulate field of powers ever responsive to human actions and spoken words.

The Storied Earth

We have begun exploring some evidence for the thesis that language, in indigenous oral cultures, is experienced not as the exclusive property of humankind, but as a property of the sensuous life-world. We've been pondering, that is, some of the ways in which the human discourse within indigenous, oral communities responds directly to the felt expressiveness of other species, of the elements, of the intelligent, animate earth. I have drawn some obvious examples from an equatorial culture embedded in the Amazonian jungle and from a society of the subarctic taiga, or boreal forest. Let's now shift our attention away from forests, whether equatorial or subarctic, toward the arid, desert ecology of the American southwest—in particular, toward the terrain inhabited by the Western Apache of Arizona.[37]

The Apache languages are, like Koyukon, part of the vast Athapaskan family of languages, but the Apachean peoples split off from the northern Athapaskans around one thousand years ago, and eventually established themselves in the American Southwest. In turning from Koyukon culture to Apache culture, we move from an indigenous community that, by virtue of its semiarctic location, has until recently been well insulated from the full impact of European civilization, to a native society that, at least since being confined to the Fort Apache Indian Reservation in 1872, has been surrounded and circumscribed by an ever-expanding population of European settlers. Yet the Apache, despite multiple generations of confrontation, confinement, and forced assimilation, have retained many of their distinct lifeways and linguistic practices. Keith Basso is a linguistic anthropologist who has worked with the Western Apache from 1959 until the present, living intermittently at Cibecue (from the Apache phrase *deeschii'bikoh*—"valley with elongated red bluffs"), a village of about eleven hundred people that has been inhabited by the Apache for centuries.

As he became conversant in the Apache language, and attuned to the rhythms of life in the village, Basso began to notice the remarkable frequency with which place-names typically arise in Western

Apache discourse.[38] The Apache seem to take great pleasure simply in uttering the native names of various locations within the Cibecue valley. For instance, while stringing a fence with two Apache cowboys, Basso noticed one of them talking quietly to himself. When he listened more closely, Basso discovered that the man was reciting a long series of place-names—"punctuated only by spurts of tobacco juice"—that went on for almost ten minutes. Later, when Basso asked him what he'd been doing, the man replied that he often "talked names" to himself. "I like to," he told the anthropologist. "I ride that way in my mind." Another Apache told Basso that his people like to pronounce place-names "because those names are good to say."[39]

The evident pleasure derived from saying these names is clearly linked to the precision with which Apache place-names depict the actual places that they name. Basso himself mapped 104 square kilometers in and around Cibecue, and within this area recorded the Apache names of 296 locations. He found that all but a few of these place-names take the form of complete sentences, each name invoking its place through a succinct yet precise visual description. Here are a few such names: "big cottonwood trees stand spreading here and there"; "coarse textured rocks lie above in a compact cluster"; "water flows down on top of a regular succession of flat rocks."[40] Upon pronouncing, or hearing, such a name, Apache persons straightaway feel themselves in the presence of that place; hence, when reciting a series of place-names, the Apache experience themselves "traveling in their minds." It would seem that the spoken place-names, by their precision, effect a direct sensorial bond between Apache persons and particular places, and we may suspect that the benefit drawn from speaking these names aloud derives not so much from the names themselves but from the nourishing power of the actual locations to which the names draw those who speak them. Place-names, that is, seem to take their particular power and magic from the actual places that they designate.

The experiential importance of geographic place for the Western Apache, and the consequent influence of particular locations in the surrounding landscape upon their everyday language, is especially evident with regard to the ethics and etiquette of contemporary Apache society. For, in a manner entirely alien to alphabetic civilization, the land itself is the ever-vigilant guardian of right behavior within traditional Apache culture. According to Mrs. Annie Peaches, a seventy-seven-year-old Apache woman:

> The land is always stalking people. The land makes people live right. The land looks after us. The land looks after people.[41]

The moral efficacy of the landscape—this power of the land to ensure mindful and respectful behavior in the community—is mediated by a whole class of stories that are regularly recounted within the village. These narratives tell of persons who underwent misfortune as a consequence of violating Apache standards for right behavior; they tell of individuals who, as a result of acting impulsively or in open defiance of Apache custom, suffered humiliation, illness, or death. Unlike the long cosmological myths told only by medicine persons, and unlike the sagas of the contemporary world told primarily for entertainment, these tales—called 'agodzaahi (literally, "that which has happened")—are typically very brief; they can usually be told in less than five minutes. More significantly, 'agodzaahi tales always begin and end with a statement that indicates, with a place-name, exactly *where* the events in the story actually occurred. Here is an example of such a story:

> It happened at "whiteness spreads out descending to water."

> Long ago, a boy went out to hunt deer. He rode on horseback. Pretty soon he saw one [a deer], standing on the side of a canyon. Then he went closer and shot it. He killed it. Then the deer rolled all the way down to the bottom of the canyon.
>
> Then the boy went down there. It was a buck, fat and muscular. There he butchered it. The meat was heavy, so he had to carry it up in pieces. He had a hard time reaching the top of the canyon with each piece.
>
> Now it was getting dark. One hindquarter was still lying at the bottom of the canyon. "I have enough meat already," he thought. So he left the hindquarter where it was lying. He left it there.

Then he packed his horse and started to ride home. Then the boy got dizzy and nearly fell off his horse. Then his nose twitched uncontrollably, like Deer's nose does. Then pain shot up behind his eyes. Then he became scared.

Now he went back to the canyon. It was dark when he got there. He walked down to where the hindquarter was lying—but it was gone! Then he returned to his horse. He rode fast to where he was living with his relatives.

The boy was sick for a long time. The people prayed for him on four separate occasions. He got better slowly.

Some time after that, when the boy had grown to manhood, he always had bad luck in hunting. No deer would present themselves to him. He said to his children: "Look at me now. I failed to be careful when I was a boy and now I have a hard time getting meat for you to eat."

It happened at "whiteness spreads out descending to water."[42]

This tale of "that which has happened" illustrates the misfortunes that might befall a hunter who neglects the respect that must be continually maintained with his animal prey, or, more broadly, the strife that attends those who fail to observe the proper etiquette in their interactions with the natural world. Yet many *'agodzaahi* tales deal solely with the right relations that must be sustained between individual persons and the larger tribal community:

It happened at "men stand above here and there."

Long ago, a man killed a cow off the reservation. The cow belonged to a Whiteman. The man was arrested by a policeman living at Cibecue at "men stand above here and there." The policeman was an Apache. The policeman took the man to the head Army officer at Fort Apache. There, at Fort Apache, the head Army officer questioned him. "What do you want?" he said. The policeman said, "I need cartridges and food." The policeman said nothing about the man who had killed the Whiteman's cow. That night some people spoke to the policeman. "It is best to report on him," they said to him. The next day the policeman returned to the head Army officer. "Now what do you want?" he said. The policeman said, "Yesterday I was going to say 'HELLO' and 'GOODBYE' [to you] but I forgot to do it." Again he said nothing about the man he arrested. Someone was working with words on his mind. The policeman returned with the man to Cibecue. He released him at "men stand above here and there."

It happened at "men stand above here and there."[43]

This particular story demonstrates the confusion that befalls an Apache person who acts too much like a white man. In the early years of the reservation, disease and malnutrition took the lives of many tribespeople. And so it is perfectly understandable to the Apache people that one of them would have killed a white man's cow for food. It was *not* acceptable, however, that *another* Apache would arrest him with the intent of taking him to jail. In other words, it is wrong to join with outsiders against members of one's own community, or to flaunt one's disrespect for the tribe by taking on the attitudes and mannerisms of white men or women. Hence, the policeman in the story found himself unable to turn in the man that he had arrested, although he twice attempted to do so. Unable to speak his purpose, he was humiliated and made to look foolish before the head officer. Finally, he released the man at the same place where he had arrested him.

Now let us see how the actual place where these events unfolded contributes to the operative potency of the 'agodzaahi tales. The telling of any such tale today is always prompted by a misdeed committed by someone in the community; the 'agodzaahi story, precisely told, acts as a remedial response to that misdeed.[44] Thus, when an Apache person offends the community by a certain action, one of his or her elders will wait for an appropriate moment—perhaps at a community gathering—and will then "shoot" the person by recounting an appropriate 'agodzaahi story. Although the offender is not identified or named aloud, he or she will know, if the "arrow" (the tale) has been well chosen and well aimed, that he is the target; he will feel the story penetrate deep beneath his skin and sap his strength, making him feel ill and weak.[45] Then the story will begin to work on him from within, making him want to change his ways, to "replace himself," to live right. And so his behavior will change. Yet the story will stay with him. For he will continually encounter the place in the land where it all happened. Perhaps, if that location is near his home. he will see it everyday. *The place,* it is said, *will keep "stalking" him.*[46]

Basso himself relates an example of such a story "going to work" on a person. In June 1977 he was present at a birthday party in Cibecue that was also attended by a young woman who two weeks earlier had gone to a girls' puberty ceremonial with her hair rolled up in a set of oversized pink plastic curlers. Although such ornamentation was no doubt considered fashionable at the off-reservation boarding school where the young woman lived, it was a clear affront to Apache custom to appear thus adorned at a traditional ceremony. Two weeks later, Basso recalls, in the midst of casual conversation at the birthday party, the young woman's maternal grandmother suddenly narrated a version of the above *'agodzaahi* tale regarding the Apache policeman who had behaved overmuch like a white man. Shortly after hearing the story, the young woman stood up and silently walked away from the party. When Basso, uncertain of what had happened, asked her grandmother if the woman was ill, the grandmother replied simply, "No. I shot her with an arrow."[47]

Two summers later Basso again met the young woman and, while helping her home with some groceries, asked if she remembered that party and why she had left so suddenly. The woman then told him that she had thrown the curlers away after hearing the story about the policeman. When Basso pointed out, as they passed it, the place where the story's events occurred ("men stand above here and there"), the woman "said nothing for several moments. Then she smiled and spoke softly in her own language: 'I know that place. It stalks me every day.'"[48]

In this uniquely oral form of community censure, a topographic place becomes the guarantor of corrected behavior, the visible presence that reminds one of past foibles and that ensures one's subsequent attentiveness. The telling of *'agodzaahi* tales establishes an almost familial bond between the persons at whom the stories are aimed and particular sites or features of the natural landscape. According to an Apache elder,

[i]t doesn't matter if you get old—that place will keep on stalking you like the one who shot you with the story. Maybe that person will die. Even so, that place will keep on stalking you. It's like that person is still alive.[49]

Hence, Apache persons often associate places with particular ancestors. Indeed, the earthly places seem to *speak* to certain persons in the voices of those grandparents who first "shot" them with stories, or even to speak in the voices of those long-dead ancestors whose follies and exploits are related in the *'agodzaahi* tales.[50] The ancestral wisdom of the community resides, as it were, in the stories, but the stories—and even the ancestors themselves—reside in the land.

We used to survive only off the land. Now its no longer that way. Now we live only with money, so we need jobs. But the land still looks after us. We know the names of the places where everything happened. So we stay away from badness.[51]

Yet to move away from the land is ultimately to lose contact with the actual sites invoked by the place-names, and so to lose touch with the spoken stories that reside in those places.

One time I went to L.A., training for mechanic. It was no good, sure no good. I start drinking, hang around bars all the time. I start getting into trouble with my wife, fight sometimes with her. It was *bad*. I forget about this country here around Cibecue. I forget all the names and stories. I don't hear them in my mind anymore. I forget how to live right, forget how to be strong.[52]

Basso, the anthropologist, presents a largely functional explanation for the native association of moral teachings with geographical sites. "Mountains and arroyos," he writes, "step in symbolically for grandmothers and uncles."[53] Persons must be continually attentive to maintaining right behavior, especially with regard to those situations in which they were once careless and impulsive, and yet the grandmothers and uncles who originally corrected such behavior necessarily grow old and perish. Since earthly sites readily outlast one's human elders, and indeed maintain their basic character across many generations, such places are perfectly suited to "step in" as ever-present symbolic reminders of the moral lessons learned in the past.[54]

Yet Basso's suggestion that the sites in the land serve a "symbolic" function (that they have come to "symbolize" moral teachings) implies an unwarranted degree of arbitrariness to the association between moral lessons and the natural landscape, by implying that the association is more conceptual or pragmatic than it is organic and unavoidable. The suggestion masks the extent to which the places themselves may be felt to be the active instigators of those painful lessons, the ultimate authors of those events and hence those stories. Note, here, Basso's own stress on the primacy of place in Western Apache storytelling:

> Nothing is considered more basic to the effective telling of a Western Apache "story" or "narrative". . . than identifying the geographical locations at which events in the story unfold. For unless Apache listeners are able to picture a physical setting for narrated events (unless, as one of my consultants said, "your mind can travel to the place and really see it"), the events themselves will be difficult to imagine. This is because events in the narrative will seem to "happen nowhere" (*dohwaa'agodzaa da*), and such an idea, Apaches assert, is both preposterous and disquieting. Placeless events are an impossibility, everything that happens must happen somewhere. The location of an event is an integral aspect of the event itself, and therefore identifying the event's location is essential to properly depicting—and effectively picturing—the event's occurrence.[55]

Basso makes evident here the central importance of place in the Western Apache experience of phenomena. Yet he provides no indication of why the Apache should put so much more stress on geographical location than we do. Surely for non-native persons, as well, "all things that happen must happen somewhere." Yet most of us do not insist on identifying the precise location of every event we hear about. Why, then, do the Apache, and native cultures in general, give so much importance to places?

The answer should by now be obvious. To members of a nonwriting culture, places are never just passive settings. Remember that in oral cultures the human eyes and ears have not yet shifted their synaesthetic participation from the animate surroundings to the written word. Particular mountains, canyons, streams, boulder-strewn fields, or groves of trees have not yet lost the expressive potency and dynamism with which they spontaneously present themselves to the senses. A particular place in the land is never, for an oral culture, just a passive or inert setting for the human events that occur there. *It is an active participant in those occurrences.* Indeed, by virtue of its underlying and enveloping presence, the place may even be felt to be the source, the primary power that expresses itself through the various events that unfold there.

It is precisely for this reason that stories are not told without identifying the earthly sites where the events in those stories occur. For the Western Apache, as for other traditionally oral peoples, human events and encounters simply cannot be isolated from the places that engender them. Thus, anthropologist Harry Hojier, speaking of another Athapaskan group—the Diné, or Navajo—notes:

> Even the most minute occurrences are described by Navajos in close conjunction with their physical settings, suggesting that unless narrated events are *spatially anchored* their significance is somehow reduced and cannot be properly assessed.[56]

Yet here again the professional anthropologist subtly misses the primary reason for this conjunction. By suggesting that narrated events must be "spatially anchored" he allows us to assume a purely external relation between events and their geographical settings; he implies that the events could be conceived as floating free of any locale before dropping anchor and binding themselves to the land. If, however, the place is itself an active element in the genesis of the event, then the metaphor of *a root* is far more precise than that of an anchor; to an oral culture, experienced events remain rooted in the particular soils, the particular ecologies, the particular places that give rise to them.

❧

FROM THE DISTANT TIME STORIES OF THE KOYUKON PEOPLE, AND from the *'agodzaahi* tales of the Western Apache, we begin to discern that storytelling is a primary form of human speaking, a mode of discourse that continually weds the human community to the land. Among the Koyukon, the Distant Time stories serve, among other things, to preserve a link between human speech and the spoken utterances of other species, while for the Western Apache the *'agodzaahi* narratives express a deep association between moral behavior and the land and, when heard, are able to effect a lasting kinship between persons and particular places.

The telling of stories, like singing and praying, would seem to be an almost ceremonial act, an ancient and necessary mode of speech that tends the earthly rootedness of human language. For narrated events, as Basso reminds us, always happen *somewhere*. And for an oral culture, that locus is never merely incidental to those occurrences. The events belong, as it were, to the place, and to tell the story of those events is to let the place itself speak through the telling.

Yet there remains another reason for the profound association between storytelling and the more-than-human terrain. It resides in the encompassing, enveloping wholeness of a story in relation to the characters that act and move within it. A story envelops its protagonists much as we ourselves are enveloped by the terrain. In other words, we are situated in the land in much the same way that characters are situated in a story. Indeed, for the members of a deeply oral culture this relation may be experienced as something more than a mere analogy: along with the other animals, the stones, the trees, and the clouds, we ourselves are characters within a huge story that is visibly unfolding all around us, participants within the vast imagination, or Dreaming, of the world.

Dreamtime

With this thought we bring ourselves very close to the Dreamtime beliefs common to the Aboriginal peoples of Australia. Their

diverse cultures—Pintupi, Pitjantjatjara, Aranda, Kaititj, Waru-
mungu, Walbiri, and a host of others—may well be the oldest
human cultures of any still in existence, cultures that have evolved
in some of the harshest of human environments for tens of thousands of years (the earliest Aboriginal remains discovered in Australia are between forty thousand and sixty thousand years old), only
to be decimated in our own time through contact with alphabetic
civilization. The astonishing endurance of the Aboriginal peoples
must be attributed, at least partially, to their minimal involvement
with technologies. Their relation to the sustaining landscape was direct and intimate, unencumbered by unnecessary mediations. They
relied upon only the simplest of tools—primarily the boomerang,
the hunting spear, and the digging stick—and thus avoided dependence upon specialized resources while maintaining the greatest
possible mobility in the face of climatic changes. Meanwhile, the
isolation of their continent, as well as its outwardly inhospitable
character, clearly protected these peoples from onslaught by more
ambitious or expansionist nations—until, that is, the British arrived
on their coast in 1788.

What, then, *is* the Dreamtime—the *Jukurrpa,* or *Alcheringa*—
that plays such a prominent part in the mythology of Aboriginal
Australia?

It is a kind of time out of time, a time hidden beyond or even
within the evident, manifest presence of the land, a magical temporality wherein the powers of the surrounding world first took up
their current orientation with regard to one another, and hence acquired the evident shapes and forms by which we now know them.
It is that time before the world itself was entirely awake (a time that
still exists just below the surface of wakeful awareness)—that dawn
when the totem Ancestors first emerged from their slumber beneath
the ground and began to sing their way across the land in search of
food, shelter, and companionship.

The earth itself was still in a malleable, half-awake state, and as
Kangaroo Dreaming Man (the ancestral progenitor not only of kan-
garoos but of all humans who are born of Kangaroo Dreaming),
Frilled Lizard Man, Tortoise Woman, Little Wallaby Man, Emu
Woman, and innumerable other Ancestors wandered, singing,
across its surface, they shaped that surface by their actions, forming

plains where they lay down, creeks or waterholes where they uri-
nated, forests where they kicked up dust, and so on.

> Gabidji, Little Wallaby, came from the West to Ooldea Soak. He
> came across the large western sand-ridge, close to a black desert-
> oak tree. He was carrying a *malu-meri* or *buda* skin waterbag,
> which was full. He crossed the ridge and came to Yuldi. There he
> put his *buda* at the base of a large sand dune to the south, and uri-
> nated in a depression which became the present-day Ooldea Soak
> ("That's the water we drink now!" said the people in 1941.) He
> stayed there for a while, and then went on to another sandhill to
> the north; from there he looked out toward the east. That sandhill
> was named Bimbali. He returned to pick up his *buda,* and then he
> spilt a little water, and that became the lake. However, he was not
> sure whether he should go farther and finally decided to return to
> Ooldea. He left his *buda* there and it was metamorphosed as the
> large southern sandhill. "That's why there is always water there."
> He camped for a while, then decided to go east again. . . .[57]

Eventually, having found an appropriate location, or simply exhausted from the work of world-shaping, each of the Ancestors went
"back in" (becoming *djang,* in Gunwinggu terminology),[58] transforming himself (or herself) into some physical aspect of the land,
and/or metamorphosing into the plant or animal species from which
he takes his name.

> [Leech Man] looked this way, that way, as he was coming. He saw
> a good place. He said, "I do this, because it's a good place. I'll set-
> tle down, I'll stay always." That man who was eating fish,
> Naberg-gaidmi, asked him, "What are you?," and he said, "I'm
> turning into Leech, I'm going to stay in one place. I'm going to
> become a rock, a little rock, and stay here, with a flat head, a short
> head. I'm Leech *djang,* Leech Dreaming!" he said. "I'm Leech!"
> and he said, "Here I sit. This is my creek flowing, this is mine,
> where I'm staying. I'm *djang,* Dreaming!"[59]

Each Ancestor thus leaves in his wake a meandering trail of geographic sites, perceivable features in the land that are the result of

particular events and encounters in that Ancestor's journey, culmi-
nating in that place where the Ancestor went "back in," metamorphosing entirely into some aspect of the world we now experience.

These meandering trails, or Dreaming tracks, are auditory as well
as visible and tactile phenomena, for the Ancestors were singing the
names of things and places into the land as they wandered through
it. Indeed, each ancestral track is a sort of musical score that winds
across the continent, the score of a vast, epic song whose verses tell
of the Ancestor's many adventures, of how the various sites along
her path came into being (and hence, indirectly, of what food plants,
water sources, or sheltering rocks may be found at those sites). The
distance between two significant sites along the Ancestor's track can
be measured, or spoken of, as a stretch of song, for the song unfolds
in an unbroken chain of couplets across the land, one couplet "for
each pair of the Ancestor's footfalls."[60] The song is thus a kind
of auditory route map through the country; in order to make her
way through the land, an Aboriginal person has only to chant the
local stanzas of the appropriate Dreaming, the appropriate Ancestor's song.

The Australian continent is crisscrossed by thousands of such
meandering "songlines" or "ways through," most of them passing
through multiple tribal areas. A given song may thus sing its way
through twenty or more different languages before reaching the
place where the Ancestor went "back in." Yet while the language
changes, the basic melody of the song remains the same, so that a
person of the Barking Lizard Clan will readily recognize distant
stretches of the Barking Lizard songline when he hears them, even
though those stanzas are being sung in a language entirely alien to
his ears. . . .[61] Knowledge of distant parts of one's song cycle—albeit in one's own language—apparently enables a person to vividly
experience certain stretches of the land even before he or she has actually visited those places. Rehearsing a long part of a song cycle together while sitting around a campfire at night, Aboriginal persons
apparently feel themselves journeying across the land in their collective imagination—much as the Apache man "talking names" to himself is "riding in his mind."[62]

Every Ancestor, while chanting his or her way across the land
during the Dreamtime, also deposited a trail of "spirit children"

along the line of his footsteps. These "life cells" are children not yet born: they lie in a kind of potential state within the ground, waiting. While sexual intercourse between a woman and a man is thought, by traditional Aboriginal persons, to *prepare* the woman for conception, the actual conception is assumed to occur much later, when the already pregnant woman is out on her daily round gathering roots and edible grubs, and she happens to step upon (or even near) a song couplet. The "spirit child" lying beneath the ground at that spot slips up into her at that moment, "works its way into her womb, and impregnates the foetus with song."[63] Wherever the woman finds herself when she feels the *quickening*—the first kick within her womb— she knows that a spirit child has just leapt into her body from the earth. And so she notes the precise *place* in the land where the quickening occurred, and reports this to the tribal elders. The elders then examine the land at that spot, discerning which Ancestor's songline was involved, and precisely which stanzas of that Ancestor's song will belong to the child.

In this manner every Aboriginal person, at birth, inherits a particular stretch of song as his private property, a stretch of song that is, as it were, his title to a stretch of land, to his conception site. This land is that part of the Dreaming from whence his life comes—it is that place on the earth where he most belongs, and his essence, his deepest self, is indistinguishable from that terrain:

> *Nyunymanu:*
> *dingo [wild dog] dreaming place*
> *Paddy Anatari's country.*
>
> *Old man squints between wrinkles*
> *drawn into a smile in the broad, red land.*
> *Played a child; walked every foot in its sand.*
>
> *"You see that rock over there?"*
>
> *(The top had been rubbed smooth and*
> *flat soft, as if it were cut by a diamond, but*
> *its been done by another rock*
> *cupped in hundreds of hands:*

increase site for birthing of dingo pup)
and
Paddy Anatari strokes the rock again,

and again. He says:
"You see this rock?

This rock's me!"[64]

The sung verses that are the tribesman's birthright, of which he is now the primary caretaker, provide him also with a kind of passport to the other lands or territories that are crossed by the same Dreaming. He is recognized as an offspring of that Ancestor whose songline he owns a part of, a descendant of the Dreamtime Being whose sacred life and power still dwells within the shapes of those lands. If, for instance, the Ancestor who walked there was Wallaby Man, then the person is said to have a Wallaby Dreaming, to be a member of the Wallaby Clan (a wallaby is a marsupial animal resembling a small kangaroo). He has allegiances to all other Wallaby Dreaming persons, both within and outside of his own tribe. He has responsibilities to the wallabies themselves; he cannot hunt them for food, since they are his brothers and sisters. And he has a profound responsibility to the land along the Wallaby Dreaming track, or songline, a responsibility to keep the land as it should be—*the way it was when it was first sung into existence.*

According to tradition, he might do this by periodically going "Walkabout," by making a ritual journey along the Dreaming track, walking in the footsteps of the clan Ancestor. As he walks, he chants the Ancestor's verses, without altering a single word, singing the land into view—and in this manner "recreates the Creation."[65]

Finally, just as each Dreamtime Ancestor metamorphosed him-or-herself, at the end of her journey, into some aspect or feature within the contemporary landscape, so also each Aboriginal person intends, at the end of his or her life, to sing himself back into the land. A traditional Pitjantjatjara or Pintupi man will return to his conception site—to his particular stretch of the Ancestral songline—to die, so that his vitality will be able to rejoin the dreaming earth at that place.[66]

The Dreamtime is not, like the Western, biblical notion of Genesis, a finished event; it is not, like the common scientific interpretation of the "Big Bang," an event that happened once and for all in the distant past. Rather, it is an ongoing process—the perpetual emerging of the world from an incipient, indeterminate state into full, waking reality, from invisibility to visibility, from the secret depths of silence into articulate song and speech. That Native Australians chose the English term "Dreaming" to translate this cosmological notion indicated their sense that the ordinary act of dreaming participates directly in the time of the clan Ancestors, and hence that that time is not entirely elsewhere, not entirely sealed off from the perceivable present.[67] Rather, the Dreaming lies in the same relation to the open presence of the earth around us as our own dream life lies in relation to our conscious or waking experience. It is a kind of depth, ambiguous and metamorphic.

> *[See there,] That tree is a digging stick*
> *left by the giant woman who was looking*
> *for honey ants;*
> *That rock, a dingo's nose;*
> *There, on that mountain, is the footprint*
> *left by Tjangara on his way to Ulamburra;*
> *Here, the rockhole of Warnampi—very dangerous—*
> *and the cave where the nyi-nyi women escaped*
> *the anger of marapulpa—the spider.*
> *Wati Kutjarra—the two brothers—travelled this way.*
> *There, you can see, one was tired*
> *from too much lovemaking—the mark of his penis*
> *dragging on the ground;*
> *Here, the bodies of the honey ant men*
> *where they crawled from the sand—*
> *no, they are not dead—they keep coming*
> *from the ground, moving toward the water at Warumpi—*
> *it has been like this for many years:*
> *the Dreaming does not end; it is not like the whiteman's way.*
> *What happened once happens again and again.*
> *This is the Law,*
> *This is the power of the Song.*

Through the singing we keep everything alive;
through the songs . . . the spirits keep us alive.[68]

What happened once happens again and again. The Dreaming, the imaginative life of the land itself, must be continually renewed, and as an Aboriginal man walks along his Ancestor's Dreaming track, singing the country into visibility, he virtually *becomes* the journeying Ancestor, and thus the storied earth is born afresh.

This identification, this bleeding of the Dreamtime into the here and now, happens not just during the solitary Walkabout, but also and especially during the collective rituals held at specific Dreaming sites, rituals wherein the Ancestors' encounters and adventures at those locations are not just sung but also *enacted* by the elders. Even an "open," greatly abbreviated version of such an enactment can display an astonishing degree of participation with the animal Ancestor (such "open" versions, or sketches, may be performed for strangers). Author Bruce Chatwin witnesses one such sketch by a late-night campfire in the outback. In response to a question from Chatwin's fellow researcher, about the significance of a nearby hill, one of the Aboriginal men

> got to his feet and began to mime (with words of pidgin thrown in) the travels of the Lizard Ancestor.
>
> It was a song of how the lizard and his lovely young wife had walked from northern Australia to the Southern Sea, and of how a southerner had seduced the wife and sent him home with a substitute.
>
> I don't know what species of lizard he was supposed to be: whether he was a "jew-lizard" or a "road-runner" or one of those rumpled, angry looking lizards with ruffs around their necks. All I do know is that the man in blue made the most lifelike lizard you could ever hope to imagine.
>
> He was male and female, seducer and seduced. He was glutton, he was cuckold, he was weary traveller. He would claw his lizard-feet sideways, then freeze and cock his head. He would lift his lower lid to cover the iris, and flick out his lizard-tongue. He puffed his neck into goiters of rage; and at last, when it was time for him to die, he writhed and wriggled, his movements growing fainter and fainter. . . .

Then his jaw locked, and that was the end.

The man in blue waved towards the hill and, with the triumphant cadence of someone who has told the best of all possible stories, shouted: "That . . . that is where he is!"[69]

The nearby hill, in other words, is that place where the Lizard Ancestor had metamorphosed back into the earth—his spirit power, or life, now inseparable from the life of the hill itself.

The enactment of such stories, songs, and ceremonies is done less for the human persons than for the land itself—upon which, of course, the humans depend. In the words of anthropologist Helen Payne:

The maintenance of a site requires both physical caring—for example the rubbing of rocks or clearing of debris—and the performance of [ritual] items aimed at caring for the spirit housed at it. Without these maintenance processes the site remains, but is said to lose the spirit held within it. It is then said to die and all those who share physical features and spiritual connections with it are then also thought to die. Thus, to endure the well-being of life, sites must be cared for and rites performed to keep alive the dreaming powers entrapped within them.[70]

Or as Bruce Chatwin writes, "an unsung land is a dead land."[71]

On certain occasions, traditionally, the elders of a particular clan would decide that it was time to sing their song cycle in all of its intricacies from start to finish. Messages would be sent up and down the Dreaming track, summoning all of the song-owners to gather at one of the important water holes along the Dreaming. Once assembled, each clan member in turn would sing his stretch of the Ancestor's footprints. The precise sequence of the chanted verses was essential; to sing one's stanzas out of order was thought to rupture the coherence of the earth itself.

It is important to realize that in Aboriginal Australia (as throughout indigenous North America) there is a high degree of differentiation between women's knowledge and men's knowledge, women's rituals and men's rituals. The power and importance of women's rites within native Australian cultures has only recently been recognized by nonaboriginal researchers, perhaps because most of the early ethnologists were male, and hence had little or no access to women's sacred knowledge. It is now apparent, as well, that Aboriginal women's song knowledge is more closely guarded than that of the men. In recent years a certain amount of innovation has occurred both in the songs sung by women and those sung by men, especially in response to changes in the landscape, and in Aboriginal society, brought about by industrial civilization. Lost segments of a song cycle, for instance, may be redreamed by qualified persons. Nevertheless, the song knowledge of women (at least in central Australia) has tended to be more conservative, more resistant to change than that of the men.[72] Another difference is this: while men's secret ceremonies seem to focus almost exclusively on renewing the vitality of the particular sites and species being celebrated, women's closed ceremonies often involve, as well, utilizing the songs to *tap* the magic power of those sites—drawing upon the power in the land for various practical purposes. Such purposes include the curing of illness (whether the sick person is female or male), as well as the practice of "love magic"—whereby the women elders influence, for the good of the community as a whole, the flows of desire between particular persons.[73]

Place and Memory

In Australia, then, among the least technological of human cultures, we find the most intimate possible relation between land and human language. Language here is inseparable from song and story, and the songs and stories, in turn, are inseparable from the shapes and features of the land. The chanting of any part of a song cycle links the human singer to one of the animals or plants or powers within the landscape, to Crocodile Man or Pandanus Tree Woman or Thunderstorm Man—to whatever more-than-human being first chanted those verses as he or she wandered across the dreaming earth. But it also binds the human singer to the land itself, to the specific hills, rocks, and streambeds that are the visible correlate of those sung stanzas.

The lived affinity between language and the land is well illustrated by an anecdote that American poet Gary Snyder tells, from a visit that he made to Australia in the fall of 1981. Snyder was traveling through part of the central desert in the back of a pickup truck, accompanied by a Pintupi elder named Jimmy Tjungurrayi. As the truck rolled down the road, the old aborigine began to speak very rapidly to Snyder, telling him a Dreamtime story about some Wallaby people and their encounter with some Lizard girls at a mountain they could see from the road. As soon as that story ended, he launched into

> another story about another hill over here and another story over there. I couldn't keep up. I realized after about half an hour of this that these were tales meant to be told while *walking,* and that I was experiencing a speeded-up version of what might be leisurely told over several days of foot travel.[74]

A similar tale is told by Chatwin. He was traveling in a Land Cruiser with several friends, including an Aboriginal man nicknamed Limpy whom they were driving to a particular place on his songline. Limpy, whose clan Ancestor was the Native Cat, or *tjilpa* (a small marsupial with a long, banded tail), had never been to this place along the Native Cat songline, yet he now wished to go there in order to see some distant relatives who were dying there. During the course of seven hours driving through the back country, bumping across shallow rivers and under gum trees, the Aboriginal man sat motionless in the front seat, squeezed between the driver, Arkady, and another passenger, except for a short burst of action when the truck crossed part of his songline. Later,

> [w]e came to the confluence of two streams: that is, we met the stream we had crossed higher up on the main road. This lesser stream was the route of the Tjilpa Men, and we were joining it at right angles.
>
> As Arkady turned the wheel to the left, Limpy bounced into

action. Again he shoved his head through both windows. His eyes rolled wildly over the rocks, the cliffs, the palms, the water. His lips moved at the speed of a ventriloquist's and, through them, came a rustle: the sound of wind through branches.

Arkady knew at once what was happening. Limpy had learnt his Native Cat couplets for walking pace, at four miles an hour, and we were travelling at twenty-five.

Arkady shifted into bottom gear, and we crawled along no faster than a walker. Instantly, Limpy matched his tempo to the new speed. He was smiling. His head swayed to and fro. The sound became a lovely melodious swishing; and you knew that, as far as he was concerned, he *was* the Native Cat. . . .[75]

Such anecdotes make vividly evident the felt correspondence between the oral language and the landscape, an alliance so thorough that the speaker must pace his stories or songs to match the speed with which he moves through the terrain. It is as though specific loci in the land release specific stories or stanzas in those Aboriginal persons who travel by them. Or as though, at such times, it is not the native person who speaks, but rather the land that speaks *through* him as he journeys across it.

This correspondence between the speaking voice and the animate landscape is an intensely felt affinity, a linkage of immense import for the survival of the people. In a land as dry as the Australian outback, where rainfall is always uncertain, the ability to *move* in response to climatic changes is indispensable. An oral Dreaming cycle, practically considered, is a detailed set of instructions for moving through the country, a safe way through the arid landscape. Anthropologist Helen Payne has analyzed a continuous series of significant Dreaming sites along a single songline, and found that each of the sites contained either a source of water, a potential shelter, a high vantage point from which to view the surrounding terrain, or a cluster of several such characteristics. Indeed, these Dreaming sites were the *only* places with such assets in an otherwise arid desert.[76]

Payne found as well that geographic sites of particular abundance were commonly crossed by more than one Dreaming—having figured in the adventures of more than one Dreamtime Ancestor—and were thus sacred to several totemic clans. The number and complexity of the rituals associated with any particular Dreaming site varied in direct proportion to the abundance of food, water, and/or shelter to be found at that place.[77]

Each person, by borrowing or trading for the right to sing distant stretches of her own or another's Dreaming tracks, may continually expand her knowledge of potential routes through the countryside along which she may travel in lean times. And since every Aboriginal band is comprised of individuals from different totemic clans, or Dreamings, it will usually have access to multiple songlines, multiple ways to move whenever lack of water or food necessitates such a move.

The Dreaming songs, in other words, provide an auditory *mnemonic* (or memory tool)—an oral means of recalling viable routes through an often harsh terrain.

Yet there is another mnemonic structure at work in the Dreaming. The two anecdotes cited above—both of them occurring in moving automobiles—indicate that the telling of specific stories or the chanting of particular songs is itself prompted by the sensible encounter with specific sites. Just as the song structure carries the memory of how to orient in the land, so the sight of particular features in the land activates the memory of specific songs and stories. The landscape itself, then, provides a *visual* mnemonic, a set of visual cues for remembering the Dreamtime stories.

The importance of this second mnemonic relation becomes apparent as soon as we acknowledge that the songs and stories carry much *more* than a set of instructions for moving through the terrain. While the topographic function of the songs is obviously of immense importance, the songs and stories also provide the codes of behavior for the community; they suggest, through multiple examples, how to act, or how *not* to act, in particular situations. The Dreamtime Ancestors depicted in the stories are neither more nor less moral than their human progeny in the contemporary world, yet the situations in which the Ancestors variously find themselves, and the often difficult results that follow from particular actions, offer a ready set of guidelines for proper behavior on the part of those who sing or hear those stories today. Social taboos, customs, interspecies etiquette—the right way to hunt particular animals or gather particular foods and medicines—all are contained in the Dreamtime songs and stories. And it is the land itself that is the most potent reminder of these teachings, since each feature in the landscape activates the memory of a particular story or cluster of stories.

We earlier encountered a similar correspondence among the Western Apache, for whom the auditory memory of particular teaching stories was triggered by contact with the specific sites where those stories unfolded.[78] One of the strong claims of this book is that the synaesthetic association of visible topology with auditory recall—the intertwining of earthly place with linguistic memory—is common to almost all indigenous, oral cultures. It is, we may suspect, a spontaneous propensity of the human organism—one that is radically transformed, yet not eradicated, by alphabetic writing.

Indeed, even within European culture there is a celebrated example of this propensity, albeit in a thoroughly altered form. In her justly famous book, *The Art of Memory,* Frances Yates describes the mnemonic technique utilized by the classical orators of Greece and Rome to remember their long speeches (a technique regularly practiced by rhetoricians up until the spread of typographic texts during the late Renaissance). The orator would imagine an elaborate palace, filled with diverse halls and rooms and intricate structural details. He would then envision himself walking through this palace, and would deposit at various places within the rooms a sequence of imagined objects associated with the different parts of his planned speech.[79] Thereafter, to recall the entire speech in its correct sequence and detail, the orator had only to envision himself once again walking the same route through the halls and rooms of the memory palace: each locus encountered on his walk would remind him of the specific phrase to be spoken or the particular topic to be addressed at that point within the discourse. Rather than striving to memorize the composed speech on its own, the orator found it much easier, and certainly much safer, to correlate the diverse parts of the speech to diverse *places* within an imaginary structure, within an envisioned topology through which he could imaginatively stroll.[80] Yet while the classical orators had to construct and move through such topological matrices in their private imaginations, the native peoples of Australia found themselves corporeally immersed in just such a linguistic-topological field, walking through a material landscape *whose every feature was already resonant with speech and song!*

In aboriginal Australia, then, we can discern two basic mnemonic relationships between the Dreamtime stories and the earthly landscape. First, the spoken or sung Dreamings provide a way of recalling viable routes through an often difficult terrain. Second, the continual encounter with various features of the surrounding landscape stirs the memory of the spoken Dreamings that pertain to those sites. While the sung stories provide an auditory mnemonic for orienting within the land, the land itself provides a visual mnemonic for recalling the Dreamtime stories. Thus, for Aboriginal peoples the Dreamtime stories and the encompassing terrain are *reciprocally* mnemonic, experientially coupled in a process of mutual invocation. The land and the language—insofar as the language is primarily embodied in the ancestral Dreamings—are inseparable.

Given this radical interdependence between the spoken stories and the sensible landscape, the ethnographic practice of writing down oral stories, and subsequently disseminating them in published form, must be seen as a peculiar form of violence, wherein the stories are torn from the visible landforms and topographic features that materially embody and *provoke* those stories. For example, *The Speaking Land,* Ronald and Catherine Berndt's published compendium of Aboriginal stories gathered over the course of four decades of research, is an honorable and meticulous piece of scholarship, yet it cannot help but disappoint those readers who hope to find therein a collection of stirring adventures and vital narratives. The printed stories seem curious at best, and very poorly plotted at worst; something seems missing, some key that would unlock the abstruse logic of these tales. And that key is nothing other than the living land itself, the expressive physiognomy of the local earth. What is missing is the silent topography, the sensuous hillsides and streambeds that pose the place-specific questions to which these stories all reply. The narratives respond directly to the land, as the land responds directly to the spoken or sung stories; here, cut off from that sensuous reference, transposed onto the flat and featureless terrain of the page, the ancient stories begin to lose their Dreaming power.

IN THIS CHAPTER WE HAVE PONDERED A FEW OF THE WAYS IN WHICH
the spoken discourse of traditionally oral, tribal cultures remains
bound to the expressive sounds, shapes, and gestures of an animate
earth. In the absence of formal writing systems, human discourse
simply cannot isolate itself from the larger field of expressive meanings in which it participates. Hence, the linguistic patterns of an oral
culture remain uniquely responsive, and responsible, to the more-
than-human life-world, or bioregion, in which that culture is embedded.

It should be easy, now, to understand the destitution of indigenous, oral persons who have been forcibly displaced from their traditional lands. The local earth is, for them, the very matrix of
discursive meaning; to force them from their native ecology (for
whatever political or economic purpose) is to render them speech-
less—or to render their speech meaningless—*to dislodge them from
the very ground of coherence*. It is, quite simply, to force them out of
their mind. The massive "relocation" or "transmigration" projects
underway in numerous parts of the world today in the name of
"progress" (for example, the forced "relocation" of oral peoples in
Indonesia and Malaysia in order to make way for the commercial
clearcutting of their forests) must be understood, in this light, as instances of cultural genocide.

Yet while such civilizational "progress" rumbles forward, a
mounting resistance is beginning to emerge within technological
civilization itself, fired in part by a new respect for oral modes of
sensibility and awareness. The kinds of studies drawn upon in this
chapter—studies that document the intimate dependence of oral
peoples and their lifeways upon the particularities of the lands that
they inhabit—are today being utilized with increasing effectiveness
to halt, on *legal* grounds, the industrial exploitation of native lands.
Keith Basso's documentation of the close relation between Western
Apache teaching stories and the perceivable landscape has already
been used successfully in litigation to protect Western Apache land
and water rights.[81] Meanwhile, documentation of the Aboriginal
Dreaming tracks is increasingly utilized in Australian courts of law
to protect vital or sacred sites from further "development."

For the Amahuaca, the Koyukon, the Western Apache, and the diverse Aboriginal peoples of Australia—as for numerous indigenous, oral cultures—the coherence of human language is inseparable from the coherence of the surrounding ecology, from the expressive vitality of the more-than-human terrain. It is the animate earth that speaks; human speech is but a part of that vaster discourse.

Time, Space, and the Eclipse of the Earth

We must stand apart from the conventions of history, even while using the record of the past, for the idea of history is itself a western invention whose central theme is the rejection of habitat. It formulates experience outside of nature and tends to reduce place to only a stage upon which the human drama is enacted. History conceives the past mainly in terms of biography and nations. It seeks causality in the conscious, spiritual, ambitious character of men and memorializes them in writing.
—PAUL SHEPARD

I wonder if the Ground has anything to say? I wonder if the ground is listening to what is said? —YOUNG CHIEF, of the Cayuses tribe
(upon signing over their lands to the U.S. government, in 1855)

PART I: ABSTRACTION

STORIES HOLD, IN THEIR NARRATIVE LAYERS, THE SEDIMENTED knowledge accumulated by our progenitors. To hear a story told and retold in one's childhood, and to recount that tale in turn when one has earned the right to do so (now inflected by the patterns of one's own experience and the rhythms of one's own voice), is to actively preserve the coherence of one's culture. The practical knowledge, the moral patterns and social taboos, and indeed the very language or manner of speech of any nonwriting culture maintain themselves primarily through narrative chants, myths, legends, and trickster tales—that is, through the telling of stories.

Yet the stories told within an oral culture are often, as we have seen, deeply bound to the earthly landscape inhabited by that culture. The stories, that is, are profoundly and indissolubly place-specific. The Distant Time stories of the Koyukon, the *'agodzaahi* tales of the Western Apache, and the Dreaming stories of the Pintupi and Pitjantjatjara present three very different ways whereby tribal stories weave the people who tell them into their particular ecologies. Or, still more precisely, three ways in which earthly locales may *speak through* the human persons that inhabit them. For meaningful speech is not—in an oral culture—experienced as an exclusively human capacity, but as a power of the enveloping earth itself, in which humans participate.

The stories of such cultures give evidence, then, of the unique power of particular bioregions, the unique ways in which different ecologies call upon the human community. Yet these stories often provide evidence, as well, about specific sites *within* those larger regions. In the oral, indigenous world, to tell certain stories without saying precisely where those events occurred (or, if one is recounting a vision or dream, to neglect to say where one was when "granted" the vision), may alone render the telling powerless or ineffective.

The singular magic of a place is evident from what happens there, from what befalls oneself or others when in its vicinity. To tell of such events is implicitly to tell of the particular power of that site, and indeed to participate in its expressive potency. The songs proper to a specific site will share a common style, a rhythm that matches the pulse of the place, attuned to the way things happen there—to the sharpness of the shadows or the rippling speech of water bubbling up from the ground. In traditional Ireland, a country person might journey to one distant spring in order to cure her insomnia, to another for strengthening her ailing eyesight, and to yet another to receive insight and protection from thieves. For each spring has its own powers, its own blessings, and its own curses. Different gods dwell in different places, and different demons. Each place has its own dynamism, its own patterns of movement, and these patterns engage the senses and relate them in particular ways, instilling particular moods and modes of awareness, so that unlettered, oral people will rightly say that each place has its own mind, its own personality, its own intelligence.

The Abstraction of Space and Time

As the technology of writing encounters and spreads through a previously oral culture, the felt power and personality of particular places begins to fade. For the stories that express and embody that power are gradually recorded in writing. Writing down oral stories renders them separable, for the first time, from the actual places where the events in those stories occurred. The tales can now be carried elsewhere; they can be read in distant cities or even on alien continents. The stories, soon, come to seem independent of any specific locale.

Previously, the power of spoken tales was rooted in the potency of the particular places where their events unfolded. While the recounting of certain stories might be provoked by specific social situations, their instructive value and moral efficacy was often dependent (as we saw with the Western Apache) upon one's visible or sensible contact with the actual sites where those stories took place. Other stories might be provoked by a direct encounter with the species of bird or animal whose exploits figure prominently in the tales, or with a particular plant just beginning to flower, or by local weather patterns and seasonal changes. In such cases, contact with the regional landscape—and the diverse sites or places within that landscape—was the primary mnemonic trigger of the oral stories, and was thus integral to the preservation of those stories, and of the culture itself.

Once the stories are written down, however, *the visible text becomes the primary mnemonic activator of the spoken stories*—the inked traces left by the pen as it traverses the page replacing the earthly traces left by the animals, and by one's ancestors, in their interactions with the local land. The places themselves are no longer necessary to the remembrance of the stories, and often come to seem wholly incidental to the tales, the arbitrary backdrops for human events that might just as easily have happened elsewhere. The transhuman, ecological determinants of the originally oral stories are no longer emphasized, and often are written out of the tales entirely. In this manner the stories and myths, as they lose their oral, performative character, forfeit as well their intimate links to the more-than-human earth. And the land itself, stripped of the particularizing stories that once sprouted from every cave and streambed and cluster of trees on its surface, begins to lose its multiplicitous power. The human senses, intercepted by the written word, are no longer gripped and fascinated by the expressive shapes and sounds of particular places. The spirits fall silent. Gradually, the felt primacy of place is forgotten, superseded by a new, abstract notion of "space" as a homogeneous and placeless void.

Of course, many factors other than, but linked to, writing, contributed to the loss of a full and differentiated sense of place. The development of writing in the Middle East, as in China and Mesoamerica, was accompanied by a large increase in the scale of human settlements, as well as by a concomitant growth in the human ability, or willingness, to manipulate and cultivate the earth. Although the earliest shifts from hunting and foraging lifestyles to more sedentary, agricultural modes of subsistence are very ancient, and may have been prompted by climatic changes at the end of the last ice age,[1] once the agricultural revolution began to accelerate, writing began to play an important role in the stabilization and subsequent spread of the new, sedentary economies. The ability to precisely measure and inventory agricultural surpluses, itself made possible by numerical and linguistic notation, enabled the new, highly centralized cities to survive and perpetuate themselves—especially through times of climatic extremity—and ultimately enabled the commercial trading of surpluses, and the rise of nation-states. The new concentration of persons within permanent towns and cities, and the increased dependence upon the regulation and manipulation of spontaneous natural processes, could only intensify the growing estrangement of the human senses from the wild, animate diversity in which those senses had evolved. But my concern in this work is neither with agriculture nor urbanization—the enormous influences of which have been elucidated in numerous volumes—but rather with the curious question of *writing;* that is, with the influence of writing upon the human senses and upon our direct sensorial experience of the earth around us.

We have seen that alphabetic writing functions to undermine the embedded, place-specific character of oral cultures in two distinct but related ways, one basically perceptual, the other primarily linguistic. First, reading and writing, as a highly concentrated form of participation, displaces the older participation between the human senses and the earthly terrain (effectively freeing human intention from the direct dictates of the land). Second, writing down the ancestral stories disengages them from particular places. This double retreat, of the senses and of spoken stories, from the diverse places that had once gripped them, cleared the way for the notion of a pure and featureless "space"—an abstract conception that has nevertheless come to seem, today, more primordial and *real* than the earthly places in which we remain corporeally embedded.

↙

BUT IF ALPHABETIC WRITING WAS AN IMPORTANT FACTOR IN THE emergence of abstract, homogeneous "space," it was no less central to the emergence of abstract, linear "time." To indigenous, oral cultures, the ceaseless flux that we call "time" is overwhelmingly cyclical in character. The senses of an oral people are still attuned to the land around them, still conversant with the expressive speech of the winds and the forest birds, still participant with the sensuous cosmos. Time, in such a world, is not separable from the circular life of the sun and the moon, from the cycling of the seasons, the death and rebirth of the animals—from the eternal return of the greening earth. According to anthropologist Åke Hultkrantz:

> Western time concepts include a beginning and an end; American Indians understand time as an eternally recurring cycle of events and years. Some Indian languages lack terms for the past and the future; everything is resting in the present.[2]

Today it is easy for most of us, living amid the ever-changing constructions of literate, technological civilization, to conceive and even *feel*, behind all the seasonal recurrences in the sensuous terrain, the inexorable thrust of a linear and irreversible time. But for cultures without writing there is simply no separate vantage point from which to view and take note of the subtle mutations and variations in the endless cycles of nature. Those changes that are noticed are often assumed to be part of other, larger cycles. For the overall trajectory of the visible, tangible world—the world disclosed to humankind by our unaided senses—is circular. Thus, in the words of Hehaka Sapa, or Black Elk, of the Oglala Sioux:

> Everything the Power of the World does is done in a circle. . . . The Wind, in its greatest power, whirls. Birds make their nests in circles, for theirs is the same religion as ours. The sun comes forth and goes down again in a circle. The moon does the same, and both are round. . . . Even the seasons form a great circle in their changing, and always come back again to where they were. The life of a man is a circle from childhood to childhood and so it is in everything where power moves. . . .[3]

The curvature of time in oral cultures is very difficult to articulate on the page, for it defies the linearity of the printed line. Yet to fully engage, sensorially, with one's earthly surroundings is to find oneself in a world of cycles within cycles within cycles. The ancestral stories of an oral culture are recounted again and again—only thus can they be preserved—and this regular, often periodic repetition serves to bind the human community to the ceaseless round dance of the cosmos. The mythic creation stories of these cultures are not, like Western biblical accounts of the world's creation, descriptions of events assumed to have happened only once in the far-off past. Rather, the very telling of these stories actively participates in a creative process that is felt to be *happening right now*, an ongoing emergence whose periodic renewal actually *requires* such participation. Mircea Eliade, in his important and enigmatic work *Cosmos and History: The Myth of the Eternal Return*, has shown as well as any scholar the extent to which indigenous peoples inhabit a cyclical time periodically regenerated through the ritual repetition of mythic events.[4] Within "archaic" cultures (Eliade's term), every effective activity—from hunting, fishing, and gathering plants, to winning a sexual partner, constructing a home, or giving birth—is the recurrence of an archetypal event enacted by ancestral or totemic powers in the mythic times.

> The myths preserve and transmit the paradigms, the exemplary models, for all the responsible activities in which men engage. By

virtue of these paradigmatic models revealed to men in mythical times, the Cosmos and society are periodically regenerated.[5]

By performing such activities with care, employing the very phrases and gestures disclosed in the Mythic Time, one actually becomes the ancestral being, and thus rejuvenates the emergent order of the world (just as the Pintupi tribesman on Walkabout, walking in the footsteps of his totem ancestor, is singing the world itself back into existence).

Even highly unusual, extraordinary events are spontaneously assimilated to recurrent mythic prototypes. Thus, Cortés's arrival on the shores of Mexico is interpreted by the Aztecs as the return of the minor god Quetzalcoatl to his kingdom (an interpretation instantly encouraged and exploited by the sly Cortés himself);[6] similarly Captain Cook's arrival in Hawaii is construed by Native Hawaiians as the return of the deity Lono.[7] To oral cultures, and even to a partially literate society like the Aztec (whose largely pictorial writing remained perceptually bound to the visible forms of surrounding nature), human events take on meaning only to the extent that they can be located within a storied universe that continually retells itself; unprecedented events, singular encounters that have no place among the cycling stories, can have no place, either, among the turning seasons or the cycles of earth and sky. The multiple ritual enactments, the initiatory ceremonies, the annual songs and dances of the hunt and the harvest—all are ways whereby indigenous peoples-of-place actively engage the rhythms of the more-than-human cosmos, and thus embed their own rhythms within those of the vaster round.

THE ALPHABET ALTERS ALL THIS. IN ORDER TO READ PHONETICALLY, we must disengage the synaesthetic participation between our senses and the encompassing earth. The letters of the alphabet, each referring to a particular sound or sound-gesture of the human mouth, begin to function as mirrors reflecting us back upon ourselves. They thus establish a new reflexivity between the human organism and its own signs, short-circuiting the sensory reciprocity between that organism and the land (the "reflective intellect" is precisely this new reflexive loop, this new "reflection" between ourselves and our written signs). Human encounters and events begin to become interesting in their own right, independent of their relation to natural cycles.

Recording mythic events in writing establishes, as well, a new experience of the permanence, fixity, and unrepeatable quality of those events. Once fixed on the written surface, mythic events are no longer able to shift their form to fit current situations. Current happenings are thus robbed of their mythic, storied resonance; when the myths are written down, contemporary events acquire a naked specificity and uniqueness hitherto unknown. As some of these naked occurrences come to be de-scribed or written down, they, too, are thereby fixed in their particularity, and so assume their singular place within the slowly accreting sequence of recorded events. Thus does oral story gradually give way to written history. The cyclical shape of earthly time gradually fades behind the new awareness of an irreversible and rectilinear progression of itemizable events. And historical, linear time becomes apparent.

But now let us step back for a moment. For by discussing in this somewhat cursory manner the influence of alphabetic writing upon the emergence of homogeneous "space" and linear "time," I have perhaps left the impression that space and time were always—for oral peoples as for ourselves—distinguishable dimensions of experience, and that the literate revolution simply altered the experiential character of these two, already distinct, phenomena. In truth, however, the very differentiation of "space" from "time" was itself born of the same perceptual and linguistic changes that we are discussing. For a time that is cyclical, or circular, is just as much *spatial* as it is *temporal*.

The Indistinction of Space and Time in the Oral Universe

We touch here upon one of the most intransigent barriers preventing genuine understanding between the modern, alphabetized West and indigenous, oral cultures. Unlike linear time, time conceived as cyclical cannot be readily abstracted from the spatial phenomena that exemplify it—from, for instance, the circular trajectories of the sun, the moon, and the stars. Unlike a straight line, moreover, a circle demarcates and encloses a spatial field. Indeed, the visible space in which we commonly find ourselves when we step outdoors is itself encompassed by the circular enigma that we have come to call "the horizon." The precise contour of the horizon varies considerably in different terrains, yet whenever we climb to a prominent vantage point, the circular character of the visible world becomes explicit. Thus cyclical time, the experiential time of an oral culture, has the same shape as perceivable space. And the two circles are, in truth, one:

> The Lakota define the year as a circle around the border of the
> world. The circle is a symbol of both the earth (with its encircling
> horizons) and time. The changes of sunup and sundown around
> the horizon during the course of the year delineate the contours
> of time, time as a part of space.[8]

On high plateaus in the Rocky Mountains, where the visible horizon is especially vast and wide, are circular arrangements of stones arrayed around a central hub. It is known that such "medicine wheels," still used by various North American tribes, once served a calendrical function. Or, rather, they enabled a person to orient herself within a dimension that was neither purely spatial nor purely temporal—the large stone that is precisely aligned with the place of the sun's northernmost emergence, marks a place that is as much in time (the summer solstice) as in space. A similar unity—of that which *to us* are two different dimensions, the spatial and the temporal—existed among the Aztecs at the time of the conquest, according to Diego Duran, a Spanish monk who arrived in Mexico in the first half of the sixteenth century:

> Duran reports that among the Aztecs, who distribute their years
> into cycles according to the cardinal points, "the years most
> feared by the people were those of the North and of the West,
> since they remembered that the most unhappy events had taken
> place under those signs."[9]

So a cyclical mode of time does not readily distinguish itself from the spatial field in which oral persons find themselves experientially immersed. We must remember, however, that this experiential space is itself very different from the static, homogeneous void that alphabetic civilization has come to call "space." As we saw above, space, for an oral culture, is directly experienced as *place,* or as *places*—as a differentiated realm containing diverse sites, each of which has its own power, its own way of organizing our senses and influencing our awareness. Unlike the abstraction of an infinite and homogeneous "space," place is from the first a qualitative matrix, a pulsing or potentized field of experience, able to move us even in its stillness. It is a mode of space, then, that is always already temporal, and we should not be surprised that oral peoples speak of what to us are purely spatial phenomena as animate, emergent processes, and of space itself as a kind of dynamism, a continual unfolding. For instance, a recent, book-length analysis of spatial concepts among the Diné, or Navajo, concludes that for them

> [s]pace, like the entities or objects within it, is dynamic. That is, all "entities," "objects," or similar units of action and perception must be considered as units that are engaged in continuous processes. In the same way, spatial units and spatial relationships are "qualitative" in this same sense and cannot be considered to be clearly defined, readily quantifiable and static in essence.[10]

The authors assert, therefore, that a complex notion of space-time (or, in their words, "time-space") would likely be a more relevant translation of Navajo experience "than clearly distinct concepts of one-dimensional time and three-dimensional space."[11]

A similar situation was discovered by the American linguist Benjamin Lee Whorf in his extensive analyses of the Hopi language during the 1930s and early 1940s. Whorf found no analog, in the Hopi language, to the linear, sequential, uniformly flowing time that Western civilization takes for granted. Indeed, Whorf found no reference to any independent temporal dimension of reality, and no terms or expressions that "refer to space in such a way as to exclude that element of extension or existence that we call time, and so by

implication leave a residue that could be referred to as time."[12] What
we call *time,* in other words, could not be isolated from the Hopi experience of *space:*

> In this Hopi view, [that which we call] time disappears and [that
> which we call] space is altered, so that it is no longer the homoge-
> neous and instantaneous timeless space of our supposed intuition
> or of classical Newtonian mechanics.[13]

Whorf's fascinating disclosures were often taken simplistically, by
researchers in other disciplines, to mean, among other things, that
the Hopi people have no temporal awareness whatsoever, or that the
Hopi language is utterly static, and has no way of distinguishing between earlier and later events, or between occurrences more or less
distant from the speaker in what *we* would call time. Such misread-
ings, doubtless encouraged by Whorf's occasional propensity for
vigorous overstatement, have led various linguists in recent years to
decry Whorf's findings. Several researchers, working closely with
the Hopi language, claim to have refuted Whorf's conclusions entirely.[14] Such refutations, however, are themselves dependent upon
an oversimplified reading of Whorf's conclusions, upon a crusading
refusal to discern that Whorf was not asserting an absence of temporal awareness among the Hopi, but rather an absence, in their discourse, of any *metaphysical* concept of time that could be isolated
from their dynamic awareness of spatiality.

While Whorf did not find separable notions of space and time
among the Hopi, he did discern, in the Hopi language, a distinction
between two basic modalities of existence, which he terms the
"manifested" and the "manifesting." The "manifested" corresponds
roughly to our notion of "objective" existence, and it comprises "all
that is or has been accessible to the senses . . . with no attempt to distinguish between present and past, but excluding everything that we
call future."[15] The "manifesting," on the other hand,

> comprises all that we call future, *but not merely this;* it includes
> equally and indistinguishably all that we call mental—everything
> that appears or exists in the mind, or, as the Hopi would prefer to

say, in the *heart,* not only the heart of man, but the heart of animals, plants, and things, and behind and within all the forms and
appearances of nature, in the heart of nature [itself]. . . .[16]

The "manifested," in other words, is that aspect of phenomena already evident to our senses, while the "manifesting" is that which is
not yet explicit, not yet present to the senses, but which is assumed
to be psychologically gathering itself toward manifestation within
the depths of all sensible phenomena. One's own feeling, thinking,
and desiring are a part of, and hence participant with, this collective
desiring and preparing implicit in all things—from the emergence
and fruition of the corn, to the formation of clouds and the bestowal
of rain. Indeed, human intention, especially when concentrated by
communal ceremony and prayer, contributes directly to the becoming-
manifested of such phenomena.

≤

WHILE THE LANGUAGE OF THE HOPI BELONGS TO THE UTO-
Aztecan family of languages, the neighboring Diné, or Navajo, speak
an Athapaskan language—like the Koyukon and other tribes of the
far Northwest, from whence the ancestors of the Apache and the
Navajo first headed south many centuries ago. (The nomadic Navajo
first came into contact with the Pueblo peoples of the Rio Grande
valley around six hundred years ago, and ultimately adopted a range
in the Arizona desert less than two hundred years ago.) Nevertheless, the Navajo language also seems to maintain a broad notion of
the influence of human desire and imagination upon a continually
emergent world, a notion very analogous to that found by Whorf
among the Hopi. In the 1983 study of Navajo semantics alluded to
earlier, the authors claim that "existence," for the Navajo, "should
be understood as a continuous manifestation . . . [as] a series of
events, rather than states or situational persistences through time."[17]
They then go on to suggest that what Western people call "the future" is experienced by the Navajo to be

like a stock of possibilities, of incompletely realized events and
circumstances. They [these circumstances] are still most of all
'becoming' (rather than being) and involved in a process of 'man-

ifesting' themselves. A human being can, through his thought and desire, exert an influence on these 'possibles.'[18]

Thus, in place of any clear distinction between space and time, we find, in examples of both the Uto-Aztecan and the Athapaskan language groups, a subtle differentiation between manifest and unmanifest spatiality—that is, a sense of space as a continual emergence from implicit to explicit existence, and of human intention as participant with this encompassing emergence.

The indistinction of space and time was also evident in our discussion, in the last chapter, of Aboriginal Australian notions of the *Alcheringa,* or Dreamtime. Like the Distant Time of the Koyukon, the Dreamtime does not refer to the past in any literal sense (to a time that is finished and done with), but rather to the temporal and psychological latency of the enveloping landscape. Different paths through the present terrain resonate with different stories from the Dreamtime, and indeed every water hole, every forest, every cluster of boulders or dry creekbed has its own Dreaming, its own implicit life. The vitality of each place, moreover, is rejuvenated by the human enactment, and en-*chant*-ment, of the storied events that crouch within it. The Dreamtime, then, is integral to the spatial surroundings. It is not a set of accomplished events located in some finished past, but is the very depth of the experiential present—the earthly sleep, or dream, out of which the visible landscape continually comes to presence. And once again human dreaming, human intention, human action and chanting participate vividly in this coming-to-presence.

Numerous other examples could be cited. These few instances, from opposite sides of the earth, should suffice at least to demonstrate that separable "time" and "space" are not absolute givens in all human experience. It is likely that without a formal system of numerical and linguistic notation it is not possible to entirely abstract a uniform sense of progressive "time" from the direct experience of the animate, emergent environment—or, what amounts to the same thing, to freeze the dynamic experience of earthly place into the intuition of a static, homogeneous "space." If this is the case, then writing must be recognized as a necessary condition for the belief in an entirely distinct space and time.

Exiled in the Word

According to Mircea Eliade, the ancient Hebrews were the first people to "discover" a linear, nonrepeating mode of time:

> [F]or the first time, the prophets placed a value on history, succeeded in transcending the traditional vision of the cycle (the conception that ensures all things will be repeated forever), and discovered a one-way time. This discovery was not to be immediately and fully accepted by the consciousness of the entire Jewish people, and the ancient conceptions were still long to survive.[19]

To the ancient Hebrews, or what we know of them through the lens of the Hebrew Bible, the cyclical return of seasonal events commanded far less attention than those happenings that were unique and without precedent (natural catastrophes, sieges, battles, and the like), for it was these nonrepeating events that signaled the will of YHWH, or God, in relation to the Hebrew people. In Eliade's terms, these unique occurrences, whose consequences were often devastating (either to the Hebrews or to their enemies), were interpreted by the prophets as "negative theophanies," as expressions of YHWH's wrath. Thus interpreted, these discordant and nonrepeating events acquired a coherence previously unknown, and so began to stand out from the cyclical unfolding of natural phenomena. And the Hebrew nation came to comprehend itself in relation to this new, nonrepeating modality of time—that is, in relation to history.

> [F]or the first time, we find affirmed, and increasingly accepted, the idea that historical events have a value in themselves, insofar as they are determined by the will of God.[20]

Yet it is crucial to recognize what Eliade does *not* mention in his discussion—that the Hebrews are, as well, the first truly alphabetic culture that we know of, the first "People of the Book." Indeed, at the founding event of the Jewish nation—the great theophany atop Mount Sinai—Moses *inscribes* the commandments dictated by

YHWH (the most sacred of God's names) upon two stone tablets, presumably in an alphabetic script.[21] (Contemporary scholars place the exodus from Egypt sometime around 1250 B.C.E.; it is just at this time that the twenty-two-letter, consonantal *aleph-beth* was coming into use in the area of Canaan, or Palestine.)

In truth, the new recognition of a nonmythological, nonrepeating time by the Hebrew scribes can only be comprehended with reference to alphabetic writing itself. Recording cultural stories in writing, as we have seen, fixes the storied events in their particularity, providing them with a new and unchanging permanence while inscribing them in a steadily accreting sequence of similarly unique occurrences. A new sense of time as a nonrepeating sequence begins to make itself felt over and against the ceaseless cycling of the cosmos. The variously scribed layers of the Hebrew Bible are the first sustained record of this new sensibility.

As we have also discerned, the ancient *aleph-beth,* as the first thoroughly *phonetic* writing system, prioritized the human voice. The increasingly literate Israelites found themselves caught up in a vital relationship not with the expressive natural forms around them, nor with the static images or idols common to pictographic or ideographic cultures, but with an all-powerful human voice. It was a voice that clearly preceded, and outlasted, every individual life—the voice, it would seem, of eternity itself—but which nevertheless addressed the Hebrew nation directly, speaking, first and foremost, through the written letters.

While the visible landscape provides an oral, tribal culture with a necessary mnemonic, or memory trigger, for remembering its ancestral stories, alphabetic writing enabled the Hebrew tribes to preserve their cultural stories intact even when the people were cut off, for many generations, from the actual lands where those stories had taken place. By carrying on its lettered surface the vital stories earlier carried by the terrain itself, *the written text became a kind of portable homeland for the Hebrew people.* And indeed it is only thus, by virtue of this portable *ground,* that the Jewish people have been able to preserve their singular culture, and thus themselves, while in an almost perpetual state of exile from the actual lands where their ancestral stories unfolded.

Yet many of the written narratives in the Bible are already stories of displacement, of exile. The most ancient stratum of the Hebrew Bible is structured, from the first, by the motif of exile—from the expulsion of Adam and Eve from the garden of Eden, to the long wandering of the Israelites in the desert. The Jewish sense of exile was never merely a state of separation from a specific locale, from a particular ground; it was (and is) also a sense of separation from the very *possibility* of being placed, from the very possibility of being entirely at home. This deeper sense of displacement, this sense of always *already* being in exile, is inseparable, I suggest, from alphabetic literacy, this great and difficult magic of which the Hebrews were the first real caretakers. Alphabetic writing can engage the human senses only to the extent that those senses sever, at least provisionally, their spontaneous participation with the animate earth. To begin to read, alphabetically, is thus already to be dis-placed, cut off from the sensory nourishment of a more-than-human field of forms. It is also, however, to feel the still-lingering savor of that nourishment, and so to yearn, to hope, that such contact and conviviality may someday return. *"Because being Jewish,"* as Edmond Jabes has written, *"means exiling yourself in the word and, at the same time, weeping for your exile."*[22]

The pain, the sadness of this exile, is precisely the trace of what has been lost, the intimation of a forgotten intimacy. The narratives in Genesis remain deeply attuned to the animistic power of places, and it is this lingering power that lends such poignancy to the motifs of exodus and exile. The stories of the patriarchs are filled with sacred place-names, and many of these narratives seem structured so as to tell how particular places came to have their specific names. While these sacred sites never seem to have an entirely autonomous power (many, for instance, take their sacredness from the fact that YHWH there speaks or otherwise reveals Himself to one of the protagonists), earthly place nevertheless remains a structuring element of biblical space.

Moreover, the trajectory of time, for the ancient Hebrews, was by no means entirely linear. The holy days described in the Bible are closely bound to the intertwined cycles of the sun and the moon. Further, the nonrepeating, historical time alluded to by Eliade seems to correlate with the sense of existential separation and exile. It is thus that, in Hebrew tradition, the expulsion from the eternity of

Eden (and, later, the destruction of the Temple) is mirrored, at the other end of sequential history, by the promised return from exile, the coming of the Messiah, and an end to separated time. The forward trajectory of time, that is, will at last open outward, flowing back into the spacious eternity of living place (the "promised land"), and so into a golden age of peace between all nations. Eternity lies not in a separated heaven (the ancient Hebrews knew of no such realm) but in the promise of a future reconciliation on the earth.

Time and space are still profoundly influenced by one another in the Hebrew Bible. They are never *entirely* distinguishable, for they are still informed, however distantly, by a participatory experience of *place*.

IT REMAINED FOR THE ANCIENT GREEKS, POSSESSED OF THEIR OWN version of the alphabet, to derive an entirely placeless notion of eternity—a strictly intelligible, nonmaterial realm of pure Ideas resting entirely outside of the sensible world. It is obvious that the Greek alphabet contributed to a kind of theoretical abstraction very different from that engaged in by the Hebrew prophets and scribes. In part, this may be attributed to the very different historical trajectories of the Hebrew and the Greek peoples, to the obvious contrasts between desert-dwelling peoples and seafaring peoples, and to a host of other influences upon Greek culture arriving, like the alphabet, from abroad. But it is also the consequence of a simple but profound structural change introduced into the alphabet by the Greek scribes when they adapted this writing system from its earlier, Semitic incarnation. We must leave to the next chapter a careful discussion of this structural change and its experiential ramifications. Here we need only observe that Greek thinkers were the first to begin to objectify space and time as entirely distinct and separable dimensions.

Yet this was a sporadic and fragmentary process, resulting from the overlapping descriptive, analytic, and speculative writings of diverse individuals and schools of thought. The earliest historians, like Hecataeus of Miletos (c. 550–489 B.C.E.), Herodotus (c. 480–425 B.C.E.), and Thucydides (c. 460–400 B.C.E.) pioneered the use of written prose, rather than poetry, to record past events. They practiced a new skepticism regarding the storied gods and goddesses of the animate environment, and by separating past events from the tradition-bound rhythms of verse and chanted story, they loosened time itself from the recurrent cycling of the sensuous earth, opening the prospect of a nonrepeating, historical time extending indefinitely into the past.

A century later Aristotle (384–322 B.C.E.) sought to *define* the dimension of time as it makes itself evident in our experience. He concluded that "time is just this: the number of a motion with respect to the prior and the posterior."[23] Time, in other words, is what is counted whenever we measure a movement between earlier and later moments of its unfolding. Time is thus inseparable from number and sequence; it appears in Aristotle's writings as a continuous linear series of points, each a punctiform "now" dividing the past from the future.

Shortly thereafter, in his remarkably influential text *Elements,* the Greek geometrician Euclid (c. 300 B.C.E.) implied by his various definitions and postulates that space itself could be conceived as an entirely homogeneous and limitless three-dimensional continuum. The homogeneous character of Euclidian space was indicated, in particular, by his assertion that parallel straight lines, no matter how far they are extended in either direction, will never meet. While this postulate holds true for a perfectly flat and featureless ideal space, the experienced world that we bodily inhabit is not so regular. Indeed, we now know that the sphericity of the earth itself— this very surface on which we dwell—confounds Euclid's parallel postulate: two straightest-possible lines that start out parallel to each other on the curved surface of a sphere will eventually converge and cross, like meridians at the North Pole. That we still commonly envision the curved surface of the earth, with all of its local irregularities (its mountains and river valleys), to be embedded within a three-dimensional space lacking any curvature of its own, is exquisite testimony to the lasting influence of Euclidean conceptions. Euclid's assumptions provided the classical basis for Western, scientific notions of space, from the Renaissance until the work of Albert Einstein, and even today our supposedly "commonsense" experience remains profoundly under the influence of such assumptions.

While evolving techniques of numerical notation and measure-

ment obviously played an explicit role in the development of these
early descriptions, the spread of alphabetic literacy was at work behind the scenes, altering the perceptual relations between the Greeks
and the sensible world around them, and thus gradually disclosing
the new, apparently independent dimensions of space and time to
which the numbers and measurements were then applied.

Absolute Space and Absolute Time

Yet a thorough description of homogeneous "space" and sequential
"time," as objectively existing entities, had to wait until the invention of the printing press. For it was the dissemination of printed
texts (texts that until then had been meticulously copied by hand
and preserved, like treasures, in monastic libraries and universities)
into the wider community of persons, and the subsequent rise of
vernacular literatures, that effectively sealed the ascendancy of alphabetic modes of thought over the oral, participatory experience of
nature. The thorough differentiation of "time" from "space" was
impossible as long as large portions of the community still experienced the surrounding terrain as animate and alive, as long as material (spatial) phenomena were still perceived by many as having their
own inherent spontaneity and (temporal) dynamism.[24] The burning
alive of tens of thousands of women (most of them herbalists and
midwives from peasant backgrounds) as "witches" during the sixteenth and seventeenth centuries may usefully be understood as the
attempted, and nearly successful, extermination of the last orally
preserved traditions of Europe—the last traditions rooted in the direct, participatory experience of plants, animals, and elements—in
order to clear the way for the dominion of alphabetic reason over a
natural world increasingly construed as a passive and mechanical set
of objects.

It was Isaac Newton, in his great *Principia Mathematica* of 1687,
who finally gave an absolute formulation to separable "time" and
"space" as the necessary frame for his clockwork universe:

Absolute, true and mathematical time, of itself and from its own
nature, flows equably without regard to anything external. . . .

Absolute space, in its own nature, without regard to anything external, remains always similar and immovable. . . .[25]

By these formulations Newton meant to distinguish "absolute time"
from that "relative time" which is simply the order of succession of
perceivable events, and to distinguish "absolute space" from that
"relative space" which is the order of coexistence between perceivable things.[26] While "relative time" is merely a relationship between
material events, and so has no existence apart from those events,
"absolute, true and mathematical time" is, for Newton, an independent reality that we cannot perceive directly, but which underlies all
material events and their relations. Similarly "absolute, true, and
mathematical space" subsists independent of all perceivable things.
In itself it is empty—a void. Like absolute time, it is infinite in extent; it can neither be created nor destroyed, and no part of it can be
distinguished from any other part.

By assuming the existence of this empty and "immovable"
space—this space that is at rest relative to any and all motion—Newton was then able to calculate the motion of the moon or the earth
relative to this absolute space; it was only by assuming these absolute
references that he was able to derive his theory of universal attrac-
tion, or "gravity." After the publication of his *Principia,* Newton's
assumptions regarding space and time were challenged by numerous
philosophers, and he found himself in extended debates with such
illustrious thinkers as Leibniz and Berkeley over the question of
whether one could rationally distinguish absolute from relative
space, or absolute from relative time.[27] However, although they challenged the absolute character of Newton's space and time, none of
these thinkers challenged the assumption of an absolute difference
between space and time—the by now commonplace assumption that
space and time were entirely distinct dimensions of experience.

In 1781, Immanuel Kant, in his *Critique of Pure Reason,* capped
the debates regarding the absolute or relative nature of time and
space. He agreed with Newton that space and time were absolute,
that they were independent of particular things and events. For

Kant, however, these distinct dimensions did not belong to the surrounding world as it exists in itself, but were necessary forms of
human awareness, the two forms by which the human mind inevitably structures the things it perceives. Thus, while he denied
that space and time necessarily exist apart from human experience,
Kant's work seemed to establish more forcefully than ever that, at
least as far as humans were concerned, "space" and "time" were distinct and inescapable dimensions.

Needless to say, Kant's writings could not be translated into
Navajo or Pintupi.

PART II: THE LIVING PRESENT

When I returned to North America from my travels among traditional peoples in Indonesia and Nepal, I quickly found myself
perplexed and confused by many aspects of my own culture. Assumptions that I had previously taken for granted, or that I had
since childhood accepted as obvious and unshakable truths, now
made little sense to me. The belief, for instance, in an autonomous
"past" and "future." Where *were* these invisible realms that had so
much power over the lives of my family and friends? Everybody that
I knew seemed to be expending a great deal of effort thinking about
and trying to hold onto the past—obsessively photographing and
videotaping events, and continually projecting and fretting about the
future—ceaselessly sending out insurance premiums for their
homes, for their cars, even for their own bodies. As a result of all
these past and future concerns, everyone appeared (to me in my raw
and newly returned state) to be strangely unaware of happenings
unfolding all around them *in the present*. They seemed utterly oblivious to all those phenomena to which I had had to sensitize myself in
order to communicate with indigenous magicians in the course of
my fieldwork: the lives of other animals, the minute gestures of insects and plants, the speech of birds, the tastes in the wind, the flux
of sounds and smells. . . . My family and my old friends all seemed
so oblivious to the sensuous presence of the world. The present, for

them, seemed nothing more than a point, an infinitesimal now separating "the past" from "the future." And indeed, the more I entered
into conversation with my family and friends, the more readily I,
too, felt my consciousness cut off, as though by a sheet of reflective
glass, from the life of the land. . . .

There is a useful exercise that I devised back then to keep myself
from falling completely into the civilized oblivion of linear time.
You are welcome to try it the next time you are out of doors. I locate
myself in a relatively open space—a low hill is particularly good, or
a wide field. I relax a bit, take a few breaths, gaze around. Then I
close my eyes, and let myself begin to feel the whole bulk of my
past—the whole mass of events leading up to this very moment.
And I call into awareness, as well, my whole future—all those projects and possibilities that lie waiting to be realized. I imagine this
past and this future as two vast balloons of time, separated from
each other like the bulbs of an hourglass, yet linked together at the
single moment where I stand pondering them. And then, very
slowly, I allow both of these immense bulbs of time to begin leaking
their substance into this minute moment between them, into the
present. Slowly, imperceptibly at first, the present moment begins to
grow. Nourished by the leakage from the past and the future, the
present moment swells in proportion as those other dimensions
shrink. Soon it is very large; and the past and future have dwindled
down to mere knots on the edge of this huge expanse. At this point
I let the past and the future dissolve entirely. And I open my
eyes. . . .

*I FIND MYSELF STANDING IN THE MIDST OF AN ETERNITY, A VAST
and inexhaustible present. The whole world rests within itself—the trees
at the field's edge, the hum of crickets in the grass, cirrocumulus clouds
rippling like waves across the sky, from horizon to horizon. In the distance I notice the curving dirt road and my rusty car parked at its
edge—these, too, seem to have their place in this open moment of vision,
this eternal present. And smells—the air is rich with faint whiffs from
the forest, the heather, the soil underfoot—so many messages mingling
between different elements in the encircling land. The jagged snag of a
single withered oak tree standing alone in the field does not, in this eter-*

nity, seem really dead. It is surrounded by an admiring clump of low bushes, and a large boulder reposes at the edge of these bushes, dialoguing with the old tree about shadows and sunlight.

Stepping closer, I see that the crumbling bark around the oak's trunk is crossed by two lines of ants, one moving up the trunk and the other heading down into the soil. From this closer vantage I see, too, that the shadows on the boulder are not really shadows at all, but patches of lichen spreading outward from various points on the rock's surface, in diverse textures and hues—dull blacks and crinkly grays and powdery, deep reds—as though through them the rock was expressing its inner moods. I scratch my leg. Strangely, the vividness of this world does not dissipate. I stomp on the ground, spin around, even stand on my head. But the open present does not disperse. Several jet black crows race out of the woods, chasing each other in swoops and sudden dives; one of them lands on the crumbling snag. "Kahhr! . . . Kahr! Kahr!" Now it glides down to the ground just in front of me—"Kahr!"—and stands there looking at me, sideways, through a purple eye. The lids blink swiftly, like shutters. It hops around me and the big beak opens. "Kawhhr!" I try to reply, "Cawr!" and the bird steps forward. Crow does not hop, I see, but walks, clumsily, on this ground. I can see the tiny feathers covering the nostrils on its beak as the breeze picks it up off the ground, feel myself swoop through the swirling breeze toward the forest edge. . . .

Things are different in this world without "the past" and "the future," my body quivering in this space like an animal. I know well that, in some time out of this time, I must return to my house and my books. But here, too, is home. For my body is at home, in this open present, with its mind. And this is no mere illusion, no hallucination, this eternity— there is something too persistent, too stable, too unshakable about this experience for it to be merely a mirage. . . .

THE UNSHAKABLE SOLIDITY OF THIS EXPERIENCE IS CURIOUS indeed. It seems to have something to do with the remarkable affinity between this temporal notion that we term "the present" and the spatial landscape in which we are embedded. When I allow the past and the future to dissolve, imaginatively, into the immediacy of the present moment, then the "present" itself expands to become an enveloping field of *presence*. And this presence, vibrant and alive, spontaneously assumes the precise shape and contour of the enveloping sensory landscape, as though this were its native shape! It is this remarkable fit between temporal concept (the "present") and spatial percept (the enveloping presence of the land) that accounts, I believe, for the relatively stable and solid nature of this experience, and that prompts me to wonder whether "time" and "space" are really as distinct as I was taught to believe. There is no aspect of this realm that is strictly temporal—for it is composed of spatial things that have density and weight, and is spatially extended around me on all sides, from the near trees to the distant clouds. And yet there is no aspect, either, that is strictly spatial or static—for every perceivable being, from the stones to the breeze to my car in the distance, seems to vibrate with life and sensation. In this open present, I am unable to isolate space from time, or vice versa. I am immersed in the world.

IN 1905, ALBERT EINSTEIN CHALLENGED THE NEWTONIAN VIEW OF absolute time and absolute space with his "special theory of relativity." Einstein's equations in this, and later in the "general theory of relativity," did not treat of time and space; they assumed, instead, the existence of a unitary continuum that Einstein termed "space-time." Space-time, however, was a highly abstract concept unthinkable apart from the complex mathematics of relativity theory. Einstein's mathematical revelations, in other words, did little to challenge the Kantian assumption that separable space and time were necessary and unavoidable forms in all ordinary perception. While space-time held sway within the *conceptual* order of relativity physics, our direct, *perceptual* experience was still assumed to be structured according to the separable dimensions of time and space.

It thus fell to the tradition of phenomenology to call into question the distinction between space and time at the level of our direct, preconceptual experience. Of course, phenomenology did not set out to undermine this distinction—only to attend, as closely as possible, to the way phenomena present themselves in our immediate, lived experience. Indeed, phenomenologists tended to assume, at the outset, a clear distinction between space and time. It was only toward the end of his investigations regarding the phenomenology of "time consciousness" that Edmund Husserl was led to suggest that the experience of time is rooted in a deeper dimension of experience that is not, in itself, strictly temporal.[28]

Husserl's assistant, the German phenomenologist Martin Heidegger, returned again and again to the analysis of temporal experience. In his massive and influential work *Being and Time,* Heidegger disclosed, underneath the commonplace Aristotelian idea of time as an infinite sequence of "now points," a forgotten sense of time as the very mystery of Being, as that strange power—essentially resistant to all objectification or representation—that nevertheless structures and makes possible all our relations to each other and to the world. This mystery cannot be represented, precisely because it is never identical to itself; primordial time, for Heidegger, is from the first outside-of-itself, or "ecstatic." Indeed, the past, the present, and the future are here described by Heidegger as the three "ecstasies" of time, the three ways in which the irreducible dynamism of existence opens us to what is outside ourselves, to that which is *other*.[29]

Yet Heidegger gradually came to suspect that this implicit, preconceptual sense of time could not be held apart from our preconceptual experience of space. Hence, in an important essay written late in his career, Heidegger alludes to a still more primordial dimension, which he calls "time-space"—a realm neither wholly temporal nor wholly spatial, from whence "time" and "space" have been artificially derived by a process of abstraction.[30]

Meanwhile, Maurice Merleau-Ponty, continually deepening his own investigations of perceptual experience, also came, in his final work, to assert an experiential realm more originary than space and time, from which these two dimensions have been derived. In the working notes to *The Visible and the Invisible,* Merleau-Ponty writes of "this very time that is space, this very space that is time, which I will have rediscovered by my analysis of the visible and the flesh."[31] Yet this analysis was cut short by his sudden death in 1961.

So all three phenomenologists—Husserl, Heidegger, and Merleau-Ponty—came independently, in the course of their separate investigations, to suspect that the conventional distinction between space and time was untenable from the standpoint of direct, preconceptual experience. Heidegger and Merleau-Ponty were both striving, toward the end of their lives, to articulate a more immediate modality of awareness, a more primordial dimension whose characteristics are neither strictly spatial nor strictly temporal, but are rather— somehow—both at once.

We have seen that such a mode of experience is commonplace for indigenous, oral peoples, for whom time and space have never been sundered. The tradition of phenomenology, it would seem, has been striving to recover such an experience from within literate awareness itself—straining to remember, in the very depths of reflective thought, the silent reciprocity wherein such reflection is born. No single one of these thinkers was entirely successful in reconciling time and space. Yet their later writings provide tantalizing clues, talismans for those who are struggling today to bring their minds and their bodies back together, and so to regain a full-blooded awareness of the present.

The Earthly Topology of Time

I remain standing on this hill under rippled clouds, my skin tingling with sensations. The expansiveness of the present holds my body enthralled. My animal senses are all awake—my ears attuned to a multiplicity of minute sounds, the tiny hairs on my face registering every lull and shift in the breeze. I am embedded in this open moment, my muscles stretching and bending with the grass. This present seems endless, inexhaustible. What, then, has become of the past and the future?

I found my way into this living expanse by dissolving past and future into the sensorial present that envelops me; did I thereby do away with them entirely? I think not. I simply did away with these dimensions as they are conventionally conceived—as autonomous realms existing apart from the sensuous present. By letting past and future dissolve into the present moment, I have opened the way for their gradual rediscovery—no longer as autonomous, mental realms, but now as aspects of the corporeal present, of this capacious terrain that bodily enfolds me. And so now I crouch in the midst of this eternity, my naked toes hugging the soil and my eyes drinking the distances, trying to discern where, in this living landscape, the past and the future might reside.

Merleau-Ponty, in one of the notes found on his desk after his death, addressed the same conundrum:

> In what sense the visible landscape under my eyes is not exterior to . . . other moments of time and the past, but has them really *behind itself* in simultaneity, inside itself, and not it and they side by side "in" time.[32]

And so we are faced with this puzzle: Where, within the visible landscape, can we locate the past and the future? Where is their place in the sensuous world?

Of course, we may say that we perceive the past all around us, in great trees grown from seeds that germinated long ago, in the eroded banks of a meandering stream, or the widening cracks in an old road. And, too, that we are peering into the future wherever we look—watching a storm cloud emerge from the horizon, or a spiderweb slowly taking shape before our eyes—since all that we perceive is already, in a sense, pregnant with the future. But how, then, can we *distinguish* these two temporal realms? We certainly have a sense that the past and the future are not the same; nevertheless, they are strangely commingled within all that we perceive. How, then, do they distinguish themselves perceptually? If we say that "the past" is where all that we see comes from and "the future" is where it is all going, we simply beg the question, naming two allegedly obvious domains that we remain unable to locate within the perceivable landscape—as though past and future are, indeed, pure intuitions of the mind, existing in some incorporeal dimension outside of the sensory world. This, presumably, is what prompts many scientists and philosophers to assert that other animals have no real awareness of time—no sense of a past or a future—since they lack any intellect that could apprehend this non-sensuous dimension.

As an animal myself, I remain suspicious of all these dodges, all these ways whereby my species lays claim to a source of truth that supposedly lies outside of the bodily world wherein plants, stones, and streams have their being, outside of this earthly terrain that we share with the other animals. And yet, as a philosopher, I feel pressed to account for these mysteries, for these "times" that are somehow *not present,* for these other "whens." And so now let us bring the human animal and the philosopher in ourselves together, and try to locate the "past" and the "future" within the sensory landscape.

⚐

FIRST, WE SHOULD TAKE SOME METHODOLOGICAL GUIDANCE FROM Merleau-Ponty, who in 1960 was already struggling to give voice to "this very time that is space, this very space that is time."[33] In his last work Merleau-Ponty describes the relation between the perceptual world and the world of our supposedly incorporeal ideals and thoughts: "it is by borrowing from the world's structure that the universe of truth and of thought is constructed for us."[34] These words assert the primacy of the bodily world relative to the universe of ideas; they suggest that the structures of our apparently incorporeal ideas are lifted, as it were, from the structures of the perceptual world. If we read Merleau-Ponty's words carefully, and accept their guidance, we discern that what we are here hunting for, in our deepening quest, are specific aspects of the perceivable landscape that have lent their particular character, or shape, to these two persistent ideas, "the past" and "the future." We are searching, that is, for a structural correspondence—an isomorphism, or match—between the conceptual structure of "the past" and "the future" and the perceptual structure of the surrounding sensory world.

If we have taken a kind of method from Merleau-Ponty, it is to Martin Heidegger that we should turn for a careful structural description of "the past" and "the future." Throughout his life, from his first to his final writings, Heidegger gave special attention to the phenomenon of time, and it is he, more than any other thinker, who developed a phenomenology of time's dimensions. In the middle of a late essay entitled "Time and Being," Heidegger asks the very question we ourselves have posed: "Where is time? *Is* time at all and does it have a place?"[35] He then goes on to distinguish that time into which he is inquiring from the common *idea* of time as a linear sequence of "nows":

> Obviously, time is not nothing. Accordingly, we maintain caution and say: there is time. We become still more cautious, and look

carefully at that which shows itself as time, by looking ahead to Being in the sense of presence, the present. However, the present in the sense of presence differs so vastly from the present in the sense of the now. . . . [T]he present as presence and everything which belongs to such a present would have to be called real time, even though there is nothing immediately about it of time as time is usually represented in the sense of a succession of a calculable sequence of nows.[36]

Heidegger's philosophical move, here, to disclose behind the present considered as "now" a deeper sense of the present as "presence," approximates our own experiential move to expand the punctiform "now" by dissolving the "past" and the "future" as conventionally experienced, thereby locating ourselves in a vast and open present—which we, too, have called "the present as presence." According to Heidegger, it is only from within this experience of the present as presence that "real time" (which, later in the essay, he will call "time-space") can begin to make itself evident. In our case the present has determined itself as presence only by taking on the precise contours of the visible landscape that enfolds us. We are now free to look around us, in this vast terrain, for the place of the past and of the future.

And Heidegger offers us a helpful clue. In *Being and Time,* he writes of past, present, and future as the three "ecstasies" of time, suggesting that the past, the present, and the future all draw us outside of ourselves. Time is ecstatic in that it opens us outward. Toward what? The three ecstasies of time, according to Heidegger, "are not simply raptures in which one gets carried away. Rather, there belongs to each ecstasy a 'whither' to which one is carried. . . ." Each of time's ecstasies carries us, Heidegger says, toward a particular "horizon."[37]

As soon as we pay heed to this curious description, we notice an obvious correspondence between the conceptual structure of time, as described by Heidegger, and the perceptual structure of the enveloping landscape. The horizon itself! Heidegger uses the term "horizon" as a structural metaphor, a way of expressing the ecstatic nature of time. Just as the power of time seems to ensure that the perceivable present is always open, always already unfolding beyond itself, so the distant horizon seems to hold open the perceivable land-scape, binding it always to that which lies beyond it.[38]

The visible horizon, that is, a kind of gateway or threshold, join-ing the presence of the surrounding terrain to that which exceeds this open presence, to that which is hidden *beyond* the horizon. The horizon carries the promise of something more, something *other*. Here we have made our first discovery: the way that other places—places not explicitly present within the perceivable landscape—are nevertheless joined to the present landscape by the visible horizon. And so let us ask: is it possible that the realms we are looking for, the place of *the past* and that of *the future*, are precisely beyond the horizon?

Certainly this is a useful first step. For clearly, neither the past nor the future are entirely out in the open of the perceivable present, *and yet they seem everywhere implied*. Since the horizon effectively implicates all that lies beyond the horizon within the present land-scape that it bounds, it seems plausible to suppose that both the past and the future reside beyond the horizon.

Yet this leaves me somewhat confused, for I am unable, then, to account for the *difference* between the past and the future. The hori-zon of the perceivable landscape is provided, I know, by the relation of my body to the vast and spherical Body of the earth. This is not merely something that I have read, or learned in school. It has be-come evident and true for me in the course of many journeys across the land, watching the horizon continually recede as I move toward it, watching it disgorge unexpected vistas that expand and envelop me even as the horizon itself maintains its distance. And yet if I glance behind me as I journey, I see that this enigmatic edge is also following me, keeping its distance behind me as well as in front, gradually swallowing those terrains that I walk, drive, or pedal away from. May I then conclude that *the future* is beyond that part of the horizon toward which I am facing, while *the past* is beyond that part of the horizon that lies behind me? Then I would need only to turn around in order for my past to become my future, and vice versa. But this does not seem quite right. If I journey toward the horizon—toward any part of that horizon—I will indeed disclose new things and places that were previously in my future, beyond the horizon. Certainly I can attempt the reverse, as when I journey back toward that distant town where I used to dwell. But in this I am never quite successful. For that town, when I arrive, is no longer as it was. The old schoolhouse now stands half-collapsed in a field overgrown with wildflowers and thistles; the marsh where each spring I used to await the arrival of herons has vanished beneath a huge shopping mall. . . . The land has changed. I cannot, it seems, journey toward the past in the same way that I can journey toward the future. For the past does not *remain* past beyond the horizon; it does not wait for me there like the future.

It is this strange asymmetry of past and future in relation to the present that Heidegger describes in his late essay "Time and Being." While in *Being and Time* Heidegger wrote of the centrifugal, ecstatic character of time—of time as that which draws us outside of ourselves, opening us to what is other—in this later essay he stresses the centripetal, inward-extending nature of time, describing time as a mystery that continually approaches us from beyond, extending and offering the gift of presence while nevertheless withdrawing behind the event of this offering. Such descriptions may sound strange, even uncanny, to our ears, and yet we should listen to them closely. For as Heidegger's thought matured, he increasingly sought to loosen human awareness from the bondage of outworn assumptions, precisely by wielding common words in highly unusual ways, shaking terms free from their conventional usages. Thus *past* and *future* are here articulated as hidden powers that approach us, offering and opening the present while nevertheless remaining withdrawn, concealed from the very present that they make possible. In Heidegger's description, both the past and the future remain hidden from the open presence that they mutually bring about.[39] And yet the way the future conceals itself in its offering is quite different from the manner in which the past is concealed in its giving. Specifically, the future, or that which is to come, *withholds* its presence, while the past, or that which has been, *refuses* its presence.[40] The future withholds, while the past refuses. In his most complete description of the vicissitudes of time, Heidegger puts the matter thus:

What has been, which, by refusing the present, lets that become present which is no longer present; and the coming toward us of what is to come, which, by withholding the present, lets that be present which is not yet present—both [make] manifest the manner of an extending opening up which gives all presencing into the open.[41]

The strange character of Heidegger's language here is part of his project: he is trying to avoid the use of nouns, of nominative forms that would freeze the temporal flux. It is precisely this strangeness that enables his words to approach, and to open us onto, the silent structuration of this mystery we call time. If we ponder these words from within the open presence of the land around us, we are led to ask: Where can we perceive this *withholding* and this *refusal* of which Heidegger speaks? Where can we glimpse this refusal and this withholding that open and make possible the sensuous presence of the world around us?

We have already noticed the magic by which the horizon encloses and yet holds open the visible landscape: precisely by concealing, or better, *withholding,* that which lies beyond it. Thus, the horizon may indeed be felt as a withholding. But it is hardly a refusal. The horizon's lips of earth and sky may touch one another, but they are never sealed; and we know that if we journey toward that horizon, it will gradually disclose to us that which it now withholds.

Where, then, can we locate the refusal to which Heidegger alludes? Do we perceive such a refusal anywhere around us? More important: how do we even know what we are looking for? Here again, Heidegger provides a clue. In "Time and Being," he writes of the past and of the future as *absences* that by their very absence concern us, and so make themselves felt within the present.[42] This description aids us a great deal. Now at least we can say what we are searching for in our attempt to locate, or place, the past and the future. We are hunting for modes of absence which, by their very way of being absent, make themselves felt within the sensuous presence of the open landscape. Or in Merleau-Ponty's terminology (the terminology of *The Visible and the Invisible*) we could say we are searching for certain *invisible* aspects of the visible environment, certain unseen regions whose very hiddenness somehow enables or makes possible the open visibility of the land around us. The *beyond-the-horizon* is just such an absent or unseen realm.

And so we must now ask: Is there *another* unseen aspect, another absent region whose very concealment is somehow necessary to the open presence of the landscape?

Of course, there are those facets that I cannot see of the things or bodies that surround me—the sides of the trees that are facing away from me, or the other side of that lichen-covered rock. Yet these concealments are all analogous, in a sense, to that which lies hidden beyond the horizon. The other side of that rock, for instance, is withheld from my gaze, but it is not refused, for I can disclose it by walking over there, just as I can disclose what lies beyond the horizon by making a longer journey.

What of my own body? Well, most of my body is present to my awareness, and visible to my gaze. I can see my limbs, my torso, and even my nose, although my back, of course, is hidden beyond the horizon of my shoulders. The back of my body is inaccessible to my vision, and yet I know that it exists, that it is visible to the crows perched behind me in the trees, as I know that the fields and forests hidden beyond the horizon are yet visible and present to those who dwell there.

Yet while pondering the unseen aspect of my body, I soon notice another unseen region: that of the whole *inside* of my body. The inside of my body is not, of course, entirely absent; but it is hidden from visibility in a manner very different from the concealment of my back, or of that which lies beyond the horizon. It is an instance, I suddenly realize, of a vast mode of absence or invisibility entirely proper to the present landscape—an absence I had almost entirely forgotten. It is the absence of what is *under the ground*.

❧

LIKE THE BEYOND-THE-HORIZON, THE ABSENCE OF THE UNDER-the-ground is an absence so familiar, and so necessary to the open presence of the world around us, that we take it entirely for granted, and so it has been very difficult for me to bring it into awareness. But once I have done so, the recognition of this hidden realm begins to clarify and balance the enigmatic power of that other unseen region beyond the horizon.

For these would seem to be the two primary dimensions from whence things enter the open presence of the landscape, and into which they depart. Sensible phenomena are continually appearing out of, and continually vanishing into, these two very different realms of concealment or invisibility. One trajectory is a passage out toward, or inward from, a vast openness. The other is a descent into, or a sprouting up from, a packed density. While the open horizon withholds the visibility of that which lies beyond it, the ground is much more resolute in its concealment of what lies beneath it. It is this resoluteness, this *refusal* of access to what lies beneath the ground, that enables the ground to solidly support all those phenomena that move or dwell upon its surface. Thus, although the absence of the beyond-the-horizon and that of the under-the-ground reciprocate one another, they contrast markedly in their relation to the perceivable present. We may describe this reciprocity and this contrast thus: *The beyond-the-horizon, by withholding its presence, holds open the perceived landscape, while the under-the-ground, by refusing its presence, supports the perceived landscape.* The reciprocity and asymmetry between these two realms bear an uncanny resemblance to the reciprocity and contrast between the *future* (or "what is to come") and the *past* (or "what has been") in Martin Heidegger's description above—the one *withholding* presence, the other *refusing* presence; both of them thus making possible the open presence of the present. Dare we suspect that these two descriptions describe one and the same phenomenon? I believe that we can, for the isomorphism is complete.

BY READING MERLEAU-PONTY AND HEIDEGGER TOGETHER, AND by setting their words in relation to our own experience, we have begun to realize that the past and the future—these curious dimensions—may be just as much spatial as they are temporal. Indeed, we have begun to *place* these dimensions, to discern their location within the sensuous world. The conceptual abstraction that we commonly term "the future" would seem to be born from our bodily awareness of that which is hidden beyond the horizon—of that which exceeds, and thus holds open, the living present. What we commonly term "the past" would seem to be rooted in our carnal sense of that which is hidden under the ground—of that which resists, and thus supports, the living present. As ground and horizon, these dimensions are no more temporal than they are spatial, no more mental than they are bodily and sensorial.

We can now discern just how close Merleau-Ponty was to this discovery by reading his aforement ˙ ɔned note of November 1960 in the light of our disclosures:

> In what sense the visible landscape under my eyes is not exterior to, and bound systematically to . . . other moments of time and the past, but has them really *behind itself* in simultaneity, *inside itself* and not it and they side by side "in" time.[43]

For we can now understand this *behind* and this *inside* in a remarkably precise manner. The visible landscape has the other moments of time "behind itself," precisely in that the future waits beyond the horizon, as well as *behind* every entity that I see, as the unseen "other side" of the many visibles that surround me. And the visible landscape has the other moments of time "inside itself," precisely in that the past preserves itself under the ground, as well as *inside* every entity that I perceive. The sensorial landscape, in other words, not only opens onto that distant future waiting beyond the horizon but also onto a near future, onto an immanent field of possibilities waiting behind each tree, behind each stone, behind each leaf from whence a spider may at any moment come crawling into our awareness. And this living terrain is supported not only by that more settled or sedimented past under the ground, but by an immanent past resting inside each tree, within each blade of grass, within the very muscles and cells of our own bodies.

It is thus that ecologists and environmental scientists may study the recent past of a particular place by "coring" several of the standing trees, in order to count their interior rings and to interpret the varying width of those rings (an extra-wide layer, fourteen rings in from the cambium, suggests a season of abundant rain fourteen years into the depth of the past, while an extra-thin layer tells of a year without rainfall). The deeper past may be pondered by digging a "soil pit" to expose the sedimented layers of the soil, and to interpret the composition and structure of those layers (a layer of charcoal, for instance, bespeaks a forest fire at that depth of the past). Meanwhile, archaeologists, paleontologists, and geologists dig still deeper beneath the ground of the present in order to unearth traces of ancient epochs and eons.

That which has been and that which is to come are not else-where—they are not autonomous dimensions independent of the encompassing present in which we dwell. They are, rather, the very depths of this living place—the hidden depth of its distances and the concealed depth on which we stand.

❧

PROMPTED BY THE PLACE-CENTERED DISCOURSE OF ORAL, INDIGE-nous peoples—which seems to lack any absolute distinction between "space" and "time"—and prompted as well by our analysis of writ-ing and its perceptual effects, we have been searching for a possible reconciliation between time and space. If the distinction between these dimensions is not a necessary distinction, then we should be able to demonstrate the possibility of another way of construing events, one in which spatial and temporal aspects are not distin-guishable.

And we have succeeded in demonstrating that there is at least one way to unify the experience of time and of space, that it is indeed possible to perceptually reconcile the temporal and the spatial in a manner that accounts for the apparent openness of what we have come to call the "future" and the apparent closedness of what we have come to call the "past." Heretofore, such a perceptual reconcil-iation was thought to be impossible, usually because space—even perceived space—was assumed to be essentially homogeneous, and so to lack any structural asymmetry that might correspond with the evident asymmetry of time. It is evident, however, that when our awareness of time is joined with our awareness of space, space itself is transformed. Space is no longer experienced as a homogeneous void, but reveals itself as this vast and richly textured field in which we are corporeally immersed, this vibrant expanse structured by both a ground and a horizon. It is precisely the ground and the hori-zon that transform abstract space into space-time. And these charac-teristics—the ground and the horizon—*are granted to us only by the earth*. Thus, when we let time and space blend into a unified space-time, we rediscover the enveloping earth.

It would seem, then, that the conceptual separation of time and space—the literate distinction between a linear, progressive time and a homogeneous, featureless space—functions to *eclipse* the enveloping earth from human awareness. As long as we structure our lives according to assumed parameters of a static space and a rectilinear time, we will be able to ignore, or overlook, our thorough dependence upon the earth around us. Only when space and time are reconciled into a single, unified field of phenomena does the encompassing earth become evident, once again, in all its power and its depth, as the very ground and horizon of all our knowing.

In the Depths of the Sensuous

The importance that our analysis has led us to place on such taken for granted phenomena as the *ground* and the *horizon* will seem strange to most readers, indeed to all of us raised in a culture that asks us to distrust our immediate sensory experience and to orient ourselves instead on the basis of an abstract, "objective" reality known only through quantitative measurement, technological instrumentation, and other exclusively human involvements. But for those indigenous cultures still participant with the more-than-human life-world, for those peoples that have not yet shifted their synaesthetic focus from the animate earth to a purely human set of signs, the riddles of the under-the-ground and the beyond-the-horizon (the inside of things and the other side of things) are felt as vast and powerful mysteries, the principal realms from whence beings enter the animate world, and into which they depart.

For instance, among most native tribes of the American Southwest, where I live—including, among others, the Hopi, the Zuñi, the Tewa, the Tiwa, the Keresan, and the Navajo nations—the people believe that they came into the world from under the ground. According to the Zuñi emergence story, all the *people* (humans and all other animals) originally lived in the fourth dark underworld within the earth. They were summoned forth from there by Sun, who, along with Moon, inhabited the bright world above Earth's surface.

And so the animal-people gathered all their sacred bundles for making rain, and for coaxing seeds to grow, and climbed upward along a reed through the four underworlds—through the soot world, the sulfur-smell world, the fog world, and the feather-wing world—until, finally, they emerged into *this* world. From the *sipapu,* or place of emergence, the people then spread out and began to settle the land.[44]

The Emergence is one of the most sacred and widely held beliefs among native North Americans today, although it is particularly evident in the Southwest.[45] In its structure the story of the people's emergence from under the ground, usually climbing up a reed or a tree, mimics the emergence from the soil of the corn and other plants harvested by the horticultural tribes of the Southwest. The people who climb up from those depths in search of sunlight and rain are like corn growing up through the soil.

But the Emergence is also akin to the process by which all mammals, including humans, are born into this world, emerging from the darkness of their mother's womb into the spaciousness of the open earth. "When we came up on this earth, it was just like a child being born from its mother."[46] In fact, earlier tellings of the Zuñi Emergence, recorded in the last century, relate that long before the existence of the people, the Sun cohabited with the Earth, and it is thus that life was conceived within the deepest, fourth womb of the Earth.[47] Hence, the Emergence may be understood as the collective *birth* of all peoples—of all animals and plants—after a prolonged period of gestation in the dark depths of the ground.

The most sacred ceremonies of the pueblo-dwelling tribes take place in the *kivas,* the underground or partially underground chambers also called "wombs" by many of the pueblo people. One enters a kiva by climbing down a ladder through a hole in the roof, and after the ceremony one leaves the kiva by climbing up through the same opening, the same *sipapu,* reexperiencing—and renewing—the primordial emergence from the underworld. In fact, all sorts of earthly openings—holes, caves, canyons, small depressions in the ground and even in stones—are considered *sipapu* by the Pueblo peoples, and so remind them of their origin under the ground that now supports them.

The individual experience of birth is thus related to the collective emergence of life from under the ground. Similarly, human death, for oral peoples, is not just a personal event but also a transformation in the land, a process whereby one's individual sensibility opens outward to rejoin the encompassing, more-than-human field of sensations. In an old Pawnee tale, a dead man returns as a ghost, saying, "I am in everything; in the grass, the water."[48] The dead do not *leave* the sensuous world, forsaking it for an immaterial heaven. Rather, the vitality of one who dies is often thought to journey just *beyond the visible horizon,* to a nearby land where all of the ancestors traditionally gather, and from whence they still influence events within the land of the living. Among the above-mentioned Pueblo peoples, for instance, the dead are thought to travel to the village of the *kachinas,* which for the Zuñi is located under a lake several days journey to the west. The kachinas, the godlike ancestors, regularly return to the various pueblos for the seasonal ceremonies at which they are impersonated, or made visible, by masked dancers. But the kachinas also visit the pueblos, whenever they wish, as rain-bearing clouds that approach from *beyond the horizon,* carrying the life-giving moisture so necessary to the corn and the other plants upon which these horticultural peoples depend:

> the Hopis—like the other Pueblos—believe their ancestors to be fertilizing clouds, bringers of rain who will nourish the crops upon which the living subsist. The necessity of death . . . becomes even more accentuated, therefore. . . . Death brings into existence the ancestors, who turn into clouds and kachinas that bring rain; moisture feeds the corn and other foods that in turn nourish the Hopi people themselves, and in the eternal cycle, death feeds life.[49]

Among nonhorticultural tribes as well, the dead are often thought to journey to a land beyond the horizon, from whence they may return among the living in the guise of animals and other natural elements. Indeed, for many hunting peoples, the realm beyond the mountains, or beyond the ocean, was where various animal species resided when they were not evident in the present landscape, a realm where the deer or the salmon were thought to remove their animal guises and to live in quasi-human form. To cite a single example, the Skagit Indians of northwestern North America held that the salmon, when they are not spawning in the rivers, live beyond the horizon in human form. Hence, in the nineteenth century, when several of these Indians traveled to the eastern coast of North America and saw the abundance of pale-skinned people living there, they reported back that they had been to salmon country and had seen salmon walking around as human beings.[50]

For the American Plains tribes, at least in the nineteenth century, the home of the dead beyond the horizon was commonly believed to be a land always abundant in edible plants and wild game—the "happy hunting ground" of popular legend. While some such indigenous notion of a fertile and abundant terrain where the ancestors dwell was likely the archaic source of even the Christian belief in a heavenly paradise, it is important to realize that for oral peoples such realms were never wholly cut off from the sensuous world of the living present. They were not projected entirely outside of the experienced world, but were felt as the mystery and hidden depth of the sensuous world itself.

If we pay close attention to the life and activity of the great celestial powers—the sun, the moon, and the clustered stars—we will see that even these entities, so commonly associated with height and vertical transcendence, seem to emerge from, and return to, the lands beyond the horizon. Hence, if the Shoshoni Indians, for example, assert that a dead person "follows the Milky Way" to the land of the dead, this need not indicate, as some anthropologists have claimed, that the Shoshoni believe in a celestial heaven.[51] For the Milky Way is but a visible trail or "way" followed by the spirits of the dead, and this trail—as we can readily see—leads precisely beyond-the-horizon.

Yet here we must acknowledge a strange ambiguity. The beyond-the-horizon is that realm where the sun goes when it leaves us, and the realm from which it emerges at dawn; it is where the moon goes to and returns from. But we could just as well say the sun sinks into the under-the-ground and the moon emerges from under-the-ground. For when we attend closely to our direct, sensory experience of the rising and the setting, we see that the moon's journey beyond the horizon is also experienced as a movement down into the ground, and indeed that the sun's rise each morning is as much an emergence from under the ground as is the emergence of a groundhog at the end of winter! Hence, for example, these words by Kiowa author N. Scott Momaday:

> "Where does the sun live?". . . [T]o the Indian child who asks the question, the parent replies, "The sun lives in the earth." The sun-watcher among the Rio Grande Pueblos, whose sacred task it is to observe, each day, the very point of the sun's emergence on the skyline, knows in the depths of his being that the sun is alive and that it is indivisible with the earth, and he refers to the far-thest eastern mesa as "the sun's house.". . . Should someone say to the sun, "Where are you going?" the sun would surely answer, "I am going home," and it is understood at once that home is the earth. All things are alive in this profound unity in which are all elements, all animals, all things. . . . [M]y father remembered that, as a boy, he had watched with wonder and something like fear the old man Koi-khan-hole, "Dragonfly," stand in the first light, his arms outstretched and his painted face fixed on the east, "praying the sun out of the ground."[52]

Phenomenologically considered, it is as though the luminous orb of the sun journeys into the ground each evening, moving all night through the density underfoot, to emerge, at dawn, at the opposite side of the visible world. For some indigenous cultures, it is precisely during this journey through the ground that the sun impregnates the earth with its fiery life, giving rise to the myriad living things—human and nonhuman—that blossom forth on earth's surface.

So the journey beyond-the-horizon can lead under-the-ground, and vice versa. We begin to glimpse here the secret identity, for oral peoples, of those topological regions that we have come to call "the past" and "the future"—the curious manner in which these two very different modes of absence can nevertheless transmute into each other, blur into one another, like moods. It is thus that many indigenous cultures have but a single term to designate the very deep past and the far distant future. Among the Inuit of Baffin Island, for example, the term *uvatiarru* may be translated both as "long ago" and "in the future."[53] The cyclical metamorphosis of the distant past into the distant future, or of that-which-has-been into that-which-is-to-come, would seem to take place continually, in the depths far below the visible present, in that place where the unseen lands beyond the horizon seem to fold into the invisible density beneath our feet.

&

MARTIN HEIDEGGER, WHOSE CAREFUL DESCRIPTIONS OF THE PAST and the future have helped us to recognize these realms as actual dimensions of the perceptual field, did not write of only two temporal dimensions, however, but of *three,* including that of the present. In *Being and Time,* Heidegger asserts that the present has its own ecstasy, its own proper transcendence, its own " 'whither' to which one is carried away."[54] The implication is that phenomena can be hidden not just within the past or the future, but also within the very thickness of the present, itself—that there is an enigmatic, hidden dimension at the very heart of the sensible present, into which phenomena may withdraw and out of which they continually emerge. Thus in "Time and Being," Heidegger writes that "even in the present itself, there always plays a kind of approach and bringing about, that is, a kind of presencing."[55] As though, paradoxically, there is a modality of absence entirely native to the present, out of which the present, itself, comes to presence: "In the present, too, presencing is given."[56]

Is there, then, yet another mode of absence or invisibility entirely endemic to the open landscape? I have already noticed, here within the perceivable present, the hidden nature of what lies behind the tree trunks and stones that surround me, which corresponds to the unseen character of that which lies on the other side of these nearby hills, and ultimately to those lands entirely beyond the horizon of the perceivable present, from whence numerous entities enter the visible terrain and into which various phenomena withdraw, recede, and finally vanish from view. I have acknowledged as well the concealed character of that which rests *inside* the trunks of these trees, inside the stones and the hills, which corresponds, ultimately, to the unseen nature of the under-the-ground, from whence beings sprout and unfurl, and into which they also crumble, decompose, and are submerged. Is there some other obvious style of absence, in the very thickness of the present, that is unique to itself, and not a mere modification of the under-the-ground or the beyond-the-horizon?

Some mode of concealment that is, paradoxically, already out in the open, from whence the visible landscape itself continually comes to presence?

Perhaps I am pushing my method too far, here, in trying to place not only the *withholding* of presence by the future and the *refusal* of presence by the past, but also this concealment of presence *from within the present itself*. For now, more than ever, I feel confused,— unable to grasp, or to conceive of, what it is that I am searching for. Even as I gaze out across the wooded hills, my mind seems muddled by these questions, by ideas and associations that keep me from directly sensing and responding to the animate earth around me. I try to relax, and so begin to breathe more deeply, enjoying the coolness of the breeze as it floods in at my nostrils, feeling my chest and abdomen slowly expand and contract. My thinking begins to ease, the internal chatter gradually taking on the rhythm of the in-breath and the out-breath, the words themselves beginning to dissolve, flowing out with each exhalation to merge with the silent breathing of the land. The interior monologue dissipates, slowly, into the rustle of pine needles and the stately gait of the clouds.

A butterfly glides by, golden wings navigating delicate air currents with a few momentary flutters before they settle on a white flower. The seedstalks of the grasses bounce in the breeze, while clustered wildflowers tremble on their stems, awaiting the humming insects that motor haphazardly from one to the other. Fragrant whiffs from new blossoms in the overgrown orchard by the creek stir not only the winged beings, but my own flaring nostrils as they reach me from afar, drifting like spiderwebs on the faint winds. My sensing body now vividly awake to the world, I gradually become conscious of a third mode of invisibility, of an unseen dimension in which I am so thoroughly and deeply immersed that even now I can hardly bring it to full awareness. . . .

It is the invisibility of the air.

The Forgetting and Remembering of the Air

Let's sit down here . . . on the open prairie, where we can't see a high-way or a fence. Let's have no blankets to sit on, but feel the ground with our bodies, the earth, the yielding shrubs. Let's have the grass for a mattress, experiencing its sharpness and its softness. Let us become like stones, plants, and trees. Let us be animals, think and feel like animals. Listen to the air. You can hear it, feel it, smell it, taste it. *Woniya wakan*—the holy air—which renews all by its breath. *Woniya, woniya wakan*—spirit, life, breath, renewal—it means all that. *Woniya*—we sit together, don't touch, but something is there; we feel it between us, as a presence. A good way to start thinking about nature, talk about it. Rather talk to it, talk to the rivers, to the lakes, to the winds as to our relatives.

—JOHN FIRE LAME DEER

WHAT A MYSTERY IS THE AIR, WHAT AN ENIGMA TO THESE human senses! On the one hand, the air is the most pervasive presence I can name, enveloping, embracing, and caressing me both inside and out, moving in ripples along my skin, flowing between my fingers, swirling around my arms and thighs, rolling in eddies along the roof of my mouth, slipping ceaselessly through throat and trachea to fill the lungs, to feed my blood, my heart, my self. I cannot act, cannot speak, cannot think a single thought without the participation of this fluid element. I am immersed in its depths as surely as fish are immersed in the sea.

Yet the air, on the other hand, is the most outrageous absence known to this body. For it is utterly invisible. I know very well that there is something there—I can feel it moving against my face and can taste it and smell it, can even hear it as it swirls within my ears and along the bark of trees, but still, I cannot see it. I can see the steady movement it induces in the shapeshifting clouds, the way it bends the branches of the cottonwoods, and sends ripples along the surface of a stream. The fluttering wing feathers of a condor soaring overheard; the spiraling trajectory of a leaf as it falls; a spider web billowing like a sail; the slow drift of a seed through space—all make evident, to my eyes, the sensuous presence of the air. Yet these eyes cannot see the air itself.

Unlike the hidden character of what lies beyond the horizon, and unlike the unseen nature of that which resides under the ground, the air is invisible *in principle*. That which today lies beyond the horizon can at least partly be disclosed by journeying into that future, as that which waits under the ground can be somewhat unearthed by excavations into the past. But the air can never be opened for our eyes, never made manifest. Itself invisible, it is the medium through which we see all else in the present terrain.

And this unseen enigma is the very mystery that enables life to live. It unites our breathing bodies not only with the under-the-ground (with the rich microbial life of the soil, with fossil and mineral deposits deep in the bedrock), and not only with the beyond-the-horizon (with distant forests and oceans), but also with the interior life of all that we perceive in the open field of the living present—the grasses and the aspen leaves, the ravens, the buzzing insects and the drifting clouds. What the plants are quietly breathing out, we animals are breathing in; what we breathe out, the plants are breathing in. The air, we might say, is the soul of the visible landscape, the secret realm from whence all beings draw their nourishment. As the very mystery of the living present, it is that most intimate absence from whence the present presences, and thus a key to the forgotten presence of the earth.

✣

NOTHING IS MORE COMMON TO THE DIVERSE INDIGENOUS CULtures of the earth than a recognition of the air, the wind, and the breath, as aspects of a singularly sacred power. By virtue of its pervading presence, its utter invisibility, and its manifest influence on all manner of visible phenomena, the air, for oral peoples, is the archetype of all that is ineffable, unknowable, yet undeniably real and efficacious. Its obvious ties to speech—the sense that spoken words are structured breath (try speaking a word without exhaling at the same time), and indeed that spoken phrases take their communicative power from this invisible medium that moves between us—lends the air a deep association with linguistic meaning and with thought. Indeed, the ineffability of the air seems akin to the ineffability of awareness itself, and we should not be surprised that many indigenous peoples construe awareness, or "mind," not as a power that resides inside their heads, but rather as a quality that they themselves *are inside of,* along with the other animals and the plants, the mountains and the clouds.

According to Robert Lawlor, a researcher who has lived and studied among the indigenous cultures of Australia, Aboriginal peoples tend to consider the visible entities around them—rocks, persons, leaves—as crystallizations of conscious awareness, while the invisible medium *between* such entities is experienced as what Westerners would call "the unconscious," the creative but unseen realm from which such conscious forms arise.[1] Thus, the *Alcheringa*, or Dreamtime—that implicit realm of dreamlike happenings from whence the visible present is continually emerging—resides not just within the hills and landforms of the surrounding terrain, but also in the invisible depths of the air itself, in the thickness of the very medium that flows within us and all around us. This leads Aboriginal Australians to accord awesome significance to various atmospheric phenomena. Flashes of lightning are experienced as violent discharges from the depths of the Dreaming. Birds, who wing their way through the invisible, are often experienced as messengers of the unconscious, while the rainbow (the Rainbow Snake, who arcs upward across the sky and then dives back into the earth) is felt to personify all the most implacable, dangerous, and yet life-giving forces in the land.[2] For the rainbow is perceived as the very *edge* of the Dreaming, as that place where the invisible, unconscious potentials begin to become visible.[3]

Wind and Spirit on the Great Plains

The omnipresent and yet invisible nature of the air ensures that the indigenous beliefs and teachings regarding this elemental mystery are among the most sacred and secret of oral traditions. Native teachings regarding the wind or the breath are exceedingly difficult to track or to record, for to give voice to them unnecessarily may violate the mystery and holiness of this enveloping power, this enigmatic presence (or absence) so obviously essential to one's life and the life of the land.

We do know that the air was an uncommonly sacred power for most of the native peoples of North America. Among the Creek Indians of the Southeast, for instance, the creator god—the only divinity equal to or exceeding the Earth and the Sun in its power—is called Hesakitumesee, the Master of Breath; it is this being who sends fog, wind, and other weather across the land, affecting the destiny of the people.[4]

For the Lakota Nation, the most sacred or *wakan* aspect of Wakan Tanka, the Great Mysterious, is Taku Škanškan, the Enveloping Sky. Known to the shamans simply as Škan, Taku Škanškan is felt to be everywhere, the omnipresent spirit that imparts life, motion, and thought to all things, yet is visible to us only as the blue of the sky. (It is this deity that contemporary Lakota persons sometimes address, in English, as the Great Spirit.) Tate (pronounced "Tah-day")—*Wind*—is created by Škan out of his own substance, to be a companion for Škan and to carry his wishes and messages throughout the world. (Škan and Tate—Sky and Wind—are thus sometimes spoken of as the same entity by the Lakota shamans.)[5] And it was Tate who mated with Ite ("Ee-day"), a beautiful woman of the Buffalo people; from this union Ite gave birth to the North Wind, the East Wind, the South Wind, and the West Wind (as well as to Yum, the little whirlwind or dust-devil). These four Winds structure, and lend their particular magics, to every Lakota ritual practiced today.[6]

Meanwhile, the peace pipe is the most *wakan* of all possessions for the Lakota. Carved from dark red pipestone found only in the northern plains—a stone considered to be the petrified blood of their ancestors—the sacred pipe is smoked in ritual fashion during all of the diverse Lakota ceremonies, from the sweat lodge to the Sun Dance. The pipe smoke makes the invisible breath visible, and as it rises from the pipe, it makes visible the flows and currents in the air itself, makes visible the unseen connections between those who smoke the pipe in offering and all other entities that dwell within the world: the winged peoples, the other walking and crawling peoples, and the multiple rooted beings—trees, grasses, shrubs, mosses.[7] Further, the rising smoke carries the prayers of the Lakota people to the sky beings—to the sun and the moon, to the stars, to the thunder beings and the clouds, to all those powers embraced by *woniya wakan*, the holy air.

> *Woniya wakan*—the holy air—which renews all by its breath. *Woniya, woniya wakan*—spirit, life, breath, renewal—it means all that. *Woniya*—we sit together, don't touch, but something is there; we feel it between us, as a presence.[8]

At the opening of any ceremony, a Lakota medicine person fills and lights the sacred pipe, and then, before smoking it himself, offers the mouthpiece to the West Wind so that the wind itself may partake of the smoke. Then, circling, he offers the pipe to be smoked by the North Wind, then to the East Wind, and finally to the South Wind. As the messengers of the gods, the winds are the first powers to be addressed in any ceremony.[9]

The winds of the four directions are also deeply associated with the cyclical, spatial sense of time. An old Lakota shaman, named Sword, interviewed early in the twentieth century, related that in any ceremony, after offering the mouthpiece of the lit pipe to each of the four winds,

> the shaman should move the pipe in the same manner until the mouthpiece again points toward the west, and say: "Circling, I complete the four quarters and the time." He should do this be-cause the four winds are the four quarters of the circle and mankind knows not where they may be or whence they may come and the pipe should be offered directly toward them. The four

quarters embrace all that are in the world and all that are in the sky. Therefore, by circling the pipe, the offering is made to all the gods. The circle is the symbol of time, for the day time, the night time, and the moon time are circles above the world, and the year time is a circle around the border of the world. Therefore the lighted pipe moved in a complete circle is an offering to all the times.[10]

After completing the circle, the shaman points the mouthpiece of the pipe toward the sky, and offers it to Wind, Tate, the father of the four Winds. Finally, then, "the shaman should smoke the pipe and while doing so should say: 'I smoke with the Great Spirit. Let us have a blue day.'"[11]

Air and Awareness Among the Diné, or Navajo

While the air is held sacred *throughout* native North America, the most extensively documented interpretation of the air is probably the Diné, or Navajo, concept of *nilch'i*—the Holy Wind. Long misunderstood by anthropologists, the Navajo term *nilch'i* refers to the whole body of the air or the atmosphere, including the air when in motion, as well as the air that swirls within us as we breathe. According to James Kale McNeley, in his meticulously documented book *Holy Wind in Navajo Philosophy*, *nilch'i*, "meaning Wind, Air, or Atmosphere," suffuses all of nature, and is that which grants life, movement, speech, and awareness to all beings. Moreover, the Holy Wind serves as the means of communication *between* all beings and elements of the animate world. *Nilch'i* is thus utterly central to the Diné, or Navajo worldview.[12]

Although *nilch'i* is conceived by the Navajo as a single, unified phenomenon, the Wind in its totality is also assumed to be comprised of many diverse aspects, a plurality of partial Winds, each of which have their own name in the Navajo language. One of these—*nilch'i hwii'siziinii*, or "the Wind within one"—refers to that part of the overall Wind that circulates within each individual. This notion was mistaken by early missionaries, and by the important missionary/ethnologist Father Berard Haile, to be a phenomenon akin to the personal soul of Christian belief. Thus, "the Wind within one" was interpreted, until recently, to be an immaterial spirit or soul, a thoroughly autonomous entity that enters the individual at birth, acts as the internal source of his or her life and behavior, and then departs from the individual at death.[13] Only recently have anthropologists like McNeley been able to break out of the interpretive blinders imposed by the Christian worldview in order to recognize that the powers attributed by Western culture to a purely internal soul or mind are experienced by the Navajo as attributes of the enveloping Wind or Atmosphere as a whole. The "Wind within one" is in no way autonomous, for it is in a continual process of interchange with the various winds that surround one, and indeed is entirely a part of the Holy Wind itself.

WE MAY BRING OURSELVES CLOSE TO THE ORAL EXPERIENCE OF THE air by consulting the words of the Navajo elders themselves, and by pondering the preeminent influence of Wind, or Air, within the Navajo universe.

> Wind existed first, as a person, and when the Earth began its existence Wind took care of it. We started existing where Darknesses, lying on one another, occurred. Here, the one that had lain on top became Dawn, whitening across. What used to be lying on one another back then, this is Wind. It (Wind) was Darkness. That is why when Darkness settles over you at night it breezes beautifully. It is this, it is a person, they say. From there when it dawns, when it dawns beautifully becoming white-streaked through the dawn, it usually breezes. Wind exists beautifully, they say. Back there in the underworlds, this was a person it seems.[14]

Already in the underworlds, in those times or realms beneath the ground, prior to the emergence of the Holy People into the world of the present, Wind existed and provided both breath and guidance to the other Holy Ones, such as First Man, First Woman, Talking

God, and Calling God. When these Holy People emerged from the ground into this world on Earth's surface, they were accompanied by Wind. Already differentiated as the Winds of Darkness and of Dawn, Wind now differentiated itself further into the Blue Wind of noon and the Yellow Wind of twilight. These four Winds spread out from the emergence place and were then placed by the Earth in the four directions, *along the horizon of the world*—Dawn Woman in the east, Horizontal Blue Girl in the south, Horizontal Yellow Boy (or evening twilight) in the west, and Darkness Man (or night) in the north (the precise names of these Winds vary from one chant to another; often they are simply spoken of as White Wind, Blue Wind, Yellow Wind, and Dark Wind). These four Winds—or four *Words*, as they are also called—are said to be the means of breath of the four sacred mountains that visibly rise at the edge of the Navajo cosmos, one in each of the cardinal directions. "They [the Winds] stand within the mountains, these [mountains] from then on being, by them, our sacred ones to the end of time."[15] Similarly, the Sun and the Moon have their own Winds, which are their means of life and breath. Other Winds surround and move between these great powers, as their means of communication with each other and with other phenomena. From its sacred home in each of the four directions, the Holy Wind is said to approach and enter into the various natural phenomena of the world, and so to provide the means of life, movement, thought, and speech to the plants, to the animals, and to all the other Earth Surface People, including the Navajo people themselves.[16]

Wind is believed by the Diné to be present within a person from the very moment of conception, when two Winds, one from the bodily fluids of the father and one from those of the mother, form a single Wind within the embryo. It is the motion of this Wind that produces the movement and growth of the developing fetus. When the baby is born, the Navajo say that the Wind within it "unfolds him"[17] and it is then, when the infant commences breathing, that another, *surrounding* Wind enters into the child. This Wind may be sent from one of the four directions along the horizon, or from the Sun, or the Moon, or from the Ground itself—indeed from *any* natural phenomenon. Of course, the particular Wind that enters with the first breath will have a powerful influence upon the whole course of that person's life. Yet other Winds will enter at later moments in the development of the child, so that, as McNeley writes, "the growing child is believed to be continually subject to the influence of Winds existing around him."[18]

Although invisible, the Holy Wind can be recognized by the swirling and spiraling traces that it continually leaves in the visible world. The Winds that enter a human being leave their trace, according to the Navajo, in the vortices or swirling patterns to be seen on our fingertips and the tips of our toes, and in the spiraling pattern made by the hairs as they emerge from our heads. As one elder explains:

There are whorls here at the tips of our fingers. Winds stick out here. It is the same way on the toes of our feet, and Winds exist on us here where soft spots are, where there are spirals. At the tops of our heads some children have two spirals, some have only one, you see. I am saying that those (who have two) live by means of two Winds. These (Winds sticking out of the) whorls at the tips of our toes hold us to the Earth. Those at our fingertips hold us to the Sky. Because of these, we do not fall when we move about.[19]

Further, it is Wind that enables us to speak. We have already noted that the four Winds of the cardinal directions are also called the "four Words." Since we speak only by means of the breath, Wind itself—the collective breath—is said to hold the power of language: "It is only by means of Wind that we talk. It exists at the tip of our tongues."[20]

Summing up these various conceptions, McNeley writes:

[A]ccording to the Navajo conception, then, Winds exist all around and within the individual, entering and departing through respiratory organs and whorls on the body's surface. *That which is within and that which surrounds one is all the same and it is holy.*[21]

Finally, and most profoundly, this invisible medium, in which we are bodily immersed, is what provides us with the capacity for conscious thought. It was mentioned above that the sacred Mountains in the four directions have various Winds that move between them as their means of communication with each other and with other entities. The invisible Wind that swirls within and around each individual person is assumed to consist, in part, of such messenger Winds from the four directions. Two of these Winds, often spoken of as Little Winds or Wind's Children, are believed to be the individual's "means of knowing."[22] These two Little Winds linger within the spiraling folds of our two ears, and it is from there that they offer guidance to us, alerting us to near and distant difficulties, helping us to plan and to make choices. When a Navajo person finds himself thinking in words, this is said to be the voice of one or both of these two Little Winds speaking into his ears.[23] Of course these Wind's Children are simply little currents or vortices within the vast body of *nilch'i*—the Holy Wind—which exists everywhere. In the words of one elder; "The one called Wind's Child, this is just like living in water"—that is, Wind's Child is inseparable from the swirling body of air in which we are thoroughly immersed.[24]

Such Little Winds from the four directions dwell not only in human ears, but in the ears or earlike aspects of all living things, providing their means of hearing, knowing, and communicating with others.[25] It is thus that other animals, for instance, know what we humans are thinking about them: "When we are thinking well of them—horses, cattle, goats, and everything that we live by—they know about it by means of Wind. They know our thinking."[26] Some elders say that nowadays Little Winds from the four directions no longer advise or speak to the Navajo as clearly as they once did, but that such Little Winds still speak clearly into the ears of other animals, telling them of what is happening in the world; and animals like Coyote and Owl often communicate such knowledge to the Navajo, warning the humans of dangerous situations by specific sounds and behaviors.[27]

Now, when referring to the multiple and diverse Winds such as Dawn Man or Dawn Woman, Sky Blue Woman, Twilight Man, Dark Wind, Wind's Child, Revolving Wind, Glossy Wind, Rolling Darkness Wind, and others, the Navajo are not speaking of abstract or ideal entities but of palpable phenomena—of the actual gusts, breezes, whirlwinds, eddies, stormfronts, crosscurrents, gales, whiffs, blasts, and breaths that they perceive in the fluid medium that surrounds and flows through their bodies. The profound belief in the overall unity of *nilch'i*, the Navajo conviction that all of these subsidiary Winds are internal expressions of a single, inexhaustible mystery, is obviously born of the observation that the multiple atmospheric vortices made by their own breathing—or by the heat rising in waves from the sun-baked cliff, or the branches of trees as they divide the surging air, or the minute trembling of a rattlesnake's tail—that all these evident currents and eddies swirling around and even inside them are not entirely autonomous forces, but rather are momentary articulations within the vast and fathomless body of Air itself.

It is clear, however, that there is a kind of *provisional* autonomy or identity to the various winds that are part of the overall atmosphere—the warm and sluggish air lingering in the sandy arroyo every afternoon is obviously different from the cool breeze blowing through the cottonwoods along the river. To the Navajo there are unpredictable Winds as well as steady Winds, helpful Winds and Harmful Winds. Certain dangerous Winds, for example, can alter the character of the good Winds within a living person, or can bring difficulty and harm to the community, or to the land. Each person must navigate through this world of diverse invisible influences with great care, strengthening her contact with the various good Winds by respecting the land itself, striving to bring her life into harmony, or *hozho*, with the four directions, into reciprocity with the Ground and the Sky, with the Sun, the Moon, and the Stars.

Like the mountains of the four directions, and like the other animals and the plants, humans are themselves one of the Wind's dwelling places, one of its multiple centers, and just as we are nourished and influenced by the Air at large, so do our actions and thoughts affect the Air in turn. The individual, that is, is not passive with respect to the Holy Wind; rather she participates *in* it, as one of its organs. Her own desire and intent (her own interior Wind) participates directly in the life of the invisible Wind all around her, and hence can engage and subtly influence events in the surrounding terrain—even, in some measure, the becoming-abundant of rain clouds, the gestation of seeds, and the seasonal procreation of animals. Hence the emphasis among the Navajo, and indeed among so many native peoples, upon concentrated thought and prayer in order to influence and aid the continual emergence of such earthly occurrences from unmanifest (implicit, invisible) to manifest (visible) existence.

It is through the ritual power of speech and song that the Navajo are enabled most powerfully to affect and alter events in the enveloping cosmos. According to Gary Witherspoon, in his landmark study of *Language and Art in the Navajo Universe*,[28] the Navajo consider the act of speech to be an externalization of thought, "an imposition of form upon the external world" in which the surrounding Air is transformed.[29] And because the Air or Wind is the very medium in which the other natural forces live and act, by transforming the Air through song, the singer is able to affect and subtly influence the activity of the great natural powers themselves.

When a Navajo person wishes to renew or reestablish, in the world, the harmonious condition of well-being and beauty expressed by the Navajo word *hozho* he must first strive, through ritual, to create this harmony and peacefulness within his own being. Having established such *hozho* within himself, he can then actively impart this state of well-being to the enveloping cosmos, through the transforming power of song or prayer. Finally, according to Witherspoon,

> [a]fter a person has projected *hozho* into the air through ritual form, he then, at the conclusion of the ritual, breathes that *hozho* back into himself and makes himself a part of the order, harmony, and beauty he has projected into the world through the ritual mediums of speech and song.[30]

This brief quote from Witherspoon makes especially evident the reciprocal, even circular character of the relation between the Navajo people and the animate cosmos that enfolds and includes them. They are not passive with respect to the other powers of this world, or rather they are both passive *and* active, inhaling *and* exhaling, receiving the nourishment of the diverse beings and actively nourishing them in turn. As it is spoken in the Blessingway ceremony:

With everything having life, with everything having the power of speech, with everything having the power to breathe, with everything having the power to teach and guide, with that in blessing we will live.[31]

For the Navajo, then, the Air—particularly in its capacity to provide awareness, thought, and speech—has properties that European, alphabetic civilization has traditionally ascribed to an interior, individual human "mind" or "psyche." Yet by attributing these powers to the Air, and by insisting that the "Winds within us" are thoroughly continuous with the Wind at large—with the invisible medium in which we are immersed—the Navajo elders suggest that that which we call the "mind" *is not ours*, is not a human possession. Rather, mind as Wind is a property of the encompassing world, in which humans—like all other beings—participate. One's individual awareness, the sense of a relatively personal self or psyche, is simply that part of the enveloping Air that circulates within, through, and around one's particular body; hence, one's own intelligence is assumed, from the start, to be entirely participant with the swirling psyche of the land. Any undue harm that befalls the land is readily felt within the awareness of all who dwell within that land. And thus the health, balance, and well-being of each person is inseparable from the health and well-being of the enveloping earthly terrain.

❧

THE NAVAJO IDENTIFICATION OF AWARENESS WITH THE AIR—THEIR intuition that the psyche is not an immaterial power that resides inside us, but is rather the invisible yet thoroughly palpable medium in which we (along with the trees, the squirrels, and the clouds) are immersed—must seem at first bizarre, even outrageous, to persons of European ancestry. Yet a few moments' etymological research will reveal that this identification is not nearly so alien to European civilization as one might assume. Indeed, our English term "psyche"—together with all its modern offspring like "psychology," "psychiatry," and "psychotherapy"—is derived from the ancient Greek word *psychê*, which signified not merely the "soul," or the "mind," but also a "breath," or a "gust of wind." The Greek noun was itself derived from the verb *psychein*, which meant "to breathe,"

238 THE SPELL OF THE SENSUOUS

or "to blow."[32] Meanwhile, another ancient Greek word for "air, wind, and breath"—the term *pneuma,* from which we derive such terms as "pneumatic" and "pneumonia"—also and at the same time signified that vital principle which in English we call "spirit."[33]

Of course, the word "spirit" itself, despite all of its incorporeal and non-sensuous connotations, is directly related to the very bodily term "respiration" through their common root in the Latin word *spiritus,* which signified both "breath" and "wind."[34] Similarly, the Latin word for "soul," *anima*—from whence have evolved such English terms as "animal," "animation," "animism," and "unanimous" (being of one mind, or one soul), also signified "air" and "breath." Moreover, these were not separate meanings; it is clear that *anima,* like *psychê,* originally named an elemental phenomenon that somehow comprised both what we now call "the air" and what we now term "the soul." The more specific Latin word *animus,* which signified "that which thinks in us," was derived from the same airy root, *anima,* itself derived from the older Greek term *anemos,* meaning "wind."[35]

We find an identical association of the "mind" with the "wind" and the "breath" in innumerable ancient languages. Even such an objective, scientifically respectable word as "atmosphere" displays its ancestral ties to the Sanskrit word *atman,* which signified "soul" as well as the "air" and the "breath." Thus, a great many terms that now refer to the air as a purely passive and insensate medium are clearly derived from words that once identified the air with life and awareness! And words that now seem to designate a strictly immaterial mind, or spirit, are derived from terms that once named the breath as the very substance of that mystery.[36]

It is difficult to avoid the conclusion that, for ancient Mediterranean cultures no less than for the Lakota and the Navajo, the air was once a singularly sacred presence. As the experiential source of both psyche and spirit, it would seem that the air was once felt to be the very matter of awareness, the subtle body of the mind. *And hence that awareness, far from being experienced as a quality that distinguishes humans from the rest of nature, was originally felt as that which invisibly **joined** human beings to the other animals and to the plants, to the forests and to the mountains.* For it was the unseen but common medium of their existence.

But how, then, did the air come to lose its psychological quality?

How did the psyche withdraw so thoroughly from the world around us, leaving the cedar trees, the spiders, the stones, and the storm clouds without that psychological depth in which they used to dwell (without, indeed, any psychological resonance or even relevance)? How did the psyche, the spirit, or the *mind* retreat so thoroughly into the human skull, leaving the air itself a thin and taken-for-granted presence, commonly equated, today, with mere empty space? Read on.

Wind, Breath, and Speech

Like so many ancient and tribal languages, Hebrew has a single word for both "spirit" and "wind"—the word *ruach*. What is remarkable here is the evident centrality of *ruach*, the spiritual wind, to early Hebraic religiosity. The primordiality of *ruach*, and its close association with the divine, is manifest in the very first sentence of the Hebrew Bible:

> When God began to create heaven and earth—the earth being unformed and void, with darkness over the surface of the deep and a wind [*ruach*] from God sweeping over the water . . .[37]

At the very beginning of creation, before even the existence of the earth or the sky, God is present as a wind moving over the waters. Remember the similar primordiality of the wind in the Navajo telling: "Wind existed first . . . and when the Earth began its existence Wind took care of it."[38] And breath, as we learn in the next section of Genesis, is the most intimate and elemental bond linking humans to the divine; it is that which flows most directly between God and man. For after God forms an earthling *(adam)*, from the dust of the earth *(adamah)*, he blows into the earthling's nostrils the breath of life, and the human awakens.[39] Although *ruach* may be used to refer to the breath, the Hebrew term used here is *neshamah*, which denotes both the breath and the soul. While *ruach* generally

refers to the wind, or spirit, at large, *neshamah* commonly signifies the more personal, individualized aspect of wind, the wind or
breath of a particular body—like the "Wind within one" of a Navajo
person. In this sense, *neshamah* is also used to signify conscious
awareness.

We moderns tend to view ancient Hebraic culture through the in-
tervening lens of Greek and Christian thought; even Jewish scholarship, and much contemporary Jewish self-understanding, has been
subtly influenced and informed by centuries of Hellenic and Christian interpretation. It is only thus that many persons today associate
the ancient Hebrews with such anachronistic notions as the belief in
an otherworldly heaven and hell, or a faith in the immateriality and
immortality of the personal soul. Yet such dualistic notions have no
real place in the Hebrew Bible. Careful attention to the evidence
suggests that ancient Hebraic religiosity was far more corporeal,
and far more responsive to the sensuous earth, than we commonly
assume.

Of course, the ancient Hebrews were, as we have seen, among the
first communities to make sustained use of phonetic writing, the
first bearers of an alphabet. Moreover, unlike the other Semitic peoples, they did not restrict their use of the alphabet to economic and
political record-keeping, but used it to record ancestral stories, traditions, and laws. They were perhaps the first nation to so thoroughly shift their sensory participation away from the forms of
surrounding nature to a purely phonetic set of signs, and so to experience the profound epistemological independence from the natural
environment that was made possible by this potent new technology.
To actively participate with the visible forms of nature came to be
considered *idolatry* by the ancient Hebrews; *it was not the land but
the written letters that now carried the ancestral wisdom.*[40]

Yet although the Hebrews renounced all animistic engagement
with the *visible* forms of the natural world (whether with the moon,
or the sun, or those animals—like the bull—sacred to other peoples
of the Middle East), they nevertheless retained a participatory relationship with the invisible medium of that world—with the wind
and the breath.

The power of this relationship may be directly inferred from the
very structure of the Hebrew writing system, the *aleph-beth*. This

ancient alphabet, in contrast to its European derivatives, had no letters for what we have come to call "the vowels." The twenty-two letters of the Hebrew *aleph-beth* were all consonants. Thus, in order to read a text written in traditional Hebrew, one had to infer the appropriate vowel sounds from the consonantal context, and add them when sounding out the written syllables.

This lack of written vowels is only partly explained by the morphological structure of the Semitic languages, in which words with the same combination of consonants (usually grouped in clusters of three) tend to have a related meaning. This morphology ensured that a person fluent in the Hebrew language could, with effort, correctly decipher a Hebrew text without the aid of written vowels. Nevertheless, additional letters for vowels would have greatly facilitated the reading of ancient Hebrew. The fact that some later Hebrew scribes, taking their lead from a standard practice of the Aramaeans, occasionally used the consonants *H, W,* and *Y* to suggest specific vowel sounds, is evidence that the lack of written vowels was indeed felt as a difficulty. When, in the seventh century C.E., vowel indicators in the form of little dots and dashes inserted below and above the letters were finally introduced into Hebrew texts, the usefulness of those marks made them a standard component of many Hebrew texts thereafter.[41]

Another, perhaps more significant, reason for the absence of written vowels in the traditional *aleph-beth* has to do with the nature of the vowel sounds themselves. While consonants are those shapes made by the lips, teeth, tongue, palate, or throat, that momentarily obstruct the flow of breath and so give form to our words and phrases, the vowels are those sounds that are made by the unimpeded breath itself. *The vowels, that is to say, are nothing other than sounded breath.* And the breath, for the ancient Semites, was the very mystery of life and awareness, a mystery inseparable from the invisible *ruach*—the holy wind or spirit. The breath, as we have noted, was the vital substance blown into Adam's nostrils by God himself, who thereby granted life and consciousness to humankind. It is possible, then, that the Hebrew scribes refrained from creating distinct letters for the vowel-sounds in order to avoid making a visible representation of the invisible. To fashion a visible representation of the vowels, of the sounded breath, would have been to concretize the ineffable, *to make a visible likeness of the divine*. It would have been to make a visible representation of a mystery whose very essence was to be invisible and hence unknowable—the sacred breath, the holy wind. And thus it was not done.

Of course, we do not know if the thought of imaging the vowels, or the sounded breath, even occurred to the ancient Semitic scribes; it is entirely possible that their reverent relation to the wind and the air—their sense of the sacredness of this element that lends its communicative magic to all spoken utterances—simply precluded such a notion from even arising. In any case, whether the avoidance of vowel notation was conscious or inadvertent, the absence of written vowels marks a profound difference between the ancient Semitic *aleph-beth* and the subsequent European alphabets.

For example, unlike texts written with the Greek or the Roman alphabets, a Hebrew text simply could not be experienced as a double—a stand-in, or substitute—for the sensuous, corporeal world. The Hebrew letters and texts were not sufficient unto themselves; in order to be read, they had to be added to, enspirited by the reader's breath. The invisible air, the same mystery that animates the visible terrain, was also needed to animate the visible letters, to make them come alive and to speak. The letters themselves thus remained overtly dependent upon the elemental, corporeal life-world—they were activated by the very breath of that world, and could not be cut off from that world without losing all of their power. In this manner the absence of written vowels ensured that Hebrew language and tradition remained open to the power of that which exceeds the strictly human community—it ensured that the Hebraic sensibility would remain rooted, however tenuously, in the animate earth. (While the Hebrew Bible would become, as we have seen, a kind of portable homeland for the Jewish people, it could never entirely take the place of the breathing land itself, upon which the text manifestly depends. Hence the persistent themes of exile and longed-for return that reverberate through Jewish history down to the present day.)

The absence of written vowels in ancient Hebrew entailed that the reader of a traditional Hebrew text had to actively *choose* the appropriate breath sounds or vowels, yet different vowels would often vary the meaning of the written consonants (much as the meaning of the consonantal cluster "RD," in English, will vary according to whether we insert a long *o* sound between those consonants, "RoaD"; or a long *i* sound, "RiDe"; a short *e* sound, "ReD"; or a long *e* sound, "ReaD"). The reader of a traditional Hebrew text must actively choose one pronunciation over another, according to the fit of that meaning within the written context, yet the precise meaning of that context would itself have been determined by the particular vowels already chosen by that reader.[42]

The traditional Hebrew text, in other words, overtly demanded the reader's conscious participation. The text was never complete in itself; it had to be actively engaged by a reader who, by this engagement, gave rise to a particular reading. Only in relation—only by being taken up and actively interpreted by a particular reader—did the text become meaningful. And there was no single, definitive meaning; the ambiguity entailed by the lack of written vowels ensured that diverse readings, diverse shades of meaning, were always possible.

Some form of active participation, as we have seen, is necessary to *all* acts of phonetic reading, whether of Greek, or Latin, or English texts such as this one. But the purely consonantal structure of the Hebrew writing system rendered this participation—the creative interaction between the reader and the text—particularly conscious and overt. It simply could not be taken for granted, or forgotten. Indeed, the willful engagement with the text that was necessitated by the absence of written vowels lent a deeply *interactive* or *interpretive* character to the Jewish community's understanding of its own most sacred teachings. The scholar Barry Holtz alludes to this understanding in his introduction to a book on the sacred texts of Judaism:

> We tend usually to think of reading as a passive occupation, but for the Jewish textual tradition, it was anything but that. Reading was a passionate and active grappling with God's living word. It held the challenge of uncovering secret meanings, unheard-of explanations, matters of great weight and significance. An active, indeed interactive, reading was their method of approaching the sacred text called Torah and through that reading process of finding something at once new and very old. . . .

244 THE SPELL OF THE SENSUOUS

By "interactive" I mean to suggest that for the rabbis of the tradition, Torah called for a living and dynamic response. The great texts in turn are the record of that response, and each text in turn becomes the occasion for later commentary and interaction. The Torah remains unendingly alive because the readers of each subsequent generation saw it as such, taking the holiness of Torah seriously, and adding their own contribution to the story. For the tradition, Torah *demands* interpretation.[43]

The reader, that is, must actively respond to the Torah, must bring his own individual creativity into dialogue with the teachings in order to reveal new and unsuspected nuances. The Jewish people must enter into dialogue with the received teachings of their ancestors, questioning them, struggling with them. The Hebrew Bible is not a set of finished stories and unchanging laws; it is not a static body of dogmatic truths but a living enigma that must be questioned, grappled with, and interpreted afresh in every generation. For, as it is said, the guidance that the Torah can offer in one generation is very different from that which it waits to offer in another.

This ongoing tradition of textual interpretation and commentary, and of commentary upon earlier commentary, has given rise to the numerous postbiblical texts of the Jewish tradition, from the Mishnah, the Talmud, and the collections of midrash, to the Zohar and other Kabbalistic works. Collectively, all these texts are known as the "Oral Torah," since they all originated in oral discussion and commentary upon the "Written Torah," upon the teachings ostensibly revealed to Moses, the first Jewish scribe, atop Mount Sinai. The process of writing down oral commentaries and interpretations, with the intent of preserving them, began in the second or third century C.E.

The first of such compilations, the Talmud, is today printed with the primary layer of text, the Mishnah, in the center of each page, and with subsequent commentaries upon that text arrayed around it—in successive layers, as it were. Thus, in its visible arrangement the Talmud displays a sense of the written text not as a definitive and finished object but as an organic, open-ended process to be entered into, an evolving being to be confronted and engaged.

The Power of Letters

Yet this sense of the written text as an animate, living mystery is nowhere more explicit than in the Kabbalah, the esoteric tradition of Jewish mysticism. For here it is not just the text as a whole but the very *letters* that are thought to be alive! Each letter of the *aleph-beth* is assumed by the Kabbalists to have its own personality, its own profound magic, its own way of organizing the whole of existence around itself. Because the written commandments were ostensibly dictated to Moses directly by God on Mount Sinai, so the written letters comprising that first Hebrew text—the twenty-two letters of the *aleph-beth*—are assumed to be the visible traces of divine utterance. Indeed, some Kabbalists claimed that it was by first generating the twenty-two letters, and then combining them into such utterances as "Let there be light," that God spoke the visible universe itself into existence. The letters, that is, are sensible concretions of the very powers of creation.[44]

By meditating, when reading, not upon the written phrases, or even upon the words, but upon the individual *letters* that gaze out at him from the surface of the page, the Jewish mystic could enter into direct contact with the divine energies. By combining and permutating the letters of particular phrases and words until the words themselves lost all evident meaning and only the letters stood forth in all their naked intensity, the Kabbalist was able to bring himself into increasingly exalted states of consciousness, awakening creative powers that previously lay dormant within his body.[45] Sometimes, when the practitioner was reading in this concentrated and magical fashion, "the letters sprang to life of their own accord," and began "speaking" directly to the mystic. At least one practitioner was alarmed to see the written letters expanding "to the size of mountains" before his eyes. Others reported that, after combining and recombining the letters, they saw the letters suddenly take wing and fly forth from the surface of the page![46]

A close acquaintance with the living letters, and a working knowledge of their individual energies, was assumed to give the Kabbalist magical abilities with which to ease suffering, illness, and discord in the world about him. The Kabbalists, in other words, considered the *aleph-beth* to be a highly concentrated and divine form of magic; therefore, they consciously cultivated their synaesthetic participation with the written letters.[47]

Since the letters of the *aleph-beth* also at times served as numbers for the Hebrew people (with the first letter, *aleph*, signifying the number 1, the second letter, *beth*, the number 2, on up through 10, and with other letters signifying 20, 30, 40, etc., and still others signifying 100, 200, 300, and 400), written words and phrases could also be compared by calculating the total numerical value of the letters that comprise them—a Kabbalistic technique called *gematria*. Through both permutating the letters and calculating their numerical values, mystics were able to demonstrate hidden equivalences and correspondences between various words and names contained in the scripture. *Elohim*, for instance, one of the most sacred names of God in the Hebrew Bible, could be shown to have the same numerical value as the Hebrew word for nature, *hateva*—evidence of the hidden unity of God and nature. (Such pantheistic notions equating God with nature—common to many practitioners of Kabbalah—would startle the various environmentalists today who charge that Hebraic religion expelled all divinity from the natural world.)

Indeed, all the diverse names of God in the Hebrew Bible, and the letters that comprise them, figure prominently in Kabbalistic theory, providing essential clues for the practitioner who seeks direct experience of the divine. Supreme among these names is the Tetragrammaton, the four-letter name, YHWH. Often written, in non-Hebrew texts, as Yahweh, the true manner of pronouncing this most powerful combination of letters is said to have been forgotten. Nevertheless, some of the most concentrated of Kabbalistic practices involved pronouncing each letter of the Tetragrammaton separately, combining it, in turn, with each of the five possible breath sounds, or vowels. A much more elaborate, and presumably dangerous, practice entailed isolating each letter of the Tetragrammaton and combining it, one at a time, with every other letter of the *aleph-beth,* pronouncing each one of *these* combinations, in turn, with each of the various vowel sounds.[48] By carefully reciting this incantation over an earthen form in the shape of a human being, it was said that one could bring the clay figure—a *golem*—to life. A clue to the sympathetic magic involved in this incantation may be found in the teaching of the great thirteenth-century Kabbalist Abraham Abulafia, who asserted that the spoker vowels and the written consonants are as interdependent "as the soul and the body."[49] To combine the vowels—the sounded breath—with the visible consonants was akin to breathing life into a clump of clay, as YHWH had lent his breath to the earthen Adam.

FINALLY, WE MUST ACKNOWLEDGE THE VAST IMPORTANCE, WITHIN the Jewish mystical tradition, of the breath itself. In the thirteenth-century *Zohar,* the most important of all Kabbalistic texts, the central figure, Rabbi Shim'on bar Yohai, insists that the union between humans and God is best effected through the medium of the breath. According to Rabbi Shim'on, King Solomon learned from his father, King David, the breathing techniques involved in invoking the holy breath, the inspiration of the divine. "By learning and practicing the secrets inherent in the breath, Solomon could lift nature's physical veil from created things and see the spirit within."[50] In a manner startlingly reminiscent of a Navajo or a Lakota ceremony, Rabbi Shim'on's son, El'azar, begins a prayer session by exhorting "the winds to come from all four directions and fill his breath," and instructs his companions to circulate the air inhaled from all four directions interchangeably within their bodies.[51] Elsewhere in the *Zohar,* one of Rabbi Shim'on's companions speaks of "the soul-breath" sent from YHWH to enter the body of the righteous person at birth. Much like the "wind within one" of the Navajo people, "the soul-breath that enters at birth directs and trains the human being and initiates him into every straight path.[52] This sense of the breath as medium between the individual and the divine is exemplified in a commentary on prayer by a nineteenth-century Hasidic master (Hasidism was a vibrant wave of Jewish mysticism that swept East European Jewry in the eighteenth and nineteenth centuries):

> *If prayer is pure and untainted,*
> *surely that holy breath*
> *that rises from your lips*

will join with the breath of heaven
that is always flowing
into you from above. . . .
Thus that part of God
which is within you
is reunited with its source.[53]

Yet the sacred breath enters not just into human beings (providing awareness and guidance), it also animates and sustains the whole of the sensible world. Like the wind itself, the breath of God permeates all of nature. In a classic text entitled "The Portal of Unity and Faith," the eighteenth-century Hasidic master Schneur Zalman of Ladi describes how the syllables and letters of God's creative utterances, such as "Let there be light," or "Let the waters bring forth swarms of living creatures," gradually generate, through a concatenated series of permutations and numerical substitutions, the exact names, and hence *the exact forms,* of all natural entities (in Hebrew a single term, *davar,* means both "word" and "thing"). Yet without the continual outflow of God's breath, which Schneur Zalman calls "the Breath of His Mouth," all of the letters that stand within the things of this world—all the letter combinations embodied in particular animals, plants, and stones—would return to their undifferentiated source in the divine Unity, and the sensible world, along with all sensing beings, would be extinguished. Just as the consonantal letters of a traditional Hebrew text depend, for their communicative power, upon the sounded breath that animates them, so the divine letters and letter combinations that structure the physical universe are dependent upon the divine breath that continually utters them forth. All things vibrate with "the Breath of His Mouth."[54]

And it is by virtue of this continual breath that nature is always new; the world around us is a continual, ongoing utterance! Thus, the activity of speech, like breathing, links humans not just to God but to all that surrounds us, from the stones to the sparrows. This is simply illustrated in another Hasidic commentary on prayer:

See your prayer as arousing the letters
through which heaven and earth
and all living things were created.

The letters are the life of all;
   when you pray through them,
   all Creation joins with you in prayer.
All that is around you can be uplifted;
   even the song of a passing bird
   may enter into such a prayer.[55]

✍

GIVEN THE SUBTLE IMPORTANCE PLACED UPON THE WIND AND THE breath within the Hebrew tradition, we may be tempted to wonder whether, long before the employment of phonetic writing and the *aleph-beth*, the monotheism of Abraham and his descendants was borne by a new way of experiencing the invisible air, a new sense of the unity of this unseen presence that flows not just within us but between all things, granting us life and speech even as it moves the swaying grasses and the gathering clouds. Is it possible that a volatile power once propitiated as a local storm god came to be generalized, by one tribe of nomadic herders, into the capricious power of the encompassing atmosphere itself? We know that the singular mystery revered by the children of Abraham was an ineffable power that could not be localized in any visible phenomenon, could not be imaged in any idol. Prior to the use of writing by Moses and the later scribes, however, it may be that this power was not intangible, but simply invisible—that it was experienced not as an abstract power entirely *outside of* sensuous nature, but as the unseen medium, the *ruach*, the ubiquitous wind or spirit that enlivens the visible world.[56]

It is remarkable that the most holy of God's names, the four-letter Tetragrammaton, is composed of the most breath-like consonants in the Hebrew *aleph-beth* (the same three letters, Y, H, and W, that were sometimes used by ancient scribes to stand in for particular vowels). The most sacred of God's names would thus seem to be the most breath-like of utterances—a name spoken, as it were, by the wind. Some contemporary students of Kabbalah suggest that the forgotten pronunciation of the name may have entailed forming the first syllable, "Y-H," on the whispered inbreath, and the second syllable, "W-H," on the whispered outbreath—the whole name thus forming a single cycle of the breath. If their suspicion is in any sense correct, then the awesome mystery invoked by the Tetragrammaton may not be separable from the mystery of *breathing*—this ebb and flow that ceaselessly binds us to the invisible.

Setting all speculations aside, however, it should be clear from the foregoing discussion that the strictly consonantal character of the Hebrew script encouraged a unique relation to the sacred texts, and to the sacred in general. In particular, the absence of written vowels fostered (1) a consciously interactive relation with the text—even, for some, an overtly animistic participation with the written letters themselves, and (2) a continued respect and reverence for the air— for the invisible medium that activates the visible letters even as it animates the visible terrain. While they certainly developed a new, literate distance from the surrounding world of nature, the Hebrews—the first "People of the Book"—nevertheless retained a profoundly oral relation to the invisible medium of that world, to the wind and the breath.

The Forgetting of the Air

It is precisely this oral awareness of the invisible depths that enfold us—this sense of the unseen air as an awesome mystery joining the human and extrahuman worlds—that was sundered by the Greek scribes.

When they adapted the ancient Semitic *aleph-beth* for their own use, probably in the eighth century B.C.E., the Greek scribes took on (with modifications) the shapes as well as the names of the early Semitic letters. Yet, as we mentioned in chapter 4, those names had no extraliterate reference for the Greeks, as they did for the Hebrews. Remember that for the Hebrews, *aleph* (Greek: *alpha*) signified not just the first letter but also, and more primordially, "ox," similarly *beth* (*beta*) meant "house," *gimmel* (*gamma*) was the word for "camel," etc. But to the Greeks, these words named only the letters themselves; they had no other significance. And as the names of the letters shed their worldly, extraliterate significance in the transfer across the Mediterranean, any pictographic resonance between the written letters and those worldly phenomena (oxen, houses, camels, etc.) was forgotten as well. In the journey to Greece, in other words, the letters of the *aleph-beth* loosened and left behind their vestigial ties to the enveloping life-world; they thereby became a much more abstract set of symbols.

But the Greeks also introduced a strange new element into the alphabet, an innovation that would ultimately increase the abstract capacity of this writing system far more than the above-mentioned factors. For the Greek scribes introduced written *vowels* into the previously consonantal system of letters.

Actually, many of the new letters were adapted from already existing Semitic letters. Certain characters in the Semitic *aleph-beth* signified consonants that had no existence in the Greek language, and it was these apparently superfluous letters that were appropriated by the Greek scribes to represent vowel sounds. The letter *aleph*, for instance, was not a vowel but a consonant in the original Hebrew usage; it signified the opening of the throat prior to all utterance. Since the Greeks had no use for this consonant, they adapted this character, which they called *alpha*, to signify the vowel sound *A*. Other Hebrew letters were altered to represent the vowels *E*, *I*, and *O*. Finally, the Greeks added the letter *upsilon*, which eventually became the Roman letter *U*.[57]

The resulting alphabet was a very different kind of tool from its earlier, Semitic incarnation—one that would have very different effects upon the senses that engaged it, and upon the various languages that adopted it as their own. For the addition of written vowels enabled a much more thorough transcription of spoken utterance onto the flat surface of the page. A text written with the new alphabet had none of the ambiguity that, as we have seen, was inherent in a traditional Hebrew text. While for any Hebrew text of sufficient length there were various possible pronunciations, or readings, each of which would yield a slightly different set of words and meanings, a comparable Greek text would likely admit of only a single correct reading. It is thus that texts written with the Greek (and later the Roman) alphabet did not invite the kind of active and ever-renewed interpretation that was demanded by the Hebrew texts. The interactive, synaesthetic participation involved in reading—in transforming a series of visible marks into a sequence of sounds—could now become entirely habitual and automatic. For there was no longer any choice in how to sound out the text; all the cues for one's participation were spelled out upon the page. Relative to Semitic texts, then, the Greek texts had a remarkable autonomy—they seemed to stand, and even to speak, on their own.[58]

Yet the apparent precision and efficiency of the new alphabet was obtained at a high price. For by using visible characters to represent the sounded breath, the Greek scribes effectively *desacralized* the breath and the air. By providing a visible representation of that which was—by its very nature—invisible, they nullified the mysteriousness of the enveloping atmosphere, negating the uncanniness of this element that was both here and yet not here, present to the skin and yet absent to the eyes, immanence and transcendence all at once.

The awesomeness of the air had resided precisely in its ubiquitous and yet unseen nature, its capacity to grant movement and life to visible nature while remaining, in itself, invisible and ungraspable. Hebraic writing had preserved this mystery by refraining from representing the air itself upon the parchment or the page—by refusing to image, or objectify, this unseen flux that sustains both the word and the visible world. By breaking this taboo, *by transposing the invisible into the register of the visible, the Greek scribes effectively dissolved the primordial power of the air.*

The effects of this perceptual dissolution were not, of course, evident all at once. In Greece, as we have seen, the new alphabet met substantial resistance in the form of a well-developed and flourishing oral culture, and so took several centuries to make itself felt within the common discourse. As late as the middle of the sixth century B.C.E., the Milesian philosopher Anaximenes could still assert:

As the *psyché*, being air, holds a man together and gives him life, so breath and air hold together the entire universe and give it life.[59]

A century and a half later, however, when the alphabet was at last being taught within the educational curriculum and was thereby spreading throughout Greek culture, Plato and Socrates were able to co-opt the term *psyché*—which for Anaximenes was fully associated with the breath and the air—employing the term now to indicate something not just invisible but utterly intangible. The Platonic *psychê* was not at all a part of the sensuous world, but was rather of another, utterly non-sensuous dimension. The *psychê*, that is, was no longer an invisible yet tangible power continually participant, by virtue of the breath, with the enveloping atmosphere, but a thoroughly abstract phenomenon now enclosed within the physical body as in a prison.[60]

We have already seen how the new relation that Plato wrote of, between the immortal *psychê* and the transcendent realm of eternal "Ideas," was itself dependent upon the new affinity between the literate intellect and the visible letters (and words) of the alphabet. We can now discern that this relation between the *psychê* and the bodiless Ideas was dependent, as well, upon a gradual forgetting of the air and the breath, itself made possible by the spread of the new technology. For it was only as the unseen air lost its fascination for the human senses that this other, more extreme invisibility came to take its place—the utterly incorporeal realm of pure "Ideas," to which the Platonic, rational *psychê* was connected much as the earlier, breathlike *psychê* was joined to the atmosphere.

🙌

THOSE WHO SPEAK FACILELY OF A "JUDEO-CHRISTIAN TRADITION" fail to discern the remarkably different approaches that distinguish the ancient Jewish and the Christian faiths, differences rooted partly in the sensorial effects of the very different writing systems employed by these two highly text-centered traditions. Unlike the Hebrew Bible, the Christian New Testament was originally written primarily in the Greek alphabet, and thus the dualistic sensibility promoted by the Greek writing system was early on allied with Christian doctrine.[61] Under the aegis of the Church, the belief in a non-sensuous heaven, and in the fundamentally incorporeal nature of the human soul—itself "imprisoned," as Plato had suggested, in the bodily world—accompanied the alphabet as it spread, first throughout Europe and later throughout the Americas. *And wherever the alphabet advanced, it proceeded by dispelling the air of ghosts and invisible influences—by stripping the air of its* anima, *its psychic depth.*

In the oral, animistic world of pre-Christian and peasant Europe, all things—animals, forests, rivers, and caves—had the power of expressive speech, and the primary medium of this collective discourse was the air. In the absence of writing, human utterance, whether embodied in songs, stories, or spontaneous sounds, was inseparable from the exhaled breath. The invisible atmosphere was thus the assumed intermediary in all communication, a zone of subtle influences crossing, mingling, and metamorphosing. This invisible yet palpable realm of whiffs and scents, of vegetative emanations and animal exhalations, was also the unseen repository of ancestral voices, the home of stories yet to be spoken, of ghosts and spirited intelligences—a kind of collective field of meaning from whence individual awareness continually emerged and into which it continually receded, with every inbreath and outbreath.

We might say that the air, as the invisible wellspring of the present, yielded an awareness of transformation and transcendence very different from that total transcendence expounded by the Church. The experiential interplay between the *seen* and the *unseen*—this duality entirely proper to the sensuous life-world—was far more real, for oral peoples, than an abstract dualism between sensuous reality as a whole and some other, utterly non-sensuous heaven.

Thus it was that the progressive spread of Christianity was largely dependent upon the spread of the alphabet, and, conversely, that Christian missions and missionaries were by far the greatest factor in the advancement of alphabetic literacy in both the medieval and the modern eras. It was not enough to preach the Christian faith: one had to induce the unlettered, tribal peoples to begin to use the technology upon which that faith depended. Only by training the senses to participate with the written word could one hope to break their spontaneous participation with the animate terrain. *Only as the written text began to speak would the voices of the forest, and of the river, begin to fade. And only then would language loosen its ancient association with the invisible breath, the spirit sever itself from the wind, the psyche dissociate itself from the environing air.* The air, once the very medium of expressive interchange, would become an increasingly empty and unnoticed phenomenon, displaced by the strange *new* medium of the written word.

Membranes and Barriers

The progressive forgetting of the air—the loss of the invisible richness of the present—has been accompanied by a concomitant internalization of human awareness. We have just seen how the ancient Greek *psychê*, or soul, was transformed from a phenomenon associated with the air and the breath into a wholly immaterial entity trapped, as it were, within the human body. In contact with the written word a new, apparently autonomous, sensibility emerges into experience, a new self that can enter into relation with its own verbal traces, can view and ponder its own statements even as it is formulating them, and can thus reflexively interact with itself in isolation from other persons and from the surrounding, animate earth. This new sensibility seems independent of the body—seems, indeed, of another order entirely—since it is borne by the letters and texts whose changeless quality contrasts vividly with the shifting life of the body and the flux of organic nature. That this new sensibility comes to view itself as an isolated intelligence located "inside" the material body can only be understood in relation to the forgetting of the air, to the forgetting of this sensuous but unseen medium that continually flows in and out of the breathing body, binding the subtle depths within us to the fathomless depths that surround us.

We may better comprehend this curious development—the withdrawal of mind from sensible nature and its progressive incarceration in the human skull—by considering that every human language secretes a kind of perceptual boundary that hovers, like a translucent veil, between those who speak that language and the sensuous terrain that they inhabit. As we grow into a particular culture or language, we implicitly begin to structure our sensory contact with the earth around us in a particular manner, paying attention to certain phenomena while ignoring others, differentiating textures, tastes, and tones in accordance with the verbal contrasts contained in the language. We simply cannot take our place within any community of human speakers without ordering our sensations in a common manner, and without thereby limiting our spontaneous access to the wild world that surrounds us. Any particular language or way of speaking thus holds us within a particular community of human speakers only by invoking an ephemeral border, or boundary, between our sensing bodies and the sensuous earth.

Nevertheless, the perceptual boundary constituted by any language may be exceedingly porous and permeable. Indeed, for many oral, indigenous peoples, the boundaries enacted by their languages are more like permeable membranes binding the peoples to their particular terrains, rather than barriers walling them off from the land. By affirming that the other animals have their own languages, and that even the rustling of leaves in an oak tree or an aspen grove is itself a kind of voice, oral peoples bind their senses to the shifting sounds and gestures of the local earth, and thus ensure that their own ways of speaking remain informed by the life of the land. Still, the membrane enacted by their language is felt, and is acknowledged as a margin of danger and magic, a place where the relations between the human and the more-than-human worlds must be continually negotiated. The shamans common to oral cultures dwell precisely on this margin or edge; the primary role of such magicians, as I suggested at the outset of this book, is to act as intermediaries between the human and more-than-human realms. By regularly shedding the sensory constraints induced by a common language, periodically dissolving the perceptual boundary in order to directly encounter, converse, and bargain with various nonhuman intelligences—with otter, or owl, or eland—and then rejoining the common discourse, the shaman keeps the human discourse from rigidifying, and keeps the perceptual membrane fluid and porous, ensuring the greatest possible attunement between the human community and the animate earth, between the familiar and the fathomless.

The emergence or adoption of a formal writing system significantly solidifies the ephemeral perceptual boundary already established by a common tongue; now the spoken language has a visible counterpart that floats, fixed and immobile, between the human body and the sensuous world. Yet while formal writing thus solidifies the linguistic-perceptual boundary, many ancient writing systems implicitly refer the human senses to that which lies *beyond* the boundary; their often pictorially derived characters cannot help but remind the reading body of its inherence in a more-than-human field of animate forms. Language is not, here, a purely human possession—it remains tied, however distantly, to the larger field of expressive powers.

The advent of *phonetic* writing further rigidifies the perceptual boundary enclosing the human community. For the written characters no longer depend, implicitly, upon the larger field of sensuous phenomena; they refer, instead, to a strictly human set of sounds. The letters, as we have said, begin to function as mirrors reflecting the human community back upon itself. Nevertheless, even this mirrored boundary may remain somewhat open to what lies beyond it. We have seen that in the original *aleph-beth* the vowels, or rather the *absence* of vowels, provided the pores, the openings in the linguistic membrane through which the invisible wind—the living breath— could still flow between the human and the more-than-human worlds.

It was only with the plugging of these last pores—with the insertion of visible letters for the vowels themselves—that the perceptual boundary established by the common language was effectively sealed, and what had once been a porous membrane became an impenetrable barrier, a hall of mirrors. The Greek scribes, that is, transformed the breathing boundary between human culture and the animate earth into a seamless barrier segregating a pure inside from a pure outside. With the addition of written vowels—with the filling of those gaps, or pores, in the early alphabet—human language became a largely self-referential system closed off from the larger world that once engendered it. And the "I," the speaking self, was hermetically sealed within this new interior.

Today the speaking self looks out at a purely "exterior" nature from a purely "interior" zone, presumably located somewhere inside the physical body or brain. Within alphabetic civilization, virtually *every* human psyche construes itself as just such an individual "interior," a private "mind" or "consciousness" unrelated to the other "minds" that surround it, or to the environing earth. For there is no longer any common medium, no reciprocity, no *respiration* between the inside and the outside. There is no longer any flow between the self-reflexive domain of alphabetized awareness and all that exceeds, or subtends, this determinate realm. Between consciousness and the unconscious. Between civilization and the wilderness.

Remembering

In the world of modernity the air has indeed become the most taken-for-granted of phenomena. Although we imbibe it continually, we commonly fail to notice that there is anything there. We refer to the unseen depth between things—between people, or trees, or clouds—as mere empty space. The invisibility of the atmosphere, far from leading us to attend to it more closely, now enables us to neglect it entirely. Although we are wholly dependent upon its nourishment for all of our actions and all our thoughts, the immersing medium has no mystery for us, no conscious influence or meaning. Lacking all sacredness, stripped of all spiritual significance, the air is today little more than a conveniently forgotten dump site for a host of gaseous effluents and industrial pollutants. Our fascination is elsewhere, carried by all these *other* media—these newspapers, radio broadcasts, television networks, computer bulletin boards—all these fields or channels of *strictly human communication* that so readily grab our senses and mold our thoughts once our age-old participation with the original, more-than-human medium has been sundered.

As a child, growing up on the outskirts of New York City, I often gazed at great smokestacks billowing dark clouds into the sky. Yet I soon stopped wondering where all that sooty stuff went: since the adults who decided such things saw fit to dispose of wastes in this manner, it must, I concluded, be all right. Later, while learning to drive, I would watch with some alarm as the trucks roaring past me on the highway spewed black smoke from their gleaming exhaust pipes, but I quickly forgave them, remembering that my car, too, offered its hot fumes to the air. Everybody did it. As the vapor trails from the jets soaring overhead seemed to disperse, perfectly, into the limitless blue, so we assumed that these wastes, these multicolored smokes and chemical fumes, would all cancel themselves, somehow, in the invisible emptiness.

It was as though after the demise of the ancestral, pagan gods, Western civilization's burnt offerings had become ever more constant, more extravagant, more acrid—as though we were petitioning some unknown and slumbering power, trying to stir some vast dragon, striving to invoke some unknown or long-forgotten power that, awakening, might call us back into relation with something other than ourselves and our own designs.

Indeed, the outpouring of technological by-products and pollutants since the Industrial Revolution could go on only so long before it would begin to alter the finite structure of the world around us, before its effects would begin to impinge upon our breathing bodies, inexorably drawing us back to our senses and our sensorial contact with the animate earth.

Today the technological media—the newspapers and radios and televisions—are themselves beginning to acknowledge and call attention to the changes underway in the air itself. It is through these secondary media that we recently learned of the massive buildup in the upper atmosphere of manufactured chemical compounds that every year burn an ever-widening hole in the stratospheric ozone layer above Antarctica, while thinning the rest of that protective layer worldwide. From these media we also learn of the drastic increase in atmospheric carbon dioxide since the onset of the Industrial Revolution, and we hear over and again that this surfeit of carbon dioxide, along with other heat-absorbing gases, is already promoting a substantial warming of the earthly climate, a change which in turn endangers the survival of numerous ecosystems, numerous animal and plant species already stressed, many to the edge of extinction, by the ever-burgeoning human population.

Nevertheless, such published and broadcast information, reaching us as it does through these technological channels, all too often remains an abstract cluster of statistics; it does little to alter our intellectual detachment from the sensuous earth until, returning from a journey, we see for ourselves the brown haze that now settles over the town where we live, until we feel the chemical breeze stinging the moist membranes that line our nose, or until we watch, with alarm, as gale-force winds rip the awning off our storefront. Or perhaps, after recovering from our fifth fevered illness in a single winter, we realize that our bodily resistance has been dampened by the increased radiation that daily pours through the exhausted sky, or by airborne fallout from the latest power-plant failure across the continent.

Phenomenologically considered—experientially considered—the changing atmosphere is not just one component of the ecological crisis, to be set alongside the poisoning of the waters, the rapid extinction of animals and plants, the collapse of complex ecosystems, and other human-induced horrors. All of these, to be sure, are interconnected facets of an astonishing dissociation—a monumental forgetting of our human inherence in a more-than-human world. Yet our disregard for the very air that we breathe is in some sense the most profound expression of this oblivion. For it is the air that most directly envelops us; the air, in other words, is that element that we are most intimately *in*. As long as we experience the invisible depths that surround us as empty space, we will be able to deny, or repress, our thorough interdependence with the other animals, the plants, and the living land that sustains us. We may acknowledge, intellectually, our body's reliance upon those plants and animals that we consume as nourishment, yet the civilized mind still feels itself somehow separate, autonomous, independent of the body and of bodily nature in general. Only as we begin to notice and to experience, once again, our immersion in the invisible air do we start to recall what it is to be fully a part of this world.[62]

For the primordial affinity between awareness and the invisible air simply cannot be avoided. As we become conscious of the unseen depths that surround us, the inwardness or interiority that we have come to associate with the personal psyche begins to be encountered in the world at large: we feel ourselves enveloped, immersed, caught up *within* the sensuous world. This breathing landscape is no longer just a passive backdrop against which human history unfolds, but a potentized field of intelligence in which our actions participate. As the regime of self-reference begins to break down, as we awaken to the air, and to the multiplicitous Others that are implicated, with us, in its generative depths, the shapes around us seem to awaken, to come alive. . . .

Coda:
Turning Inside Out

> Ah, not to be cut off,
> not through the slightest partition
> shut out from the law of the stars.
> The inner—what is it?
> if not intensified sky,
> hurled through with birds and deep
> with the winds of homecoming.
>
> —RAINER MARIA RILKE

NOT TO BE CUT OFF, AS RILKE SAYS. AND YET WE SEEM, today, so estranged from the stars, so utterly cut off from the world of hawk and otter and stone. This book has traced some of the ways whereby the human mind came to renounce its sensuous bearings, isolating itself from the other animals and the animate earth. By writing these pages I have hoped, as well, to *renew* some of those bearings, to begin to recall and reestablish the rootedness of human awareness in the larger ecology.

Each chapter has disclosed the subtle dependence of various "interior," mental phenomena upon certain easily overlooked or taken-for-granted aspects of the surrounding sensuous world. Language was disclosed as a profoundly bodily phenomenon, sustained by the gestures and sounds of the animate landscape. The rational intellect so prized in the West was shown to rely upon the external, visible letters of the alphabet. The presumably interior, mental awareness of the "past" and the "future" was shown to be dependent upon our sensory experience of that which is hidden beneath the ground and concealed beyond the horizon. Finally, the experience of awareness itself was related to mysteries of the breath and the air, to the tangible but invisible atmosphere in which we find ourselves immersed.

The human mind is not some otherworldly essence that comes to house itself inside our physiology. Rather, it is instilled and provoked by the sensorial field itself, induced by the tensions and participations between the human body and the animate earth. The invisible shapes of smells, rhythms of cricketsong, and the movement of shadows all, in a sense, provide the subtle body of our thoughts. Our own reflections, we might say, are a part of the play of light and *its* reflections. "The inner—what is it, if not intensified sky?"

By acknowledging such links between the inner, psychological world and the perceptual terrain that surrounds us, we begin to turn inside-out, loosening the psyche from its confinement within a strictly human sphere, freeing sentience to return to the sensible world that contains us. Intelligence is no longer ours alone but is a property of the earth; we are in it, of it, immersed in its depths. And indeed each terrain, each ecology, seems to have its own particular intelligence, its unique vernacular of soil and leaf and sky.

Each place its own mind, its own psyche. Oak, madrone, Douglas fir, red-tailed hawk, serpentine in the sandstone, a certain scale to the topography, drenching rains in the winter, fog off-shore in the summer, salmon surging in the streams—all these together make up a particular state of mind, a place-specific intelligence shared by all the humans that dwell therein, but also by the coyotes yapping in those valleys, by the bobcats and the ferns and the spiders, by all beings who live and make their way in that zone. Each place its own psyche. Each sky its own blue.

THE SENSE OF BEING IMMERSED IN A SENTIENT WORLD IS preserved in the oral stories and songs of indigenous peoples—in the belief that sensible phenomena are all alive and aware, in the assumption that all things have the capacity of speech. Language, for oral peoples, is not a human invention but a gift of the land itself.

I do not deny that human language has its uniqueness, that from a certain perspective human discourse has little in common with the sounds and signals of other animals, or with the rippling speech of the river. I wish simply to remember that this was not the perspective held by those who first acquired, for us, the gift of speech. Human language evolved in a thoroughly animistic context; it necessarily functioned, for many millennia, not only as a means of communication between humans, but as a way of propitiating, praising, and appeasing the expressive powers of the surrounding terrain. Human language, that is, arose not only as a means of attunement between persons, but also between ourselves and the animate landscape. The belief that meaningful speech is a purely human property was entirely alien to those oral communities that first evolved our various ways of speaking, and by holding to such a belief today we may well be inhibiting the spontaneous activity of language. By denying that birds and other animals have their own styles of speech, by insisting that the river has no real voice and that the ground itself is mute, we stifle our direct experience. We cut ourselves off from the deep meanings in many of our words, severing our language from that which supports and sustains it. We then wonder why we are often unable to communicate even among ourselves.

IN ELUCIDATING THE PROCESS WHEREBY CIVILIZATION HAS TURNED in upon itself, isolating itself from the breathing earth, I have concentrated upon the curious perceptual and linguistic transformations made possible by the advent of formal writing systems, and in particular by the advent of *phonetic* writing. I do not, however, wish to imply that writing was the sole factor in this process—a complex process that, after all, has been under way for several thousand years. Many other factors could have been chosen. I have hardly alluded, in this work, to the emergence of agriculture at the dawn of the Neolithic era, although the spread of agricultural techniques radically transformed the experienced relation between humans and other species. Nor have I addressed the development of formal numbering systems, and the consequent influence of numerical measurement, and quantification, upon our interactions with the land. And of course I have said little or nothing regarding the countless technologies spawned by alphabetic civilization itself, from telephones to televisions, from automobiles to antibiotics. By concentrating upon the written word, I have wished to demonstrate less a particular thesis than a particular stance, a particular way of pondering and of questioning *any* factor that one might choose.

It is a way of thinking that strives for rigor without forfeiting our animal kinship with the world around us—an attempt to think in accordance with the senses, to ponder and reflect without severing our sensorial bond with the owls and the wind. It is a style of thinking, then, that associates *truth* not with static fact, but with a quality of relationship.

Ecologically considered, it is not primarily our verbal statements that are "true" or "false," but rather the kind of relations that we sustain with the the rest of nature. A human community that lives in a mutually beneficial relation with the surrounding earth is a community, we might say, that lives in truth. The ways of speaking common to that community—the claims and beliefs that enable such reciprocity to perpetuate itself—are, in this important sense, *true*. They are in accord with a right relation between these people and their world. Statements and beliefs, meanwhile, that foster violence toward the land, ways of speaking that enable the impairment or ruination of the surrounding field of beings, can be described as *false* ways of speaking—ways that encourage an unsustainable relation with the encompassing earth. A civilization that relentlessly destroys the living land it inhabits is not well acquainted with *truth,* regardless of how many supposed facts it has amassed regarding the calculable properties of its world.

Hence I am less concerned with the "literal" truth of the assertions that I have made in this work than I am concerned with the kind of relationships that they make possible. "Literal truth" is entirely an artifact of alphabetic literacy: to be *literally true* originally meant to be true to "the letter of scripture"—to "the letter of the law." In this work I have tried to reacquaint the reader with a mode of awareness that precedes and underlies the literate intellect, to a way of thinking and speaking that strives to be faithful not to the written record but to the sensuous world itself, and to the other bodies or beings that surround us.

For such an oral awareness, to *explain* is not to present a set of finished reasons, but to tell a story. That is what I have attempted in these pages. It is an unfinished story, told from various angles, sketchy in some parts, complete with gaps and questions and unrealized characters. But it is a story, nonetheless, not a wholly determinate set of facts.

Of course, not all stories are successful. There are good stories and mediocre stories and downright bad stories. How are they to be judged? If they do not aim at a static or "literal" reality, how can we discern whether one telling of events is any better or more worthy than another? The answer is this: a story must be judged according to whether it *makes sense*. And "making sense" must here be understood in its most direct meaning: to make sense is *to enliven the senses*. A story that makes sense is one that stirs the senses from their slumber, one that opens the eyes and the ears to their real surroundings, tuning the tongue to the actual tastes in the air and sending chills of recognition along the surface of the skin. To *make sense* is to release the body from the constraints imposed by outworn ways of speaking, and hence to renew and rejuvenate one's felt awareness of the world. It is to make the senses wake up to where they are.

⚘

THE APPARENTLY AUTONOMOUS, MENTAL DIMENSION ORIGINALLY opened by the alphabet—the ability to interact with our own signs in utter abstraction from our earthly surroundings—has today blossomed into a vast, cognitive realm, a horizonless expanse of virtual interactions and encounters. Our reflective intellects inhabit a global field of information, pondering the latest scenario for the origin of the universe as we absently fork food into our mouths, composing presentations for the next board meeting while we sip our coffee or cappuccino, clicking on the computer and slipping into cyberspace in order to network with other bodiless minds, exchanging information about gene sequences and military coups, "conferencing" to solve global environmental problems while oblivious to the moon rising above the rooftops. Our nervous system synapsed to the terminal, we do not notice that the chorus of frogs by the nearby stream has dwindled, this year, to a solitary voice, and that the song sparrows no longer return to the trees.

In contrast to the apparently unlimited, global character of the technologically mediated world, the sensuous world—the world of our direct, unmediated interactions—is always local. The sensuous world is the particular ground on which we walk, the air we breathe. For myself as I write this, it is the moist earth of a half-logged island off the northwest coast of North America. It is this dark and stone-rich soil feeding the roots of cedars and spruces, and of the alders that rise in front of the cabin, their last leaves dangling from the branches before being flung into the sky by the early winter storms. And it is the salty air that pours in through the loose windows, spiced with cedar and seaweed, and sometimes a hint of diesel fumes from a boat headed south tugging a giant raft of clear-cut tree trunks. Sometimes, as well, there is the very faint, fishy scent of otter scat. Each day a group of otters slips out of the green waters onto the nearby rocks at high tide, one or two adults and three smaller, sleek bodies, at least one of them dragging a half-alive fish between its teeth. The otters, too, breathe this wild air, and when the storm winds batter the island, they stretch their necks into the invisible surge, drinking large drafts from the tumult.

In the interior of this island, in the depths of the forest, things are quieter. Huge and towering powers stand there, unperturbed by the winds, their crusty bark fissured with splitting seams and crossed by lines of ants, inchworms, and beetles of varied shapes and hues. A single woodpecker is thwacking a trunk somewhere, the percussive rhythm reaching my ears without any echo, absorbed by the mosses and the needles heavy with water drops that have taken hours to slide down the trunks from the upper canopy (each drop lodging itself in successive cracks and crevasses, gathering weight from subsequent drips, then slipping down, past lichens and tiny spiders, to the next protruding ridge or branch). Fallen firs and hemlocks, and an old spruce tree tunneled by termites, lie dank and rotting in the ferns, the jumbled branches of the spruce blocking the faint deer trail that I follow.

The deer on this island have recently molted, forsaking their summer fur for a thicker, winter coat. I watch them in the old orchard at dusk. No longer the warm brown color of sunlight on soil, their fur is now grey against the shadowed trunks and the all-grey sky. These quiet beings seem entirely a part of this breathing terrain, their very texture and color shifting with the local seasons.

Human persons, too, are shaped by the places they inhabit, both individually and collectively. Our bodily rhythms, our moods, cycles of creativity and stillness, and even our thoughts are readily engaged and influenced by shifting patterns in the land. Yet our organic attunement to the local earth is thwarted by our ever-increasing intercourse with our own signs. Transfixed by our technologies, we short-circuit the sensorial reciprocity between our breathing bodies and the bodily terrain. Human awareness folds in upon itself, and the senses—once the crucial site of our engagement with the wild and animate earth—become mere adjuncts of an isolate and abstract mind bent on overcoming an organic reality that now seems disturbingly aloof and arbitrary.

The alphabetized intellect stakes its claim to the earth by *staking it down,* extends its dominion by drawing a grid of straight lines and right angles across the body of a continent—across North America, across Africa, across Australia—defining states and provinces, counties and countries with scant regard for the oral peoples that already live there, according to a calculative logic utterly oblivious to the life of the land.

If I say that I live in the "United States" or in "Canada," in "British Columbia" or in "New Mexico," I situate myself within a purely human set of coordinates. I say very little or nothing about the earthly place that I inhabit, but simply establish my temporary location within a shifting matrix of political, economic, and civilizational forces struggling to maintain themselves, today, largely at the expense of the animate earth. The great danger is that I, and many other good persons, may come to believe that our breathing bodies really inhabit these abstractions, and that we will lend our lives more to consolidating, defending, or bewailing the fate of these ephemeral entities than to nurturing and defending the actual places that physically sustain us.

The land that includes us has its own articulations, its own contours and rhythms that must be acknowledged if the land is to breathe and to flourish. Such patterns, for instance, are those traced by rivers as they wind their way to the coast, or by a mountain range that rises like a backbone from the plains, its ridges halting the passage of clouds that gather and release their rains on one side of the range, leaving the other slope dry and desertlike. Another such contour is the boundary between two very different kinds of bedrock formed by some cataclysmic event in the story of a continent, or between two different soils, each of which invites a different population of plants and trees to take root. Diverse groups of animals arrange themselves within such subtle boundaries, limiting their movements to the terrain that affords them their needed foods and the necessary shelter from predators. Other, more migratory species follow such patterns as they move with the seasons, articulating routes and regions readily obscured by the current human overlay of nations, states, and their various subdivisions. Only when we slip beneath the exclusively human logic continually imposed upon the earth do we catch sight of this other, older logic at work in the world. Only as we come close to our senses, and begin to trust, once again, the nuanced intelligence of our sensing bodies, do we begin to notice and respond to the subtle logos of the land.

There is an intimate reciprocity to the senses; as we touch the bark of a tree, we feel the tree *touching us;* as we lend our ears to the local sounds and ally our nose to the seasonal scents, the terrain gradually tunes us in in turn. The senses, that is, are the primary way that the earth has of informing our thoughts and of guiding our actions. Huge centralized programs, global initiatives, and other "top down" solutions will never suffice to restore and protect the health of the animate earth. *For it is only at the scale of our direct, sensory interactions with the land around us that we can appropriately notice and respond to the immediate needs of the living world.*

Yet at the scale of our sensing bodies the earth is astonishingly, irreducibly diverse. It discloses itself to our senses not as a uniform planet inviting global principles and generalizations, but as this forested realm embraced by water, or a windswept prairie, or a desert silence. We can know the needs of any particular region only by participating in its specificity—by becoming familiar with its cycles and styles, awake and attentive to its other inhabitants.

OF COURSE, THE INTENSELY PLACE-CENTERED CHARACTER OF THE older, oral cultures was not without its drawbacks. Exquisitely integrated into their surrounding ecologies, indigenous, oral cultures were often so bound to their specific terrains that other, neighboring ecologies—other patterns of flora, fauna, and climate—could seem utterly incongruous, threatening, even monstrous. While such uncanniness may have helped to limit territorial incursions into neighboring bioregions, and thus may have minimized the potential for intertribal conflict, still there were times when human bands were displaced from their familiar lands—whether by climatic changes, by changes in the migration routes of prey, or simply by accident—and suddenly found themselves in a world where their ritual gestures, their prayers, and their stories seemed to lose all meaning, where the shapes of the landforms lacked coherence, *where nothing seemed to make sense.*

Without a set of stories and songs appropriate to the new surroundings, without an etiquette matched to *this* land and its specific affordances of food, fuel, and shelter, the displaced and often frightened newcomers could easily disrupt and even destroy a large part of the biotic community. The extinctions of various large animals that occurred immediately after migrating humans first crossed the Bering Strait and spread throughout North and South America may well have been precipitated by just such a situation—by a lack of cultural and linguistic patterns tuned to the diverse ecologies of this continent. A similar wave of extinctions appears to have occurred much earlier, during the first centuries of human incursion into Australia, while other extinctions have marked the arrival of our species in various island ecologies, including New Zealand, Hawaii, and Madagascar.[1] Such events suggest that the deep attunement to place characteristic of so many oral peoples emerges only after several generations in one general terrain.

It is also evident that encounters between human groups from entirely different bioregions could at times precipitate violence—in some cases quite bloody violence—merely as a result of the incommensurability of cultural universes and the consequent terror that each group might induce in the other. Such considerations must lead us to wonder whether the strange sense of human commonality made possible by the spread of formal writing systems is not something very worthy after all. Is there not something terrifically valuable about the modern faith in human equality? Although achieved at the cost of our cultural attunement to the particular places we inhabit, is there not something wondrous about the spreading recognition that we are part of a single, unitary earth?

Perhaps there is. And yet it is a precarious value. For at the very moment that human populations on every continent have come to recognize the planet as a unified whole, we discover that so many other species are rapidly dwindling and vanishing, that the rivers are choking from industrial wastes, that the sky itself is wounded. At the very moment that the idea of human equality has finally spread, via the printed word or the electronic media, into every nation, it becomes apparent that it is indeed nothing more than an idea, that in some of the most "developed" of nations humans are nevertheless destroying each other, physically and emotionally, in unprecedented numbers—whether through warfare, through the callousness of corporate greed, or through a rapidly spreading indifference.

Clearly, something is terribly missing, some essential ingredient has been neglected, some necessary aspect of life has been dangerously overlooked, set aside, or simply forgotten in the rush toward a common world. In order to obtain the astonishing and unifying image of the whole earth whirling in the darkness of space, humans, it would seem, have had to relinquish something just as valuable—the humility and grace that comes from being fully a part of that whirling world. We have forgotten the poise that comes from living in storied relation and reciprocity with the myriad things, the myriad *beings,* that perceptually surround us.

Only if we can renew that reciprocity—grounding our newfound capacity for literate abstraction in those older, oral forms of experience—only then will the abstract intellect find its real value.[2] It is surely not a matter of "going back," but rather of coming full circle, uniting our capacity for cool reason with those more sensorial and mimetic ways of knowing, letting the vision of a common world root itself in our direct, participatory engagement with the local and the particular. If, however, we simply persist in our reflective cocoon, then all of our abstract ideals and aspirations for a unitary world will prove horribly delusory. If we do not soon remember ourselves to our sensuous surroundings, if we do not reclaim our solidarity with

the other sensibilities that inhabit and constitute those surroundings, then the cost of our human commonality may be our common
extinction.

Indeed, many persons and communities, both within and outside
of the industrialized nations, are already engaged in such a process
of remembering. Individuals with the most varied backgrounds and
skills—farmers, physicists, poets, professors, herbalists, engineers,
mapmakers—have all been drawn toward the practice that some call
"reinhabitation." They have begun to apprentice themselves to their
particular places, to the ecological regions they inhabit. Many, for
instance, have become careful students of the plants and trees that
grow in their terrain, learning each plant's nutritive and/or medicinal properties, and its associations with specific insects and animals.
Others have taken as teachers the local animals themselves, spending
their spare time monitoring migrations, or learning the life cycle and
behavior of particular species. They work to restore damaged habi-
tats, and gradually to restore native species that had been locally
eradicated by human recklessness. Working together, they shut
down the factory that pollutes the estuary, and they woo the salmon
back into the streams. In the heart of the city they plant collective
gardens with endemic species, and hold equinox feasts with the
homeless. At every juncture they strive to discern those modes of
human community that are most appropriate to the region, most responsive and responsible to the earthly surroundings.

In North America this spontaneous and quietly growing movement goes by many names. In truth, it is less a movement than
a common sensibility shared by persons who have, in Robinson
Jeffers's phrase, "fallen in love outward" with the world around
them. As their compassion for the land deepens, they choose to resist
the contemporary tendency to move always elsewhere for a better
job or more affluent lifestyle, and resolve instead to dedicate themselves to the terrain that has claimed them, to meet the generosity of
the land with a kind of wild faithfulness. They rejuvenate their
senses by entering into reciprocity with the sensuous surroundings.
This does not prevent them from engaging in the political realities of
counties and countries, from supporting statewide initiatives and
voting in national elections. They are aware, however, that political
and economic institutions not aligned with earthly realities are not

likely to last, that such structures are like ephemeral phantoms to which we must attend without letting them distract us from what is really *here*. Such persons ally themselves not with the ever-expanding human monoculture, nor with the abstract vision of a global economy, but with the far more sustainable prospect of a regionally diverse and interdependent web of largely self-sufficient communities—a multiplicity of technologically sophisticated, vernacular cultures tuned to the structure and pulse of particular places. They know well that if humankind is to flourish without destroying the living world that sustains us, then we must grow out of our adolescent aspiration to encompass and control all that is. Sooner or later, they suspect, our technological ambition must begin to scale itself down, allowing itself to be oriented by the distinct needs of specific bioregions. Sooner or later, that is, technological civilization must accept the invitation of gravity and settle back into the land, its political and economic structures diversifying into the varied contours and rhythms of a more-than-human earth.

✒

YET THE PRACTICE OF REALIGNMENT WITH REALITY CAN HARDLY afford to be utopian. It cannot base itself upon a vision hatched in our heads and then projected into the future. Any approach to current problems that aims us toward a mentally envisioned future implicitly holds us within the oblivion of linear time. It holds us, that is, within the same illusory dimension that enabled us to neglect and finally to forget the land around us. By projecting the solution somewhere outside of the perceiveable present, it invites our attention away from the sensuous surroundings, induces us to dull our senses, yet again, on behalf of a mental ideal.

A genuinely ecological approach does not work to attain a mentally envisioned future, but strives to enter, ever more deeply, into the sensorial present. It strives to become ever more awake to the other lives, the other forms of sentience and sensibility that surround us in the open field of the present moment. For the other animals and the gathering clouds do not exist in linear time. We meet them only when the thrust of historical time begins to open itself outward, when we walk out of our heads into the cycling life of the land around us. This wild expanse has its own timing, its rhythms of dawning and dusk, its seasons of gestation and bud and blossom. It is here, and not in linear history, that the ravens reside.

Of course, if we live in the thick of the city, or even among the sprawling malls of suburbia, the sensuous world itself seems to surge toward a transcendent future, as high-rise buildings spring up from vacant lots, as wetlands give way to highways and billboard advertisements become 3-D holograms. Yet this restless progression takes place only within the encircling horizon of the breathing earth. New York City remains, first and foremost, an island settlement in the Hudson River estuary, subject to the coastal weather of that geography. For all the international commerce that goes on within its glassy walls, Manhattan could not exist without its grounding amid the waters with their tidal surges. Meanwhile, the inhabitants of Los Angeles awaken, often enough, to the trembling power of their own terrain. To return to our senses is to renew our bond with this wider life, to feel the soil beneath the pavement, to sense—even when indoors—the moon's gaze upon the roof.

❧

BUT WHAT, THEN, OF WRITING? THE PRECEDING PAGES HAVE CALLED attention to some unnoticed and unfortunate side-effects of the alphabet—effects that have structured much of the way we now perceive. Yet it would be a perilous mistake for any reader to conclude from these pages that he or she should simply relinquish the written word. Indeed, the story sketched out herein suggests that the written word carries a pivotal magic—the same magic that once sparkled for us in the eyes of an owl and the glide of an otter.

For those of us who care for an earth not encompassed by machines, a world of textures, tastes, and sounds other than those that we have engineered, there can be no question of simply abandoning literacy, of turning away from all writing. Our task, rather, is that of *taking up* the written word, with all of its potency, and patiently, carefully, writing language back into the land. Our craft is that of releasing the budded, earthly intelligence of our words, freeing them to respond to the speech of the things themselves—to the green uttering-forth of leaves from the spring branches. It is the practice of spinning stories that have the rhythm and lilt of the local soundscape, tales for the tongue, tales that want to be told, again and again, sliding off the digital screen and slipping off the lettered page to inhabit these coastal forests, those desert canyons, those whispering grasslands and valleys and swamps. Finding phrases that place us in contact with the trembling neck-muscles of a deer holding its antlers high as it swims toward the mainland, or with the ant dragging a scavenged rice-grain through the grasses. Planting words, like seeds, under rocks and fallen logs—letting language take root, once again, in the earthen silence of shadow and bone and leaf.

*

AN ALDER LEAF, LOOSENED BY WIND, IS DRIFTING OUT WITH THE tide. As it drifts, it bumps into the slender leg of a great blue heron staring intently through the rippled surface, then drifts on. The heron raises one leg out of the water and replaces it, a single step. As I watch I, too, am drawn into the spread of silence. Slowly, a bank of cloud approaches, slipping its bulged and billowing texture over the earth, folding the heron and the alder trees and my gazing body into the depths of a vast breathing being, enfolding us all within a common flesh, a common story now bursting with rain.

CHAPTER 1: THE ECOLOGY OF MAGIC

1. This work was done at the Philadelphia Association, a therapeutic community directed by Dr. R. D. Laing and his associates.

2. A simple illustration of this may be found among many of the indigenous peoples of North America, for whom the English term "medicine" commonly translates a word meaning "power"—specifically, the sacred power received by a human person from a particular animal or other nonhuman entity. Thus, a particular *medicine person* may be renowned for her "badger medicine" or "bear medicine," for his "eagle medicine," "elk medicine," or even "thunder medicine." It is from their direct engagement with these nonhuman powers that medicine persons derive their own abilities, including their ability to cure human ailments.

3. To the Western mind such views are likely to sound like reckless "projections" of human consciousness into inanimate and dumb materials, suitable for poetry perhaps, but having nothing, in fact, to do with those actual birds or that forest. Such is our common view. This text will examine the possibility that it is civilization that has been confused, and not indigenous peoples. It will suggest, and provide evidence, that one perceives a world at all only by projecting oneself into that world, that one makes con-

ıth things and others only by actively participating in them, lending e's sensory imagination to things in order to discover how they alter and transform that imagination, how they reflect us back changed, how they are different from us. It will suggest that perception is *always* participatory, and hence that modern humanity's denial of awareness in nonhuman nature is borne not by any conceptual or scientific rigor, but rather by an inability, or a refusal, to fully perceive other organisms.

4. The similarity between such animistic worldviews and the emerging perspective of contemporary ecology is not trivial. Atmospheric geochemist James Lovelock, elucidating the well-known Gaia hypothesis—a theory stressing the major role played by organic life in the ceaseless modulation of the earth's atmospheric and climatic conditions—insists that the geological environment is itself constituted by organic life, and by the products of organic metabolism. In his words, we inhabit "a world that is the breath and bones of our ancestors." See, for instance, "Gaia: the World as Living Organism," in the *New Scientist,* December 18, 1986, as well as *Scientists on Gaia,* ed. Stephen Schneider and Penelope Boston (Cambridge: M.I.T. Press, 1991).

CHAPTER 2: PHILOSOPHY ON THE WAY TO ECOLOGY

1. Galileo Galilei, cited in Edwin Jones, *Reading the Book of Nature* (Athens: Ohio University Press, 1989), p. 22.

2. "Phenomenon," in *Merriam-Webster's Collegiate Dictionary,* 10th ed., signifies "an object or aspect known through the senses rather than by thought or intuition." It is commonly contrasted with the term "noumenon" (from the Greek *nooumenon:* "that which is apprehended by thought"—itself derived from the Greek term *nous,* for "mind").

3. Maurice Merleau-Ponty, *Phenomenology of Perception,* trans. Colin Smith (London: Routledge & Kegan Paul, 1962), pp. viii–ix.

4. Edmund Husserl, *Cartesian Meditations: An Introduction to Phenomenology,* trans. Dorion Cairns (The Hague: Martinus Nijhoff Publishers, 1960). (Husserl completed the original text in 1929.)

5. Edmund Husserl, "Epilogue," in *Ideas Pertaining to a Pure Phenomenology II,* trans. Richard Rozcewicz and André Schuwer, 1989, p. 421. The notion of intersubjectivity did not reach the American popular awareness until the 1960s, when various authors began to describe objective reality as the "consensus reality" of the cultural mainstream.

6. Husserl's notion of the life-world was developed in his last, unfinished book, *The Crisis of European Sciences* and *Transcendental Phenome-*

nology, written from 1934 to 1937, in the shadow of the impending world war. As a German Jew, Husserl was denied any public platform from which to lecture, teach, or publish in his own country; hence, the lectures from which *The Crisis* grew were presented on journeys to Vienna and to Prague, and the first installments of the book were published in Yugoslavia shortly before Husserl's death in 1938. The "Crisis" of the title, which he wrote of as "the loss of science's meaning for life," was soon to be exemplified in the supreme indifference to life of many of Germany's scientists and medical doctors as they wrote numerous scientific articles on the biological inferiority of particular races, and later, in the objective and technological efficiency of the death factories at Auschwitz, Dachau, Buchenwald, and Treblinka. Although the gas chambers are no more, the same crisis—the same estrangement of a presumably "objective" rationality from living, sensuous reality—continues today in the reckless poisoning of the waters and the winds, and the forced extinction of countless forms of life, by a technological "progress" utterly oblivious to the living world on which it feeds.

7. Husserl, "Foundational Investigations of the Phenomenological Origin of the Spatiality of Nature," trans. Fred Kersten, in Peter McCormick and Frederick A. Elliston, eds., *Husserl: Shorter Works* (Brighton, Eng.: Harvester Press, 1981).

8. Ibid., p. 227.

9. Ibid., p. 231.

10. See Maurice Merleau-Ponty, *Signs,* trans. Richard McCleary (Evanston, Ill.: Northwestern University Press, 1964), pp. 180–81.

11. In this chapter I will be intertwining Merleau-Ponty's conclusions with my own experiential illustrations of those conclusions. I am less interested in merely repeating Merleau-Ponty's insights thirty years after his death than I am in demonstrating the remarkable usefulness of those insights for a deeply philosophical (and psychological) ecology. While my explications will at times move beyond the exact content of Merleau-Ponty's writings, they are nonetheless inspired by a close and long-standing acquaintance with those writings, and they remain faithful, I trust, to the unfinished and open-ended character of his thinking.

12. Aristotle, *The Politics of Aristotle,* trans. E. Barker (Oxford: Oxford University Press, 1946), p. 13 (1254b).

13. Merleau-Ponty, *Phenomenology of Perception,* p. 214.

14. Ibid.

15. Ibid., p. 317.

16. Ibid., pp. 211–12.

17. Ibid., pp. 320, 322.

18. Lucien Lévy-Bruhl, *How Natives Think,* (reprint, Princeton: Princeton University Press, 1985), p. 77.

19. Merleau-Ponty, *Phenomenology of Perception,* p. 227.

20. Ibid., p. 229.

21. Ibid., p. 228.

22. Genuine art, we might say, is simply human creation that does not stifle the nonhuman element but, rather, allows whatever is Other in the materials to continue to live and to breathe. Genuine artistry, in this sense, does not impose a wholly external form upon some ostensibly "inert" matter, but rather allows the form to emerge from the participation and reciprocity between the artist and his materials, whether these materials be stones, or pigments, or spoken words. Thus understood, art is really a cooperative endeavor, a work of cocreation in which the dynamism and power of earth-born materials is honored and respected. In return for this respect, these materials contribute their more-than-human resonances to human culture.

23. Maurice Merleau-Ponty, *The Visible and the Invisible,* trans. Alphonso Lingis, (Evanston, Ill.: Northwestern University Press, 1968).

24. Ibid., p. 127.

25. Richard K. Nelson, *Make Prayers to the Raven: A Koyukon View of the Northern Forest* (Chicago: University of Chicago Press, 1983), p. 14.

26. Ibid., p. 241.

27. Kenneth Lincoln, "Native American Literatures," in *Smoothing the Ground: Essays on Native American Oral Literature,* Brian Swann, ed., (Berkeley: University of California Press, 1983), p. 18.

28. Ibid., p. 22.

CHAPTER 3: THE FLESH OF LANGUAGE

1. Merleau-Ponty, *Phenomenology of Perception,* p. 184.

2. Ibid.

3. James M. Edie, introduction to Merleau-Ponty, *Consciousness and the Acquisition of Language* (Evanston, Ill.: Northwestern University Press, 1973), p. xviii.

4. Giambattista Vico, *The New Science of Giambattista Vico,* trans. Thomas G. Bergin and Max H. Fisch, 3rd ed. (Garden City, N.Y.: Doubleday & Co., 1961).

5. Jean-Jacques Rousseau, "Essay on the Origin of Languages," trans. John H. Moran; and Johann Gottfried Herder, "Essay on the Origin of

Language," trans. Alexander Gode in Rousseau and Herder, *On the Origin of Language* (Chicago: University of Chicago Press, 1966). Wilhelm von Humboldt later took up and extended Herder's views on language, contesting the mainstream view of language as an objective and determinate system. He insisted that we must think of language primarily as *speech,* and of speech as a dynamic and creative *activity,* not as a finished phenomenon—as *energeia,* not *ergon.* See Charles Taylor, *Human Agency and Language* (New York: Cambridge University Press, 1985), p. 256.

6. Merleau-Ponty, *Phenomenology of Perception,* p. 184.

7. Ample evidence for such a view may be found by studying the phonetic texture of particular words. To present a single example: Philosopher Peter Hadreas has sampled the words for "sea" and for "earth" (or "ground") in fifteen European and Asian languages currently in use, and found that the words for "sea" consistently depend upon continuant consonants, while the words for "earth" or "ground" depend upon plosive consonants. (Continuant consonants are those consonants that do not involve a stoppage of air flow. With such consonants—*n, m, ng, s, z, f, v, h, sh*—the breath is shaped by the vocal organs without being obstructed by them. Plosives, on the other hand, involve a momentary stoppage of the air flow and a subsequent, slightly explosive, release. Such are *t, d, ch, j, p, b, and g.*) Here is Hadreas's chart:

language	"sea"	"earth" or "ground"
French	mer	terre
Italian	mare	terra
Spanish	mer	tierra
German	meer	erde
Dutch	zee	aarde
Russian	more	potshva
Polish	morze	gleba
Czech	more	puda
Lithuanian	jura	padas
Latvian	jura	augsne
Turkish	deniz	toprak
Arabic	bahar	trab
Japanese	umi	dai chi
Korean	hoswu	taeji
Chinese	hoi	tati

Hadreas offers this explanation of the findings: "The sea as we move over or through it does not involve an obstruction of movement; whereas the earth or ground, at least insofar as it breaks a fall, always does." Accordingly, the words for "earth" or "ground" all employ plosives, while the words for "sea" employ only continuants. (Even in the apparent exceptions of Turkish and Arabic, the words for "sea" are relatively less plosive than those for "earth.") See Peter J. Hadreas, *In Place of the Flawed Diamond* (New York: Peter Lang Publishers, 1986); pp. 100–102.

8. Although an almost dogmatic insistence upon the arbitrariness of the relation between linguistic signs and that which they signify has been common among linguists throughout the twentieth century, several major researchers have dared to challenge this profoundly dualistic assumption, and have undertaken careful studies of the implicit significance carried by particular speech sounds, or "phonemes." Among those theorists who have stressed the importance of this layer of meanings immanent in the speech sounds themselves are the German linguist Hans Georg von der Gabelentz (1840–93); the French linguist Maurice Grammont (1866–1946), whose work focused on the evocative significance of the different vowel sounds; the well-known American linguist Edward Sapir (1884–1939); and Sapir's correspondent, the outstanding Danish linguist Otto Jesperson (1860–1943), who accomplished substantial research on the role of onomatopoeias and "sound symbolism" in the ongoing evolution of spoken languages (see, for instance, chap. 20 of Jesperson's book *Language—Its Nature, Development, and Origin* [New York: Henry Holt, 1922]). Finally, I must acknowledge the great Russian investigator of languages, Roman Jacobson (1896–1982), whose wonderful chapter "The Spell of Speech Sounds," from a late book written with Linda R. Waugh entitled *The Sound Shape of Language* (Bloomington: Indiana University Press, 1979), was my initial encounter with the first two linguists mentioned above.

9. Merleau-Ponty, *Phenomenology of Perception,* p. 197.

10. Ferdinand de Saussure, *Course in General Linguistics,* ed. Charles Bally and Albert Sechehaye, trans. Wade Baskin (New York: McGraw-Hill, 1966).

11. Merleau-Ponty, *Signs,* p. 39.

12. Ibid., pp. 40, 42.

13. Merleau-Ponty, *The Visible and the Invisible.* See, for instance, the note on "Perception and Language," p. 213.

14. Ibid., p. 125.

15. Ibid., p. 194. Compare these well-known lines from Dogen, the great thirteenth-century Japanese Zen teacher: "That the self advances and

realizes the ten thousand things is delusion. That the ten thousand things advance and realize the self is enlightenment" (from the *Genjo Koan* by Dogen).

16. Merleau-Ponty, *The Visible and the Invisible,* p. 155.

17. Merleau-Ponty's approach to language and to meaning, disclosing their source in a carnal field of participation that subtends the strictly human universe of instituted and inert meanings, provides a powerful response to the significant challenge posed to Western rationality by the postmodern "deconstructionist" thinkers. While these theorists aim to effect a deconstruction of *all* philosophical foundations, Merleau-Ponty's work suggests that, underneath all those admittedly shaky foundations, there remains the actual ground that we stand on, the earthly ground of rock and soil that we share with the other animals and the plants. This dark source, to which we can readily point even in the silence, will outlast all our purely human philosophies as it outlasts all the other artificial structures we erect upon it. We would do well, then, to keep our thoughts and our theories close to this nonarbitrary ground that already supports all our cogitations. The density beneath our feet is a depth we cannot fathom, and it spreads out on all sides into the horizon, and beyond. Unlike all the human-made foundations we construct upon its surface, the silent and stony ground itself can never be grasped in a purely human act of comprehension. For it has, from the start, been constituted (or "constructed") by many organic entities besides ourselves.

18. See Marcel Griaule, *Conversations with Ogotemmêli* (London: Oxford University Press, 1965), pp. 16–21.

19. See, for instance, Howard Norman, "Crow Ducks and Other Wandering Talk," in David M. Guss, ed., *The Language of the Birds* (San Francisco: North Point Press, 1985), p. 19.

20. Translated by Edward Field, in Jerome and Diane Rothenberg, eds., *Symposium of the Whole* (Berkeley: University of California Press, 1983), p. 3.

21. Norman, "Crow Ducks," p. 20.

22. See, for instance, Richard Nelson, *Make Prayers to the Raven: A Koyukon View of the Northern Forest* (Chicago: University of Chicago Press, 1983).

23. Mircea Eliade, *Shamanism: Archaic Techniques of Ecstasy,* trans. Willard R. Trask (Princeton: Princeton University Press, 1964), pp. 96–98.

24. Brian Swann, ed., *Smoothing the Ground: Essays on Native American Oral Literature* (Berkeley: University of California Press, 1983), p. 28.

25. Merleau-Ponty, *The Visible and the Invisible,* p. 213.

26. Edward Sapir, "The Status of Linguistics as a Science," in David G. Mandelbaum, ed., *Selected Writings of Edward Sapir* (Berkeley: University of California Press, 1949), p. 162.

Chapter 4: Animism and the Alphabet

1. Perhaps the most influential of such analyses has been historian Lynn White Jr.'s much-reprinted essay "The Historical Roots of Our Ecologic Crisis," originally published in *Science* 155 (1967), pp. 1203–1207.

The Genesis quote is from *Tanakh: The Holy Scriptures,* translated by the Jewish Publication Society according to the traditional Hebrew text (Philadelphia: Jewish Publication Society, 1985).

2. Jacques Derrida and other theorists have claimed that there is no self-identical author or subject standing behind any text that one reads, legislating its "actual" meanings; the precise meaning of a text, like its real origin, can only be indicated by referring to other texts to which this one responds, and since those, in turn, mark divergences from still other texts, the clear source, or the true meaning, is always deferred, always elsewhere. Since neither the origin nor the precise meaning of a text can ever be made wholly explicit, there can be no real meeting between the reader and the writer, at least not in the traditional sense of a pure coinciding of one's "self" with the exact intention of a supposed "author."

My equation of "meaning" with "meeting" would seem, at first blush, to fall easy prey to this critique. Yet Derrida's critique has bite only if one maintains that the other who writes is an exclusively *human* Other, only if one assumes that the written text is borne by an exclusively human subjectivity. Here, however, I am asserting a homology between the act of reading and the ancestral, indigenous act of *tracking.* I am suggesting that that which lurks behind all the texts that we read is not a human subject but another animal, another shape of awareness (ultimately the otherness of animate nature itself). The meeting that I speak of, then, is precisely the encounter with a presence that can never wholly coincide with our own, the confrontation with an enigma that cannot be dispelled by thought, an otherness that can never be fully overcome.

3. J. Gernet, quoted in Jacques Derrida, *Of Grammatology,* trans. Gayatri Spivak (Baltimore: Johns Hopkins University Press, 1976), p. 123.

4. The approximate dates referred to in this paragraph are drawn from several texts, including Albertine Gaur, *A History of Writing* (New York: British Library/Cross River Press, 1992); J. T. Hooker et al., *Reading the Past: Ancient Writing from Cuneiform to the Alphabet* (Berkeley: British Museum/University of California Press, 1990); and Jack Goody, *The Inter-*

face Between the Written and the Oral (Cambridge: Cambridge University Press, 1987).

5. The written characters or glyphs that I have referred to as ideograms are sometimes called logograms (word signs) by contemporary linguists, in order to emphasize that these characters are regularly used to transcribe or invoke particular words. The term "logogram," however, hides or masks the pictorial element that remains subtly operative in many of these written characters, and it is for this reason that I, like many others, have retained the popular terminology. The pictorial, "iconic" nature of many characters within a script inevitably influences the experience of language and linguistic meaning common to those who use that script. In the Mayan languages, for instance, the words for "writing" and "painting" were and are the same—the same artisans practiced both crafts, and the patron deities of both crafts were twin monkey gods. As Dennis Tedlock informs us in his introduction to the Mayan *Popol Vuh,* "In the books made under the patronage of these twin gods . . . the writing not only records words but sometimes has elements that picture or point to their meaning without the necessity of a detour through words." Dennis Tedlock, trans., *Popul Vuh: The Mayan Book of the Dawn of Life* (New York: Simon & Schuster, 1985), p 30.

6. That the contemporary Chinese word for "writing," as we saw earlier, also applies to the tracks of animals and the marks on a turtle shell may well be attributed to the fact that China has retained a somewhat iconic or pictorially derived mode of writing down to the present day.

7. Jack Goody, *The Interface Between the Written and the Oral,* pp. 34, 38.

8. It is important to realize that many pictorially derived writing systems commonly assumed by Western thinkers to be largely ideographic—like Egyptian hieroglyphs, the Chinese script, and even the recently deciphered Mayan system—utilize a host of conventional rebuses as phonetic indicators in combination with ideographic signs. These phonetic characters, however, commonly retain pictorial ties to the sensuous world. Although a hasty reader might choose to read these phonetic symbols without giving thought to their pictorial significance, according to Dennis Tedlock "the other meanings were still there for a reader who could see and hear them—even the same reader perhaps, in a different mood." A striking demonstration of the imagistic logic that animates such nonalphabetic writing systems may be found in the chapter entitled "Eyes and Ears to the Book" in Tedlock's remarkable study of Mayan culture, *Breath on the Mirror* (San Francisco: HarperCollins, 1993, pp. 109–14).

9. Walter J. Ong, *Orality and Literacy: The Technologizing of the Word* (New York: Methuen, 1982), pp. 87–88.

10. Ibid.

11. J. A. Hawkins, "The Origin and Dissemination of Writing in Western Asia," in P. R. S. Moorey, ed., *Origins of Civilization* (London: Oxford University Press, 1979), p. 132.

12. Ong, p. 89. See also Hooker et al., pp. 210–11; Gaur, p. 87.

13. However, the *aleph* in the Hebrew *aleph-beth* does not represent a vowel sound—rather, it signifies the opening of the throat prior to any sound.

14. Another common version of the early Semitic 'qoph' consisted of a *semicircle* intersected by a vertical line: Φ. Linguist Geoffrey Sampson writes that "no-one familiar with the look of heavy simian eyebrows ought . . . to find it difficult to see ['qoph'] as a full-face view of an ape." Likewise, the Semitic letter 'gimel' (which means camel in Hebrew) consisted of a rising and descending line: ∧—Sampson believes that this may be a stylized image of a camel's most prominent feature: its hump. Other letters took their forms from a hand, mouth, a snake. See Geoffrey Sampson, *Writing Systems: A Linguistic Introduction* (Stanford: Stanford University Press, 1985), pp. 78–81.

These letter shapes are from the original Hebrew *aleph-beth,* known in the later Jewish tradition as *Ksav Ivri* (literally: "script of the Hebrews"). These letters were eventually replaced, between the fifth and the third century B.C.E., by the square Hebrew letters used today, themselves borrowed from a late Aramaic version of the *aleph-beth.* See Hooker, et al., pp. 226–27; also Gaur, p. 92.

15. David Diringer, *The Alphabet* (New York: Philosophical Library, 1948), p. 159.

16. Plato, *Phaedrus,* trans. R. Hackforth, in *Plato: The Collected Dialogues,* ed. Edith Hamilton and Huntington Cairns (Princeton: Princeton University Press, 1982), sec. 230d.

17. Homer, *The Odyssey,* trans. Robert Fitzgerald (Garden City, N.Y.: Doubleday & Co., 1961); and Homer, *The Iliad,* trans. Robert Fitzgerald (Garden City, N.Y.: Doubleday & Co., 1974).

18. Eric Havelock, *The Muse Learns to Write: Reflections on Orality and Literacy from Antiquity to the Present* (New Haven: Yale University Press, 1986), pp. 19, 83, 90. See also Havelock's seminal text *Preface to Plato* (Cambridge: Harvard University Press, 1963).

19. The earliest Greek inscriptions of an alphabetic nature yet to be discovered are from around 740 or 730 B.C.E. (Hooker et al., pp. 230–32). See also Rhys Carpenter, "The Antiquity of the Greek Alphabet," *American Journal of Archaeology* 37 (1933); Havelock, *Preface to Plato,* pp. 49–52; Havelock, *The Muse Learns to Write,* pp. 79–97; Goody, *The Interface Between the Written and the Oral,* pp. 40–47.

20. The evidence for this resistance is carefully documented by Eric A. Havelock, the most accomplished scholar of the transition from orality to literacy in ancient Greece, particularly in his essay "The Special Theory of Greek Orality," in *The Muse Learns to Write*.

21. Havelock, *The Muse Learns to Write*, p. 87.

22. There is a linguistic parallel here with the Vedic *sutras,* so named because they, too, are sewn, or *sutured,* together.

23. See Adam Parry, ed., *The Making of Homeric Verse: The Collected Papers of Milman Parry* (Oxford: Clarendon Press, 1971). See also Albert Lord, *The Singer of Tales* (Cambridge: Harvard University Press, 1960).

24. Ivan Illich and Barry Sanders, *The Alphabetization of the Popular Mind* (San Francisco: North Point Press, 1988), p. 18.

25. See Ong, p. 35: "Fixed, often rhythmically balanced, expressions of this sort and of other sorts can be found occasionally in print, indeed can be 'looked up' in books of sayings, but in oral cultures they are not occasional. They are incessant. They form the substance of thought itself. Thought in any extended form is impossible without them, for it consists in them."

26. Today these disks are housed in the Parry Collection at Harvard University.

27. See especially "Whole Formulaic Verses in Greek and Southslavic Heroic Song," as well as other essays in Adam Parry, *The Making of Homeric Verse*.

28. Ibid., p. 378.

29. Ong, p. 59. In recent years Milman Parry's conclusion that the Homeric epics originated in a completely oral context has been disputed by Jack Goody, another careful student of oral-literate contrasts. Goody points out that while the Yugoslavian bards recorded by Parry and Lord were themselves nonliterate, the culture in which they sang and improvised their epic poems was not entirely untouched by literacy. Goody himself has worked among the LoDagaa people of northern Ghana—a tribe unacquainted with literacy until quite recently—and he undertook to record their oral myth, "the Bagre," which is ritually recited during the course of a long series of initiatory ceremonies. (Jack Goody, *The Myth of the Bagre* (Oxford: Clarendon Press, 1972). Along with many obvious similarities, he has found marked differences between the LoDagaa recitation and both the Slavic and the Homeric epics. The epic poems of Yugoslavia and of ancient Greece seem much more formal and tightly composed than their African counterparts (see "Africa, Greece and Oral Poetry," in Goody, *The Interface Between the Written and the Oral*). Further, according to Goody, the epic mode of the bardic tales, centered on the legendary acts of a human hero or a group of heroes, is foreign both to the Bagre and to other oral composi-

tions of indigenous Africa (on this, see also Ruth Finnegan, *Oral Literature in Africa* [London: Oxford University Press, 1970]). Goody's evidence suggests that the epic mode is more proper to the poetry of cultures in the earliest stages of literacy, rather than to that of purely oral peoples. He argues from this that the culture in which the *Iliad* and the *Odyssey* took shape should not be considered a pristinely oral culture, since even if the culture was without writing it had nevertheless been influenced (1) by the much earlier existence of nonalphabetic writing systems (Linear A and Linear B, which had been used, for economic and military accounting, by the Minoan and Mycenaean cultures on the island of Crete, until such writing vanished around 1100 B.C.E.), and (2) by the literacy of the neighboring societies of the Near East, societies with which the Greek merchants must have been in frequent contact ("Africa, Greece and Oral Poetry," pp. 98, 107–9). Goody's premise, that pre-Homeric Greece may have been influenced by the limited literacy of its Minoan and Mycenaean forebears, or by the protophonetic literacy of some cultures across the Mediterranean, may help us to understand why the Homeric gods and goddesses are as anthropomorphic as they are, much more human in form than are the deities of most cultures entirely untouched by literacy. We may, however, accept Goody's argument for the *indirect* influence of literacy without concluding that mainland Greece from 1100 to 750 B.C.E. made any *direct* use of writing, or had any wish to do so. For a lively debate on the orality of the Homeric epics, see "Becoming Homer: An Exchange," in the *New York Review of Books,* May 14, 1992.

30. Havelock, *The Muse Learns to Write,* p. 112.

31. Philip Wheelwright, ed., *The Presocratics* (New York: Macmillan Publishing Co., 1985), p. 45.

32. Illich and Sanders, pp. 22–23.

33. Plato, *Meno,* trans. W. K. C. Guthrie, in *Plato: The Collected Dialogues,* ed. Hamilton and Cairns sec. 72a (Princeton: Princeton University Press, 1982).

34. The reader may object that the alphabet gave a fixed and visible form *not* to the actual quality we call "justice," but only to the word, to the verbal label that "stands for" that quality. Surely Socrates was asking his discussants to ponder the quality itself, not the mere word. However, the clear distinction assumed by this objection, between words and what they "stand for," is a fairly recent distinction, itself made possible by the spread of phonetic writing. Only after spoken words were fixed in writing could they begin to be thought of as arbitrary "labels." In the Athens of Socrates and Plato, however—a society only emerging into literacy—the word was still directly participant with the phenomenon that it invoked, the phenom-

enon still participant with the spoken word. If the new technology of writing imparted to the spoken word "virtue" a new sense of autonomy and permanence, it brought a new sense of changelessness to the quality itself.

35. Ernest Fenollosa, cited in Ezra Pound, *ABC of Reading* (New York: New Directions Press, 1960), pp. 19–22.

36. Jacques Derrida has explored at great length the consequences of this curious vanishing throughout the trajectory of Western (alphabetic) philosophy, a tradition that ceaselessly forgets, or represses, its dependence upon writing. See, for instance, *Of Grammatology,* trans. Gayatri Spivak (Baltimore: Johns Hopkins University Press, 1976). Derrida, however, does not notice some of the most glaring differences between alphabetic and nonalphabetic modes of thought, differences that make themselves evident in our experienced relation to the animate earth. While Derrida assimilates all language to writing *(l'écriture),* my approach has been largely the reverse, to show that all discourse, even written discourse such as this, is implicitly sensorial and bodily, and hence remains bound, like the sensing body, to a world that is never exclusively human.

37. By suggesting that the relation, in Plato's writing, between the immortal psyche and the intelligible Ideas is dependent upon the experienced relation between the new, literate intellect and the visible letters of the alphabet, my intention is not to effect a reduction of transcendent, philosophic notions to banal, mundane experience, but rather to reawaken a sense of the profoundly magical, transcendent activity that reading *is*. In this I am simply practicing the method of wakefulness urged by Merleau-Ponty, whose phrase "the primacy of perception" expressed an intuition that even the most transcendental philosophies remain rooted in, and dependent upon, the very corporeal, sensuous world that they seek to forget.

38. *Phaedrus,* 275a.

39. Ibid., 275b.

40. Ibid., 277e.

41. Ibid., 278a.

42. Ibid., 230d.

43. Two reputable and accessible firsthand accounts of how visions and "medicine power" were and sometimes still are invoked among the Plains tribes are *Lame Deer, Seeker of Visions* by John Fire Lame Deer and Richard Erdoes, and *Black Elk Speaks,* by John Neihardt. Both books exist in numerous editions.

44. *Phaedrus,* 236e.

45. Ibid., 275b.

46. Ibid., 259a–d.

47. Ibid., 259b–c.

48. Richard Nelson, *Make Prayers to the Raven* (Chicago: University of Chicago, 1983), p. 17.

49. Jack Goody, in *The Domestication of the Savage Mind* (Cambridge: Cambridge University Press, 1977), has shown the dependence of such "mental" lists upon visible, written lists. See also Walter Ong: "Primary oral cultures commonly situate their equivalent of lists in narrative, as in the catalogue of the ships and captains in the *Iliad* (Book 11, lines 461–879). . . . In the text of the Torah, which set down in writing thought forms still basically oral, the equivalent of geography (establishing the relationship of one place to another) is put into a formulary action narrative (Numbers 33:16ff.): 'Setting out from the desert of Sinai, they camped at Kibroth-hattaavah. Setting out from Kibroth-hattaavah, they camped at Hazeroth. Setting out from Hazeroth, they camped at Rithmah . . .' and so on for many more verses. Even genealogies out of such orally framed tradition are in effect commonly narrative. Instead of a recitation of names, we find a sequence of 'begats,' of statements of what someone did: 'Irad begat Mahajael, Mahajael begat Methusael, Methusael begat Lamech' (Genesis 4:18)." Ong, p. 99.

50. Walter Ong writes of this as the "agonistic" requirement in oral storytelling. See Ong, pp. 43–45.

51. *Phaedrus,* 262d.

52. Ibid., 247c.

53. For instance, the research of Milman Parry and Albert Lord (see n. 23 above).

54. Such is the focus of the research undertaken by such diverse scholars as Eric Havelock, Marshall McLuhan, Walter Ong, Jack Goody, and, most recently, Ivan Illich. See Havelock, *Preface to Plato* and *The Muse Learns to Write: Reflections on Orality and Literacy from Antiquity to the Present;* Marshall McLuhan, *The Gutenberg Galaxy: The Making of Typographic Man* (Toronto: University of Toronto Press, 1962); Ong, *Interfaces of the Word* (London: Cornell University Press, 1977) and *Orality and Literacy: The Technologizing of the Word;* Goody, *The Interface Between the Written and the Oral* and *The Domestication of the Savage Mind* (Cambridge: Cambridge University Press, 1977); Illich and Sanders, *The Alphabetization of the Popular Mind.*

55. This is a special concern in Illich and Sanders, and in Goody, *The Interface Between the Written and the Oral.*

56. Ivan Illich, *In the Vineyard of the Text* (Chicago: University of Chicago Press, 1993). Also Illich and Sanders, pp. 45–51.

57. This reciprocity, the circular manner in which a nuanced sense of

self emerges only through a deepening relation with other beings, is regularly acknowledged in Buddhism as the "dependent co-arising of self and other."

58. Indeed, Merleau-Ponty takes the visual focus to be paradigmatic for synaesthesia in general: ". . . the senses interact in perception as the two eyes collaborate in vision." *Phenomenology of Perception,* pp. 233–34.

59. It is important to realize that the focused structure of perception ensures that I am able to participate with any phenomenon only by *not* participating with other phenomena. I cannot directly perceive a particular entity, in all its synaesthetic depth and otherness, without forfeiting, for the moment, a direct encounter with other entities, which must therefore remain part of the indeterminate background—at least until they themselves succeed in winning the focus of my senses. Thus, among many indigenous, oral peoples, for whom all things are potentially animate, it is nonetheless clear that *not all phenomena are experienced as animate all the time.* Indeed, certain phenomena, certain plants or insects that we ask about, may have little or no overt significance to the tribal community; they may not even have names within the storied language of the culture. Since these phenomena do not solicit the focused attention of the human community, they are rarely, if ever, experienced by them as unique entities with their own intensity and depth. Only those phenomena that regularly engage our synaesthetic attention stand out from the body of the land as autonomous powers in their own right. If there is no focus, no juxtaposition of diverse sensory modalities, then the phenomenon has no chance to move us, no chance to play one part of our experience off another, no chance to teach us. It thus remains flat, without much depth or dynamism, a purely background phenomenon.

60. A Carrier Indian, quoted in Diamond Jenness, *The Carrier Indians of the Bulkley River,* Bureau of American Ethnology: Bulletin 133 (Washington, D.C.: Smithsonian Institution, 1943), p. 540 (emphasis added).

61. Tzvetan Todorov, *The Conquest of America,* trans. Richard Howard (New York: Harper & Row, 1984).

62. Ibid., p. 89.

63. Ibid., pp. 61–62.

Chapter 5: In the Landscape of Language

1. *Phaedrus,* 275d.

2. See especially Elizabeth Eisenstein's two-volume work, *The Printing Press as an Agent of Change: Communications and Cultural Transforma-*

tions in *Early Modern Europe* (New York: Cambridge University Press, 1979). An older, more iconoclastic source is McLuhan's *The Gutenberg Galaxy: The Making of Typographic Man.*

3. For an auditory example of such tuning, the reader may wish to listen to a compact disc entitled *Voices of the Rainforest* (Rykodisk, 1991), a compilation of field recordings of the Kaluli people of Papua New Guinea made by ethnomusicologist Steven Feld. The Kaluli people sing with birds, with insects, with tree frogs and tumbling waterfalls, with the rain itself. "And when the Kaluli sing with them, they sing *like* them. Nature is music to the Kaluli ears. And Kaluli music is naturally part of the surrounding soundscape. . . . In this rainforest musical ecology, the world really is a tuning fork." The songful language of the Kaluli is rich with onomatopoeic words that echo the speech of animals as well as mimic the diverse swirling, bubbling, and plopping sounds made by water in the rain forest. But like all oral languages, the participatory songs of the Kaluli people are now threatened with extinction, in this case due to the encroachment of oil-drilling operations: the new voices in the forest are those of helicopters and drilling rigs. See also Steven Feld's book, *Sound and Sentiment: Birds, Weeping, Poetics and Song in Kaluli Expression,* rev. ed. (Philadelphia: Temple University Press, 1991).

4. F. Bruce Lamb, *Wizard of the Upper Amazon: The Story of Manuel Córdova-Rios,* (Boston: Houghton Mifflin, 1971).

5. Ibid., pp. 63–64.

6. Ibid., p. 51.

7. Ibid., pp. 48–49.

8. See, for instance, the works of Otto Jesperson and Roman Jacobson cited in chap. 3, n. 8. Late in his life, Jacobson claimed that the reluctance of linguists to acknowledge the inner significance of speech sounds arose simply because early attempts to document this significance had failed to dissect the speech sounds into their most basic constituents. Jacobson and Waugh, *The Sound Shape of Language* (Bloomington: Indiana University Press, 1979), p. 185.

9. Richard Nelson, *Make Prayers to the Raven: A Koyukon View of the Northern Forest* (Chicago: University of Chicago Press, 1983), p. 2.

10. Ibid., p. 20.

11. Richard Nelson, *The Island Within* (San Francisco: North Point Press, 1989), p. 110.

12. Nelson, *Make Prayers to the Raven,* p. 172.

13. Ibid., p. 86.

14. Ibid., p. 87.

15. Ibid.

16. Ibid., p. 109.
17. Ibid., p. 115.
18. Ibid., p. 110.
19. Ibid., p. 116.
20. Ibid., p. 111.
21. Ibid., p. 106.
22. Ibid.
23. Ibid.
24. Ibid., p. 115.
25. Ibid., p. 119.
26. Ibid., p. 16.
27. Nelson, *Make Prayers to the Raven,* p. 118.
28. John Bierhorst, *The Mythology of North America* (New York: William Morrow & Co., 1985), pp. 6–7. See also, for instance, Gerald Vizenor, *Anishnabe Adisokan: Tales of the People* (Minneapolis: Nodin Press, 1970), p. 9.
29. Ibid., p. 127.
30. Ibid., p. 148.
31. Ibid., p. 155.
32. Ibid., p. 176.
33. Ibid., p. 177.
34. Nelson, *The Island Within,* p. 117.
35. Ibid., p. 69.
36. A Koyukon elder, quoted in Nelson, *Make Prayers to the Raven,* p. 26.
37. The choice of cultures here is determined both by my intention to present examples from contrasting biotic regions as well as by my wish to suggest, in the short space of a chapter, the wildly variant ways in which oral languages display their earthly dependence.
38. Keith Basso, "'Stalking with Stories': Names, Places, and Moral Narratives Among the Western Apaches" (henceforth Basso, "Stalking") in Daniel Halpern, ed., *On Nature: Nature, Landscape, and Natural History* (San Francisco: North Point Press, 1987).
39. Ibid., p. 101.
40. Ibid., pp. 105–6. See also Keith H. Basso, "'Speaking with Names': Language and Landscape Among the Western Apache" (henceforth Basso, "Speaking"), in *Cultural Anthropology,* May 1988, p. 111.
41. Basso, "Stalking," p. 95.
42. Basso, "Speaking," pp. 117–18. I have, however, transcribed the story into the form used by Basso in Basso, "Stalking."
43. Basso, "Stalking," p. 107.
44. Ibid., p. 108.

45. Ibid., pp. 111–12.

46. Ibid., p. 112.

47. Ibid., p. 110.

48. Ibid.

49. Nick Thompson, quoted in Basso, "Stalking," p. 112.

50. Basso, "Stalking," p. 113; Basso, "Speaking," pp. 118, 121–22.

51. Nick Thompson, quoted in Basso, "Stalking," p. 96.

52. Wilson Lavender, quoted in Basso, "Stalking," p. 97.

53. Basso, "Stalking," p. 112.

54. Ibid., pp. 112–14.

55. Basso, "Speaking," p. 110.

56. Quoted in Basso, "Stalking," pp. 100–101.

57. Ronald M. Berndt and Catherine H. Berndt, "How Ooldea Soak Was Made," in *The Speaking Land: Myth and Story in Aboriginal Australia* (London: Penguin Books, 1989), p. 42.

58. Berndt and Berndt, p. 213.

59. "Leech at Mamaraawiri," in Berndt and Berndt, p. 211.

60. Bruce Chatwin, *The Songlines* (London: Penguin Books, 1987), p. 60.

61. The Pintupi people say that they recognize a song by its smell *(mayu)* or taste *(ngurru)*—a remarkable example of synaesthesia.

62. See Gary Snyder, *The Practice of the Wild* (San Francisco: North Point Press, 1990), p. 83, as well as Basso, "Stalking," p. 101.

63. Chatwin, p. 60. See also T. G. H. Strehlow, *Aranda Traditions* (Melbourne: Melbourne University Press, 1947), p. 17.

64. Billy Marshall-Stoneking, "Paddy: A Poem for Land Rights," in *Singing the Snake: Poems from the Western Desert* (Pymble, Austral.: Angus & Robertson, 1990).

65. Chatwin, p. 14.

66. Colin Tatz, ed., *Black Viewpoints: the Aboriginal Experience* (Sydney: Australia and New Zealand Book Co., 1975), p. 29. On this point, see also an interview with aboriginal writer and educator Eric Willmot in *Omni,* June 1987.

67. W. E. H. Stanner, "The Dreaming," in Jerome Rothenberg and Diane Rothenberg, eds., *Symposium of the Whole* (Berkeley: University of California Press, 1983), pp. 201–5. See also Nancy Munn, *Walbiri Iconography: Graphic Representation and Cultural Symbolism in a Central Australian Society* (Ithaca, N.Y.: Cornell University Press, 1973), pp. 131–33.

68. From Marshall-Stoneking, "Passage," in *Singing the Snake,* p. 30.

69. Chatwin, pp. 105–6.

70. Helen Payne, "Rites for Sites or Sites for Rites? The Dynamics of Women's Cultural Life in the Musgraves," in Peggy Brock, ed., *Women,*

Rites, and Sites: Aboriginal Women's Cultural Knowledge (North Sydney, Austral.: Allen & Unwin Limited, 1989), p. 56.

71. Chatwin, p. 52.

72. Catherine J. Ellis and Linda Barwick, "Antikirinja Women's Song Knowledge 1963–1972," in *Women, Rites, and Sites,* pp. 31–32.

73. Ibid., pp. 34–36. While I have spoken of various aboriginal traditions in the present tense, the reader should be aware that many of these traditions are rapidly being lost under the influence of alphabetic civilization.

74. Gary Snyder, *The Practice of the Wild,* p. 82.

75. Chatwin, pp. 293–94.

76. Payne, "Rites for Sites or Sites for Rites?" in *Women, Rites, and Sites,* p. 45.

77. Ibid.

78. Basso, "Speaking," pp. 110–13.

79. The gender specificity here is intentional: almost all orators were men.

80. Frances A. Yates, *The Art of Memory* (Chicago: University of Chicago Press, 1966).

81. Basso, "Stalking," pp. 115–16.

CHAPTER 6:
TIME, SPACE, AND THE ECLIPSE OF THE EARTH

1. See Charles A. Reed, ed., *Origins of Agriculture* (The Hague: Mouton & Co., 1977).

2. Åke Hultkrantz, *Native Religions of North America* (San Francisco: Harper & Row, 1987), pp. 32–33.

3. T. C. McLuhan, *Touch the Earth* (New York: Outerbridge and Dienstfrey, 1971), p. 42.

4. Mircea Eliade, *The Myth of the Eternal Return* (New York: Harper & Row, 1959).

5. Ibid., p. vii.

6. See Todorov, pp. 116–19.

7. Marshall Sahlins, *Historical Metaphors and Mythical Realities* (Ann Arbor: University of Michigan Press, 1981).

8. Hultkrantz, p. 33.

9. Todorov, p. 85.

10. Rik Pinxten, Ingrid Van Doren, and Frank Harvey, *Anthropology of Space: Explorations into the Natural Philosophy and Semantics of the Navajo* (Philadelphia: University of Pennsylvania Press, 1983), p. 168.

11. Ibid., p. 36.

12. Benjamin Lee Whorf, "An American Indian Model of the Universe," in Dennis Tedlock and Barbara Tedlock, eds., *Teachings from the American Earth* (New York: Liveright, 1975), p. 122.

13. Ibid.

14. See especially Ekkehart Malotki, *Hopi Time: A Linguistic Analysis of the Temporal Concepts in the Hopi Language* (New York: Mouton Publishers, 1983).

15. Whorf, "An American Indian Model," p. 124.

16. Ibid.

17. Pinxten et al., p. 18.

18. Ibid., pp. 20–21.

19. Eliade, *The Myth of the Eternal Return,* p. 104.

20. Ibid.

21. Indeed, the *original* tablets, smashed by Moses in anger upon seeing the golden calf, were according to the Hebrew Bible inscribed directly "by the finger of God." Exodus 31:18. See also Rabbi Michael L. Munk, *The Wisdom in the Hebrew Alphabet: The Sacred Letters as a Guide to Jewish Deed and Thought* (Brooklyn: Mesorah Publications, 1983).

22. Edmond Jabes, *Elya* (Berkeley, Calif.: Tree Books, 1974), p. 72.

23. Aristotle, *Physics,* trans. Hippocrates G. Apostle (Bloomington: Indiana University Press, 1969), book IV.

24. By the era of the printing press, the mechanical clock was slowly exerting its influence throughout Europe. The presence of alphabetic writing may help explain why the mechanical clock was invented in Europe and had spread throughout European culture long before taking hold in the more ideographic world of the Orient. Actually, a few elaborate clocklike machines had been designed and built for the private use of Chinese emperors as early as the eleventh century, yet these were intended strictly as calendrical devices modeling the movements of the heavens—machines that would allow the emperor to *align* his intentions and decrees more precisely with astrological events. The order of time remained inseparable from such cosmic, spatial phenomena.

In the West, on the contrary, the mechanical clock functioned to *sever* the experience of time from the spatial cycles of the sun, moon, and stars, marking out a series of determinate intervals that paid little heed to the heavens or to the shifting lengths of daylight and darkness. Mechanical clocks originated in monasteries (the strongholds of alphabetic literacy throughout the Middle Ages), where they were used to regulate the times for prayer. But by the middle of the fourteenth century, large clocks in the belfries of churches and town halls rang the equal hours for the whole pop-

ulace, regulating the daily activities of the community according to an artificially determined and unvarying measure. Because the fixed hours of the
clock were ultimately independent of the sun, independent of its rising and
setting and the length of the daylight (all of which might vary not just in
different seasons but in different locations), clock-time could ultimately be
used to regulate transactions *between* different villages and towns, eventually establishing the sense of a wholly objective, quantitative time impervious to the particular rhythms of different locales and seasons. The voice of
this objective time was the implacable "tick-tock" of the clock's internal
mechanism, which lent auditory force to the Aristotelian sense of time as a
countable series of discrete now-points. See Daniel Boorstin, *The Discov-
erers* (New York: Random House, 1983), pp. 36–46, 56–78.

25. Quoted in Alexandre Koyré, *From the Closed World to the Infinite
Universe* (New York: Harper & Brothers, 1958), pp. 161, 162.

26. Ibid., pp. 161–62, 245.

27. Ibid., pp. 221–72.

28. Edmund Husserl, *Phenomenology of Internal Time-Consciousness,*
trans. James S. Churchill (Bloomington: Indiana University Press, 1964),
pp. 104, 150. See also David Wood, *The Deconstruction of Time* (Atlantic
Highlands, N.J.: Humanities Press, 1989), pp. 106–9.

29. Martin Heidegger, *Being and Time,* trans. John Macquarrie and Edward Robinson (Oxford: Basil Blackwell, 1967).

30. Martin Heidegger, "Time and Being," in *On Time and Being,* trans.
Joan Stambaugh (New York: Harper & Row, 1972).

31. Merleau-Ponty, *The Visible and the Invisible,* p. 259. It is worthy of
note that these words were written by Merleau-Ponty on June 1, 1960, less
than a year before his death, and more than a year and a half before Heidegger's introduction of "time-space" in his January 1962 lecture "Time
and Being."

32. Ibid., p. 267.

33. Ibid., p. 259.

34. Ibid., p. 13.

35. Heidegger, "Time and Being," p. 11.

36. Ibid., pp. 11–12.

37. Heidegger, *Being and Time,* p. 416.

38. In truth, the idea of time is a thoroughly horizon-laden thought for
Heidegger; in *Being and Time* he can hardly mention the phenomenon of
time in any capacity without linking it to the horizon metaphor. Thus,
when explicating the genesis of our ordinary conception of time as a linear
sequence, Heidegger translates Aristotle's definition of time in the following manner: "For this is time: that which is counted in the movement which

we encounter within the horizon of the earlier and later" (*Being and Time,* p. 473). And indeed, the entire book ends with the question "Does *time* itself manifest as the horizon of *Being?*" (*Being and Time,* p. 488).

39. Heidegger, "Time and Being," p. 13.

40. Ibid., pp. 16–17.

41. Ibid., p. 17.

42. Ibid., pp. 13, 17.

43. Merleau-Ponty, *The Visible and the Invisible,* p. 267.

44. John Bierhorst, *The Mythology of North America* (New York: William Morrow & Co., 1985), pp. 77–92. See also Åke Hultkrantz, *Native Religions of North America,* pp. 91–94.

45. One finds resonances throughout the Americas: "The people came 'out of the ground' (Nez Percé); 'the people grew up from the soil' (Tarahumara); 'the people came out of the hills' (Tzotzil); 'the first man emerged from the earth' (Toba)." See John Bierhorst, *The Way of the Earth* (New York: William Morrow & Co., 1994), p. 98.

46. A Jicarilla Apache storyteller, quoted in Bierhorst, *Mythology of North America,* 1985, p. 82.

47. Hultkrantz, pp. 91–92.

48. George B. Grinell, *Pawnee Hero Stories and Folk-tales* (1889) (Lincoln: University of Nebraska Press, 1961), pp. 149–50.

49. Christopher Vecsey, *Imagine Ourselves Richly: Mythic Narratives of North American Indians* (San Francisco: HarperCollins, 1991), p. 45. See also Dennis Tedlock, "An American Indian View of Death" in Dennis Tedlock and Barbara Tedlock, eds., *Teachings from the American Earth: Indian Religion and Philosophy* (New York: Liveright, 1975), especially pp. 264–70.

50. June McCormick Collins, "The Mythological Basis for Attitudes Towards Animals Among Salish-Speaking Indians," *Journal of American Folklore* 65, no. 258 (1952), p. 354.

51. Åke Hultkrantz, for instance, asserts that the belief among the Wind River Shoshoni that the dead must follow the Milky Way to "the land of the dead" conflicts with "another belief" according to which the dead dwell beyond the mountains (Hultkrantz, p. 59). Examined phenomenologically, however, the two beliefs are not in conflict at all, since the visible path of the Milky Way leads precisely beyond the mountains.

52. N. Scott Momaday, "Personal Reflections," in Calvin Martin, ed., *The American Indian and the Problem of History* (New York: Oxford University Press, 1987), pp. 156–61.

53. See, for instance, John James Houston, "Songs in Stone: Animals in Inuit Sculpture," in *Orion Nature Quarterly* 4, no. 4 (Autumn 1985), p. 8.

54. Heidegger, *Being and Time,* p. 416.
55. Heidegger, "Time and Being," p. 15.
56. Ibid., p. 13.

CHAPTER 7:
THE FORGETTING AND REMEMBERING OF THE AIR

1. Robert Lawlor, *Voices of the First Day: Awakening in the Aboriginal Dreamtime* (Rochester, Vt.: Inner Traditions, 1992), p. 41.

2. See, for instance, Berndt and Berndt, pp. 73–125.

3. Lawlor, p. 42.

4. See Christopher Vecsey, *Imagine Ourselves Richly: Mythic Narratives of North American Indians* (San Francisco: HarperCollins, 1991), chap. 7.

5. See, for instance, the words of the Lakota medicine man, Finger, recorded by Dr. James R. Walker in Tedlock and Tedlock, pp. 208–13.

6. See D. M. Dooling, ed., *The Sons of the Wind: The Sacred Stories of the Lakota* (New York: Parabola Books, 1984), for a beautiful and carefully researched telling of the sacred Lakota stories. Precise insights into the nature of the *wakan* beings may be gleaned from these stories, aided by the very useful glossary at the front of the book. The stories should be supplemented by the words of the old Lakota holy men—Sword, Finger, One-Star, and Tyon—recorded early in the twentieth century by Dr. James R. Walker and excerpted in chap. 13, "Oglala Metaphysics," in Tedlock and Tedlock, pp. 205–18. Dr. Walker's own essential research may be found in J. R. Walker, *The Sun Dance and Other Ceremonies of the Teton Dakota,* Anthropological Papers of the American Museum of Natural History 16 (1917); and in Elaine Jahner, *Lakota Myth* (Lincoln: University of Nebraska Press, 1983).

7. The peace pipe was given to the Lakotas by White Buffalo Woman as a gift from the buffalo, whose sacred breath is also visible when it is seen on a cold day. Yet it is not only animals and plants that are assumed to breathe and to partake of the air: in the *inipi,* or sweat lodge, ceremony, water is poured on the red-hot rocks to release the living breath of the rocks themselves: "You pray to the Great Spirit, to the sacred rocks, the *tunka,* the *inyan.* They have no mouth, no eyes, no arms or legs, but they exhale the breath of life." From John Fire Lame Deer and Richard Erdoes, *Lame Deer, Seeker of Visions* (New York: Simon & Schuster, 1972), p. 180.

8. John Fire Lame Deer, in Lame Deer and Erdoes, p. 119.

9. See Tedlock and Tedlock, pp. 217–18.

10. Ibid., p. 218.

11. Ibid., p. 218.

12. James Kale McNeley, *Holy Wind in Navajo Philosophy* (Tucson: University of Arizona Press, 1981), p. 1. This book is the fruit of twenty years of association with the Navajo. McNeley is married to a Diné woman, and the two of them teach on the Navajo Reservation in Arizona. Although the Navajo commonly refer to themselves as "Diné"—the People—I have mostly used the more familiar term "Navajo," for convenience' sake, in this work.

13. Ibid., p. 2.

14. A Navajo singer and healer quoted in McNeley, pp. 9–10. Most of the elders interviewed by McNeley requested that their identities remain unpublished.

15. Ibid., pp. 16, 21.

16. Ibid., pp. 14–31.

17. Ibid., pp. 23, 33–34.

18. Ibid., pp. 34–35.

19. Ibid., p. 35.

20. Ibid., p. 35.

21. Ibid., p. 35. Emphasis added.

22. Ibid., p. 36.

23. Ibid., pp. 11, 36–37.

24. Ibid., p. 36.

25. Ibid., p. 24.

26. Ibid., p. 24.

27. Ibid., pp. 37–38.

28. Gary Witherspoon, *Language and Art in the Navajo Universe* (Ann Arbor: University of Michigan Press, 1977).

29. Witherspoon, p. 31; McNeley, p. 57.

30. Witherspoon, p. 61.

31. Leland C. Wyman, *Blessingway* (Tucson: University of Arizona Press, 1970), p. 616. These words are translated from River Junction Curly's version of the Blessingway.

32. C. T. Onions, ed., *The Oxford Dictionary of English Etymology* (Oxford: Clarendon Press, 1966), p. 720.

33. Ibid., p. 691.

34. Eric Partridge, *Origins: A Short Etymological Dictionary of Modern English* (London: Routledge & Kegan Paul, 1958), pp. 651–52.

35. Onions, p. 38; Partridge, p. 18.

36. Here is how the British linguist and historian Owen Barfield addressed these curious evidences embedded in our words:

such a purely material content as "wind". . . and . . . such a purely abstract content as "the principle of life within man or animal" are both *late* arrivals in human consciousness. Their abstractness and their simplicity are alike evidence of long ages of intellectual evolution. So far from the psychic meaning of "spiritus" having arisen because someone had the idea, "principle of life . . ." and wanted a word for it, the abstract idea "principle of life" is itself a *product* of the old concrete meaning of "spiritus," which contained within itself the germs of both later significations. We must, therefore, imagine a time when "spiritus" or "pneuma," or older words from which these had descended, meant neither *breath*, nor *wind*, nor *spirit*, nor yet all three of these things, but when they simply had their own peculiar meaning, which has since, in the course of the evolution of consciousness, crystallized into the three meanings specified. . . .

See Owen Barfield, *Saving the Appearances* (Middletown, Conn., Wesleyan University Press, 1965), pp. 80–81.

37. *Tanakh: The Holy Scriptures* (Philadelphia: Jewish Publication Society, 1985), Genesis 1:2. This is the most authoritative English translation of the Hebrew Bible from the traditional Hebrew text. The traditional Hebrew name for the Bible, *Tanakh,* is an acronym formed by the first letters of the three sections of the Hebrew text: *T*orah (Instruction), *N*evi'im (Prophets), and *K*ethuvim (Writings). Although the relevant phrase in the first sentence of the Torah is commonly translated into English as "the spirit of God," "a wind from God" is actually a more direct rendering of the original Hebrew.

38. McNeley, p. 10.

39. Genesis 2:7. Just as the Hebrew term for human *(adam)* relates directly to the word for earth *(adamah),* so also the English term "human" relates directly to the word "humus"—the earth or soil. Thus, both the Hebrew *adam* and the English "human" can be precisely translated as "earthling," or "earthborn one."

40. This is not to suggest that all of the ancient Hebrews were able, or even allowed, to read—far from it. Yet to the extent that they took the written commandments as their supreme laws, and to the extent that the story about receiving those scribed commandments, at Mount Sinai, became their foundational story, *every* Hebrew life was structured in accordance with Scripture—with writing—whether the individual was literate or not.

41. An excellent analysis of the extent to which the lack of vowel letters in the Hebrew writing system can or cannot be thoroughly explained by the structure of the Hebrew language is found in Geoffrey Sampson's masterful text, *Writing Systems: A Linguistic Introduction* (Stanford: Stanford

University Press, 1985), pp. 77–98. Sampson's analysis shows that even a reader fluent in Hebrew encounters a relatively high degree of ambiguity when reading a traditional text without vowel marks; it is this ambiguity that forces the reader of Hebrew to actively grapple with conflicting meanings, conflicting ways of sounding the text.

42. While Hebrew words that share the same group of consonants tend to have a related meaning, meanings can still change drastically with different vowel sounds. For instance, while the word "TSaHaK" means "sexual intercourse," the word "TSaHoK" means "laughter." Or consider the Hebrew words "DĪR" (a stable), "DāR" (mother-of-pearl), "DōR" (generation), "DūR" (ruin), "DōR" (to dwell).

43. Barry W. Holtz, ed., *Back to the Sources: Reading the Classic Jewish Texts* (New York: Summit Books, 1984), pp. 16–17.

44. See, for instance, Lawrence Kushner, *The Book of Letters: A Mystical Alef-bait* (New York: Harper & Row, 1975). Also Rabbi Michael L. Munk, *The Wisdom in the Hebrew Alphabet: The Sacred Letters as a Guide to Jewish Deed and Thought* (New York: Mesorah Publications, 1983). See also Aryeh Kaplan, *Sefer Yetzirah: The Book of Creation*.

45. Moshe Idel, *Kabbalah: New Perspectives* (New Haven: Yale University Press, 1988), pp. 234–37.

46. Perle Epstein, *Kaballah: The Way of the Jewish Mystic* (Boston: Shambhala, 1988), pp. 98–99.

47. The voluminous research on Kabbalah conducted by the great twentieth-century scholar Gershom Scholem has led many to believe that the Kabbalah was something of an anomaly within traditional Judaism, sparked by non-Jewish influences, like Gnosticism, which ostensibly infiltrated Jewish circles early on and combined with other, Neoplatonic influences during the Middle Ages. However, more recent scholarship—particularly the extensive and ongoing research of the brilliant Israeli scholar Moshe Idel—has called into question some of Scholem's assumptions, and has begun to suggest the profoundly endemic relation of Kabbalah to the very core of ancient and medieval Judaism. Idel's carefully reasoned scholarship suggests that many Kabbalistic beliefs and practices were preserved and transmitted orally long before being written down, and that the fragmentary written teachings that first surfaced during the twelfth century were expressions of a coherent tradition of esoteric Jewish praxis that likely extended back to the archaic origins of Judaism itself. See especially Idel, *Kabbalah,* particularly chaps. 2, 5, and 7. See also Gershom Scholem, *Major Trends in Jewish Mysticism* (New York: Schocken Books, 1961).

48. Idel, pp. 97–103; Epstein, pp. 93–94.

49. Idel, p. 100; Epstein, p. 88; Gershom Scholem, *Kabbalah* (New York: New American Library, 1974), pp. 351–55.

50. Quoted in Epstein, pp. 59–60. The *Zohar* was almost certainly written in the latter half of the thirteenth century by Moses de León of Guadalajara. De León himself, however, ascribed authorship to the second-century sage who figures as the central character in the text, Rabbi Shim'on bar Yohai.

51. Quoted in Epstein, p. 66.

52. Daniel Chanan Matt, ed. and trans., *Zohar, The Book of Enlightenment* (New York: Paulist Press, 1983), pp. 60–62. In the *Zohar* the soul-breath, or *neshamah,* also has intermediary aspects resembling the Messenger Winds of the Navajo, as is evident from this quote: "The *neshamah* of a human being . . . leaves him every single night. In the morning she returns to him and dwells in his nostrils." See p. 219n.

53. Arthur Green and Barry W. Holtz, eds., *Your Word Is Fire: The Hasidic Masters on Contemplative Prayer* (New York: Schocken Books, 1987), p. 48.

54. Shneur Zalman of Ladi, "The Portal of Unity and Faith," in *An Anthology of Jewish Mysticism,* trans. Raphael Ben Zion (New York: Judaica Press, 1981), pp. 83–128. For a book-length commentary on this important text, see Adin Steinsaltz, *The Sustaining Utterance,* trans. Yehuda Hanegbi (London: Jason Aronson, 1974).

55. Green and Holtz, p. 43.

56. Even in the written narratives of the Bible, YHWH typically manifests himself in atmospheric phenomena, from the rains that flood the earth for forty days in Genesis, to the tumultuous whirlwind that addresses Job in the later writings. In the pivotal theophany atop Mount Sinai, YHWH displays himself to the assembled tribes as a storm cloud, thundering and lightning, and it is as a cloud that YHWH accompanies the Israelites in their subsequent wanderings through the desert.

57. The rest of Europe inherited these Greek innovations only by way of the Romans, who modified the Greek shapes into the capital letter forms used today throughout Western Europe and the Americas. See David Diringer's excellent, if somewhat dated, overview, *The Alphabet: A Key to the History of Mankind* (New York: Philosophical Library, 1953).

58. Plato provides a remarkably precise description of this new situation when he has Socrates state, in the *Phaedrus,* that written words "seem to talk to you as though they were intelligent, but if you ask them anything about what they say, from a desire to be instructed, they go on telling you just the same thing forever" (*Phaedrus,* 275d). Socrates' description clearly indicates the apparent autonomy of Greek texts, yet at the same time makes

evident the monotonous, almost mechanical efficiency of the new alphabet. A Hebrew reader could never claim that a traditional text "goes on telling you just the same thing forever," for the simple reason that the consonantal text may subtly vary its words, and hence its meanings, each time that the reader engages it!

59. Philip Wheelwright, ed., *The Pre-Socratics* (New York: Macmillan Publishing Co., 1985), pp. 60, 288. Anaximenes, it is reported, also claimed that the air was the immortal and ever-moving source of all phenomena; that even the gods themselves were born of the air! See Wheelwright, pp. 61–63.

60. *Phaedrus,* 250c.

61. The explicit fusion of Christian theology with Platonic philosophy was accomplished by the early Church theologians—first by Justin Martyr; later by Clement of Alexandria and Origen; finally, and most profoundly, by Augustine. For an accessible and engaging discussion of Christianity's alliance with Greek philosophy, see Richard Tarnas's sweeping work *The Passion of the Western Mind* (New York: Ballantine Books, 1991).

62. Thus it was that two decades ago a careful scientific study of the atmosphere, using new, highly sensitive instruments, yielded a new astonishment at the anomalous chemical makeup of the medium. The chemical composition of the earthly atmosphere was very far from any stable equilibrium, and yet, remarkably, this composition seemed to be actively and quite sensitively maintained by some unknown and enigmatic set of processes. This disclosure led several scientists to hypothesize that the composition of the atmosphere was being actively monitored and modulated by all of the earth's organic constituents acting collectively, as a vast, planetary metabolism. The Gaia hypothesis—named for the ageless mother of the gods in the oral mythology of ancient Greece—proposed that the earthly world in which we find ourselves must be reconceptualized as a living entity.

Whatever the scientific fate of the Gaia hypothesis, its emergence provides a striking illustration of the way in which a renewed awareness of the air forces us to recognize, ever more vividly, our interdependence with the countless organisms that surround us, and ultimately encourages us to speak of the encompassing earth in the manner of our oral ancestors, as an animate, living presence. See David Abram, "The Perceptual Implications of Gaia" in *The Ecologist* (Summer 1985); reprinted in *Dharma Gaia: A Harvest of Essays in Buddhism and Ecology,* edited by A. H. Badiner (San Francisco: Parallax Press, 1990). Also see Stephen Schneider and Penelope Boston, eds., *Scientists on Gaia* (Cambridge: M.I.T. Press, 1991).

CODA: TURNING INSIDE OUT

1. Paul S. Martin, "40,000 Years of Extinction on the 'Planet of Doom,'" in *Paleogeography, Paleoclimatology, Paleoecology* 82 (1990), pp. 187–201. See also Paul Martin and Richard Klein, eds., *Quaternary Extinctions* (Tucson: University of Arizona Press, 1984).

2. In contrast to a long-standing tendency of Western social science, this work has not attempted to provide a rational explanation of animistic beliefs and practices. On the contrary, it has presented an animistic or participatory account of rationality. It has suggested that civilized reason is sustained only by a deeply animistic engagement with our own signs. To tell the story in this manner—to provide an animistic account of reason, rather than the other way around—is to imply that animism is the wider and more inclusive term, and that oral, mimetic modes of experience still underlie, and support, all our literate and technological modes of reflection. When reflection's rootedness in such bodily, participatory modes of experience is entirely unacknowledged or unconscious, reflective reason becomes dysfunctional, unintentionally destroying the corporeal, sensuous world that sustains it.

Bibliography

Abram, David. "The Perceptual Implications of Gaia." *The Ecologist* (Summer 1985); reprinted in *Dharma Gaia: A Harvest of Essays in Buddhism and Ecology*. Edited by A. H. Badiner. San Francisco: Parallax Press, 1990.

————. "Merleau-Ponty and the Voice of the Earth." *Environmental Ethics,* Summer 1988.

————. "The Mechanical and The Organic: On the Impact of Metaphor in Science," in *Scientists on Gaia*. Edited by Stephen Schneider and Penelope Boston. Cambridge: M.I.T. Press, 1991.

Aristotle. *The Politics of Aristotle*. Translated by E. Barker. London: Oxford University Press, 1946.

————. *Physics*. Translated by Hippocrates G. Apostle. Bloomington: Indiana University Press, 1969.

Astrov, Margot, ed. *The Winged Serpent: American Indian Prose and Poetry*. Boston: Beacon Press, 1992. Originally published in 1946.

Barfield, Owen. *Saving the Appearances*. Middletown, Conn.: Wesleyan University Press, 1965.

Basso, Keith. "'Stalking with Stories': Names, Places, and Moral Narratives Among the Western Apaches." In *On Nature: Nature, Landscape, and Natural History*. Edited by Daniel Halpern. San Francisco: North Point Press, 1987.

305

————. "'Speaking with Names': Language and Landscape Among the Western Apache." *Cultural Anthropology,* May 1988.

Berndt, Ronald M., and Catherine H. Berndt. *The Speaking Land: Myth and Story in Aboriginal Australia.* London: Penguin Books, 1989.

Bierhorst, John. *The Mythology of North America.* New York: William Morrow & Co., 1985.

————. *The Way of the Earth.* New York: William Morrow & Co., 1994.

Brock, Peggy, ed. *Women, Rites, and Sites: Aboriginal Women's Cultural Knowledge.* North Sydney, Austral.: Allen & Unwin, 1989.

Carpenter, Rhys. "The Antiquity of the Greek Alphabet." *American Journal of Archaeology* 37 (1933).

Carr, David. *Interpreting Husserl.* The Hague: Martinus Nijhoff Publishers, 1987.

Cassirer, Ernst. *The Philosophy of Symbolic Forms.* Translated by Ralph Manheim. New Haven: Yale University Press, 1953.

Chatwin, Bruce. *The Songlines.* London: Penguin Books, 1987.

Collins, June M. "The Mythological Basis for Attitudes Towards Animals Among Salish-Speaking Indians." *Journal of American Folklore* 65, no. 258 (1952).

Derrida, Jacques. *Of Grammatology.* Translated by Gayatri Spivak. Baltimore: Johns Hopkins University Press, 1976.

Diringer, David. *The Alphabet: A Key to the History of Mankind.* New York: Philosophical Library, 1948.

Dooling, D. M., ed. *The Sons of the Wind: The Sacred Stories of the Lakota.* New York: Parabola Books, 1984.

Duerr, Hans Peter. *Dreamtime: Concerning the Boundary Between Civilization and the Wilderness.* Translated by Felicitas Goodman. Oxford: Basil Blackwell, 1985.

Edie, James M. Introduction to Maurice Merleau-Ponty, *Consciousness and the Acquisition of Language.* Evanston, Ill.: Northwestern University Press, 1973.

Eisenstein, Elizabeth. *The Printing Press as an Agent of Change: Communications and Cultural Transformations in Early Modern Europe.* New York: Cambridge University Press, 1979.

Eliade, Mircea. *The Myth of the Eternal Return.* Translated by Willard R. Trask. New York: Harper & Row, 1959.

————. *Shamanism: Archaic Techniques of Ecstasy.* Translated by Willard R. Trask. Princeton: Princeton University Press, 1964.

Ellis, Catherine J., and Linda Barwick. "Antikirinja Women's Song Knowledge 1963–1972." In *Women, Rites, and Sites.* Edited by Peggy Brock. North Sydney, Austral.: Allen & Unwin, 1989.

Epstein, Perle. *Kaballah: The Way of the Jewish Mystic*. Boston: Shambhala, 1988.

Feld, Steven. *Sound and Sentiment: Birds, Weeping, Poetics and Song in Kaluli Expression,* rev. ed. Philadelphia: Temple University Press, 1991.

Finnegan, Ruth. *Oral Literature in Africa*. London: Oxford University Press, 1970.

Goody, Jack. *The Myth of Bagre*. London: Oxford University Press, 1972.

―――. *The Domestication of the Savage Mind*. Cambridge: Cambridge University Press, 1977.

―――. *The Interface Between the Written and the Oral*. Cambridge: Cambridge University Press, 1987.

Green, Arthur, and Barry W. Holtz, eds. *Your Word Is Fire: The Hasidic Masters on Contemplative Prayer*. New York: Schocken Books, 1987.

Griaule, Marcel. *Conversations with Ogotemmêli*. London: Oxford University Press, 1965.

Grinell, George B. *Pawnee Hero Stories and Folk-tales*. Originally published 1889. Lincoln: University of Nebraska Press, 1961.

Guss, David M., ed. *The Language of the Birds*. San Francisco: North Point Press, 1985.

Hadreas, Peter J. *In Place of the Flawed Diamond*. New York: Peter Lang Publishers, 1986.

Halpern, Daniel. *On Nature: Nature, Landscape, and Natural History*. San Francisco: North Point Press, 1987.

Havelock, Eric. *Preface to Plato*. Cambridge: Harvard University Press, 1963.

―――. *The Muse Learns to Write: Reflections on Orality and Literacy from Antiquity to the Present*. New Haven: Yale University Press, 1986.

―――. "The Special Theory of Greek Orality." In *The Muse Learns to Write: Reflections on Orality and Literacy from Antiquity to the Present*. New Haven: Yale University Press, 1986.

Hawkins, J. A. "The Origin and Dissemination of Writing in Western Asia." In *Origins of Civilization*. Edited by P. R. S. Moorey. London: Oxford University Press, 1979.

Heidegger, Martin. *Being and Time*. Translated by John Macquarrie and Edward Robinson. Oxford: Basil Blackwell, 1967.

―――. "Time and Being." In *On Time and Being*. Translated by Joan Stambaugh. New York: Harper & Row, 1972.

―――. "The Origin of the Work of Art." In *Basic Writings*. Edited by David Farrell Krell. New York: Harper & Row, 1977.

Herder, Johann G. *On the Origin of Language*. Translated by John H.

Moran and Alexander Gode. Chicago: University of Chicago Press, 1986.

Holtz, Barry W. *Back to the Sources: Reading the Classic Jewish Texts*. New York: Summit Books, 1984.

Homer. *The Odyssey*. Translated by Robert Fitzgerald. Garden City, N.Y.: Doubleday & Co., 1961.

Horowitz, Edward. *How the Hebrew Language Grew*. New York: Jewish Education Committee Press, 1960.

Houston, John J. "Songs in Stone: Animals in Inuit Sculpture." In *Orion*, Autumn 1985.

Hultkrantz, Åke. *Native Religions of North America*. San Francisco: Harper & Row, 1987.

Husserl, Edmund. *Cartesian Meditations: An Introduction to Phenomenology*. Translated by Dorion Cairns. The Hague: Martinus Nijhoff Publishers, 1960.

―――. *Phenomenology of Internal Time-Consciousness*. Translated by James S. Churchill. Bloomington: Indiana University Press, 1964.

―――. *The Crisis of the European Sciences and Transcendental Phenomenology: An Introduction to Phenomenological Philosophy*. Translated by David Carr. Evanston, Ill.: Northwestern University Press, 1970.

―――. "Foundational Investigations of the Phenomenological Origin of the Spatiality of Nature." Translated by Fred Kersten. In *Husserl: Shorter Works*. Edited by Peter McCormick and Frederick A. Elliston. Brighton, Eng.: Harvester Press, 1981.

―――. "Epilogue." In *Ideas Pertaining to a Pure Phenomenology II*. Translated by Richard Rozcewicz and André Schuwer, 1989.

Idel, Moshe. *Kabbalah: New Perspectives*. New Haven: Yale University Press, 1988.

Illich, Ivan. *In the Vineyard of the Text*. Chicago: University of Chicago Press, 1993.

Illich, Ivan, and Barry Sanders. *ABC: The Alphabetization of the Popular Mind*. San Francisco: North Point Press, 1988.

Jabes, Edmond. *Elya*. Berkeley, Calif.: Tree Books, 1974.

Jacobson, Roman, and Linda Waugh. *The Sound Shape of Language*. Bloomington, Ind.: Indiana University Press, 1979.

Jahner, Elaine. *Lakota Myth*. Lincoln: University of Nebraska Press, 1983.

Jenness, Diamond. *The Carrier Indians of the Bulkley River*. Bureau of American Ethnology, Bulletin 133. Washington, D.C.: Smithsonian Institution, 1943.

Jesperson, Otto. *Language—Its Nature, Development, and Origin*. New York: Henry Holt, 1922.

Jones, Edwin. *Reading the Book of Nature*. Athens: Ohio University Press, 1989.

Kockelman, Joseph J., ed. *Phenomenology: The Philosophy of Edmund Husserl and Its Interpretation*. Garden City, N.Y.: Doubleday & Co., 1967.

Koyré, Alexandre. *From the Closed World to the Infinite Universe*. New York: Harper & Row, 1958.

Kushner, Lawrence. *The Book of Letters: A Mystical Alef-Bait*. New York: Harper & Row, 1975.

Lamb, Bruce F. *Wizard of the Upper Amazon: The Story of Manuel Córdova-Rios*. Boston: Houghton Mifflin Co., 1971.

Lame Deer, John Fire, and Richard Erdoes. *Lame Deer, Seeker of Visions*. New York: Simon & Schuster, 1972.

Lawlor, Robert. *Voices of the First Day: Awakening in the Aboriginal Dreamtime*. Rochester, Vt.: Inner Traditions, 1992.

Lévy-Bruhl, Lucien. *How Natives Think*. Princeton: Princeton University Press, 1985.

Lincoln, Kenneth. "Native American Literatures." In *Smoothing the Ground: Essays on Native American Oral Literature*. Edited by Brian Swann. Berkeley: University of California Press, 1983.

Littleton, C. Scott. "Lucien Lévy-Bruhl and the Concept of Cognitive Relativity." Introduction to Lucien Lévy-Bruhl, *How Natives Think*. Princeton: Princeton University Press, 1985.

Lord, Albert. *The Singer of Tales*. Cambridge: Harvard University Press, 1960.

Lovelock, James. "Gaia: The World as Living Organism." *New Scientist*, 1986.

McLuhan, Marshall. *The Gutenberg Galaxy: The Making of Typographic Man*. Toronto: University of Toronto Press, 1962.

McLuhan, T. C. *Touch the Earth*. New York: Outerbridge & Dienstfrey, 1971.

McNeley, James K. *Holy Wind in Navajo Philosophy*. Tucson: University of Arizona Press, 1981.

Malotki, Ekkehart. *Hopi Time: A Linguistic Analysis of the Temporal Concepts in the Hopi Language*. New York: Mouton Publishers, 1983.

Marshall-Stoneking, Billy. *Singing the Snake: Poems from the Western Desert*. Pymble, Austral.: Angus & Robertson, 1990.

Martin, Calvin, ed. *The American Indian and the Problem of History*. New York: Oxford University Press, 1987.

Matt, Daniel C., ed. and trans. *Zohar, the Book of Enlightenment*, New York: Paulist Press, 1983.

Merleau-Ponty, Maurice. *Phenomenology of Perception*. Translated by Colin Smith. London: Routledge & Kegan Paul, 1962.

————. *The Primacy of Perception*. Evanston, Ill.: Northwestern University Press, 1964.

————. *Signs*. Translated by Richard McCleary. Evanston, Ill.: Northwestern University Press, 1964.

————. *The Visible and the Invisible*. Translated by Alphonso Lingis. Evanston, Ill.: Northwestern University Press, 1968.

Mishara, Aaron L. "Husserl and Freud: Time, Memory, and the Unconscious." *Husserl Studies* 7 (1990).

Momaday, N. Scott. "Personal Reflections." In Calvin Martin, *The American Indian and the Problem of History*. New York: Oxford University Press, 1987.

Munk, Michael L. *The Wisdom in the Hebrew Alphabet: The Sacred Letters as a Guide to Jewish Deed and Thought*. Brooklyn: Mesorah Publications, 1983.

Neihardt, John. *Black Elk Speaks*. Lincoln: University of Nebraska Press, 1968.

Nelson, Richard. *Make Prayers to the Raven: A Koyukon View of the Northern Forest*. Chicago: University of Chicago Press, 1983.

————. *The Island Within*. San Francisco: North Point Press, 1989.

Norman, Howard. "Crows Ducks and Other Wandering Talk." In *The Language of the Birds*. Edited by David M. Guss. San Francisco: North Point Press, 1985.

Ong, Walter J. *Orality and Literacy: The Technologizing of the Word*. New York: Methuen, 1982.

————. *Interfaces of the Word*. London: Cornell University Press, 1977.

Onions, C. T., ed. *The Oxford Dictionary of English Etymology*. Oxford: Oxford University Press, 1966.

Parry, Adam, ed. *The Making of Homeric Verse: The Collected Papers of Milman Parry*. Oxford: Clarendon Press, 1971.

Parry, Milman. "Whole Formulaic Verses in Greek and Southslavic Heroic Song." In *The Making of Homeric Verse: The Collected Papers of Milman Parry*. Edited by Adam Parry. Oxford: Clarendon Press, 1971.

Partridge, Eric. *Origins: A Short Etymological Dictionary of Modern English*. London: Routledge & Kegan Paul, 1958.

Payne, Helen. "Rites for Sites or Sites for Rites? The Dynamics of Women's Cultural Life in the Musgraves." In *Women, Rites, and Sites: Aboriginal Women's Cultural Knowledge*. Edited by Peggy Brock. North Sydney, Austral.: Allen & Unwin, 1989.

Pinxten, Rik; Ingrid Van Doren; and Frank Harvey. *Anthropology of Space: Explorations into the Natural Philosophy and Semantics of the Navajo*. Philadelphia: University of Pennsylvania Press, 1983.

Pirsig, Robert. *Zen and the Art of Motorcycle Maintenance*. New York: William Morrow & Co., 1974.

Plato. *Phaedrus*. Translated by R. Hackforth. In Edith Hamilton and Huntington Cairns, eds., *Plato: The Collected Dialogues*. Princeton: Princeton University Press, 1982.

Pound, Ezra. *ABC of Reading*. New York: New Directions Press, 1960.

Reed, Charles A., ed. *Origins of Agriculture*. The Hague: Mouton & Co., 1977.

Rothenberg, Jerome, and Diane Rothenberg, eds. *Symposium of the Whole*. Berkeley: University of California Press, 1983.

Rousseau, Jean-Jacques. "Essay on the Origin of Languages." Translated by John H. Moran, in Rousseau and Herder, *On the Origin of Language*. Chicago: University of Chicago Press, 1986.

Sahlins, Marshall. *Historical Metaphors and Mythical Realities*. Ann Arbor, Mich.: University of Michigan Press, 1981.

Sampson, Geoffrey. *Writing Systems, A Linguistic Introduction*. Stanford: Stanford University Press, 1985.

Sapir, Edward. "The Status of Linguistics as a Science." In *Selected Writings of Edward Sapir in Language, Culture, and Personality*. Edited by David G. Mandelbaum. Berkeley: University of California Press, 1949.

Saussure, Ferdinand de. *Course in General Linguistics*. Edited by Charles Bally and Albert Sechehaye. Translated by Wade Baskin. New York: McGraw-Hill, 1966.

Schneider, Stephen, and Penelope Boston, eds., *Scientists on Gaia*. Cambridge: M.I.T. Press, 1991.

Scholem, Gershom. *Major Trends in Jewish Mysticism*. New York: Schocken Books, 1961.

————. *Kabbalah*. New York: New American Library, 1974.

Snyder, Gary. *The Practice of the Wild*. San Francisco: North Point Press, 1990.

Spiegelberg, Herbert. *The Phenomenological Movement*. The Hague: Martinus Nijhoff Publishers, 1960.

Stanner, W. E. H. "The Dreaming." In Jerome Rothenberg and Diane Rothenberg, eds., *Symposium of the Whole*. Berkeley: University of California Press, 1983.

Swann, Brian, ed. *Smoothing the Ground: Essays on Native American Oral Literature*. Berkeley: University of California Press, 1983.

Tanakh: The Holy Scriptures. Philadelphia: Jewish Publication Society, 1985.

Tarnas, Richard. *The Passion of the Western Mind*. New York: Ballantine, 1991.

Taylor, Charles. *Human Agency and Language*. New York: Cambridge University Press, 1985.

————. *Sources of the Self*. Cambridge: Harvard University Press, 1989.

Tedlock, Dennis. "An American Indian View of Death." In *Teachings from the American Earth: Indian Religion and Philosophy*. New York: Liveright, 1975.

————. *Breath on the Mirror*. San Francisco: HarperCollins, 1993.

————, translator. *Popul Vuh: The Mayan Book of the Dawn of Life*. New York: Simon & Schuster, 1985.

Tedlock, Dennis, and Barbara Tedlock, eds. *Teachings from the American Earth*. New York: Liveright, 1975.

Todorov, Tzvetan. *The Conquest of America*. Translated by Richard Howard. New York: Harper & Row, 1984.

Vecsey, Christopher. *Imagine Ourselves Richly: Mythic Narratives of North American Indians*. San Francisco: HarperCollins, 1991.

Vico, Giambattista. *The New Science of Giambattista Vico*, 3rd ed. Translated by Thomas G. Bergin and Max H. Fisch. Garden City, N.Y.: Doubleday & Co., 1961.

Vizenor, Gerald. *Anishnabe Adisokan: Tales of the People*. Minneapolis: Nodin Press, 1970.

Walker, J. R. *The Sun Dance and Other Ceremonies of the Teton Dakota*. Anthropological Papers of the American Museum of Natural History 16 (1917).

Wheelwright, Philip, ed. *The Presocratics*. New York: Macmillan Publishing Co., 1985.

Whorf, Benjamin Lee. "An American Indian Model of the Universe." In Dennis Tedlock and Barbara Tedlock, eds., *Teachings from the American Earth*. New York: Liveright, 1975.

Witherspoon, Gary. *Language and Art in the Navajo Universe*. Ann Arbor: University of Michigan Press, 1977.

Wood, David. *The Deconstruction of Time*. Atlantic Highlands, N.J.: Humanities Press International, 1989.

Wyman, Leland C. *Blessingway*. Tucson: University of Arizona Press, 1970.

Yates, Frances A. *The Art of Memory*. Chicago: University of Chicago Press, 1966.

Zalman, Shneur. *The Portal of Unity and Faith*. In *An Anthology of Jewish Mysticism*. Translated by Raphael Ben Zion. New York: Judaica Press, 1981.

Permissions Acknowledgments

Chapter One, "The Ecology of Magic," was originally published in somewhat different form in *Orion Magazine*.

Grateful acknowledgment is made to the following for permission to reprint previously published material:

The Ecco Press: Excerpt from "From March '79" by Tomas Transtromer and translated by John F. Deane, from *Selected Poems 1954–1986*, edited by Robert Hass. Copyright © 1987 by Tomas Transtromer and John F. Deane. Published by The Ecco Press in 1987. Excerpt from "Stalking with Stories" by Keith Basso from *Antaeus: On Nature*, edited by Daniel Halpern, copyright © 1986 by *Antaeus*, New York. First published by The Ecco Press in 1986. Reprinted by permission of The Ecco Press.

ETT Imprint: Excerpts from "Passage" and "Paddy: A Poem for Land Rights" from *Singing the Snake* by Billy Marshall-Stoneking (Angus & Robertson, Pymble, Australia, 1990). Reprinted by permission of ETT Imprint.

Barry W. Holtz: Excerpts from *Your Word Is Fire*, edited and translated by Arthur Green and Barry W. Holtz (Schocken Books, New York, 1987). Reprinted by permission of Barry W. Holtz.

Index

Scholem, Gershom, 300*n*47
science, 32, 35
conventional division between
subject and object, 66–67
Copernican worldview, 42–43
life-world and, 41
phenomenology and, 36, 43
subjective experience and, 33–
34
scribes, 98–99
senses: *see* perception; synaesthesia
sensuous world, ix–x
language's connection to, 84–89
modern man's alienation from,
22–23, 25–28, 255–57,
265–68, 270–71
recuperation of the sensuous,
62–65, 69–70, 268–71
shaman's connection with, 6–11
shamanism:
consciousness-altering and, 9
"developed world's" interest in,
21–22
familiars, 23
harmful magic, 5–6
healing function, 4, 7–8, 275*n*2
language and, 88–89
learning shaman's skills, 116
mediation between human and
more-than-human realms,
6–11, 256
sleight-of-hand magic and, 4–5
spirits, propitiation of, 11–13
Shepard, Paul, 181
Sherpa people, 23–24
Shim'on bar Yohai, Rabbi, 247,
301*n*50
Shoshoni people, 220, 296*n*51
"silent" reading, 124–25
Skagit people, 219–20
Slavic singers, 106–7
sleep, 55

sleight-of-hand magic, 4–5
perception and, 5, 57–59
smells, 26–27
smoke, 229
Snyder, Gary, 93, 173
Socrates, 102, 103, 109–11, 112–14,
115–16, 117, 118, 121–22,
138, 252, 301*n*58
Socratic dialectic, 109
Solomon, King, 247
songlines, 166–68
*Sons of the Wind: The Sacred Sto-
ries of the Lakota* (Dooling),
297*n*6
sorcery: *see* shamanism
soul, 231, 238: *see also psychê*
space, 184, 185
absolute space, 199–201, 204
Euclidian space, 198
as "place," 182–83, 190
see also space-time
space-time, 204–6
Einstein's views on, 204
enveloping earth and, 216–17
gradual separation of space
from time, 187–88, 193,
194–95, 197–201
in Hebrew culture, 196–97
in indigenous, oral cultures,
188–93, 217–22
past and future as aspects of
sensory landscape, 206–17
perceptual reconciliation of
time and space, 216
phenomenology and, 42–43,
204–6
presence and, 204
Spanish conquest of the Americas,
133–35, 187
Speaking Land (Berndt and
Berndt), 165, 177
"spell," ambiguous meaning of, 133